AF469075

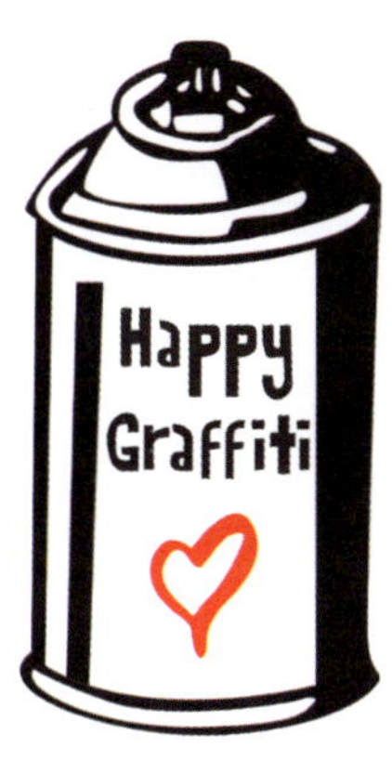
Happy
Graffiti

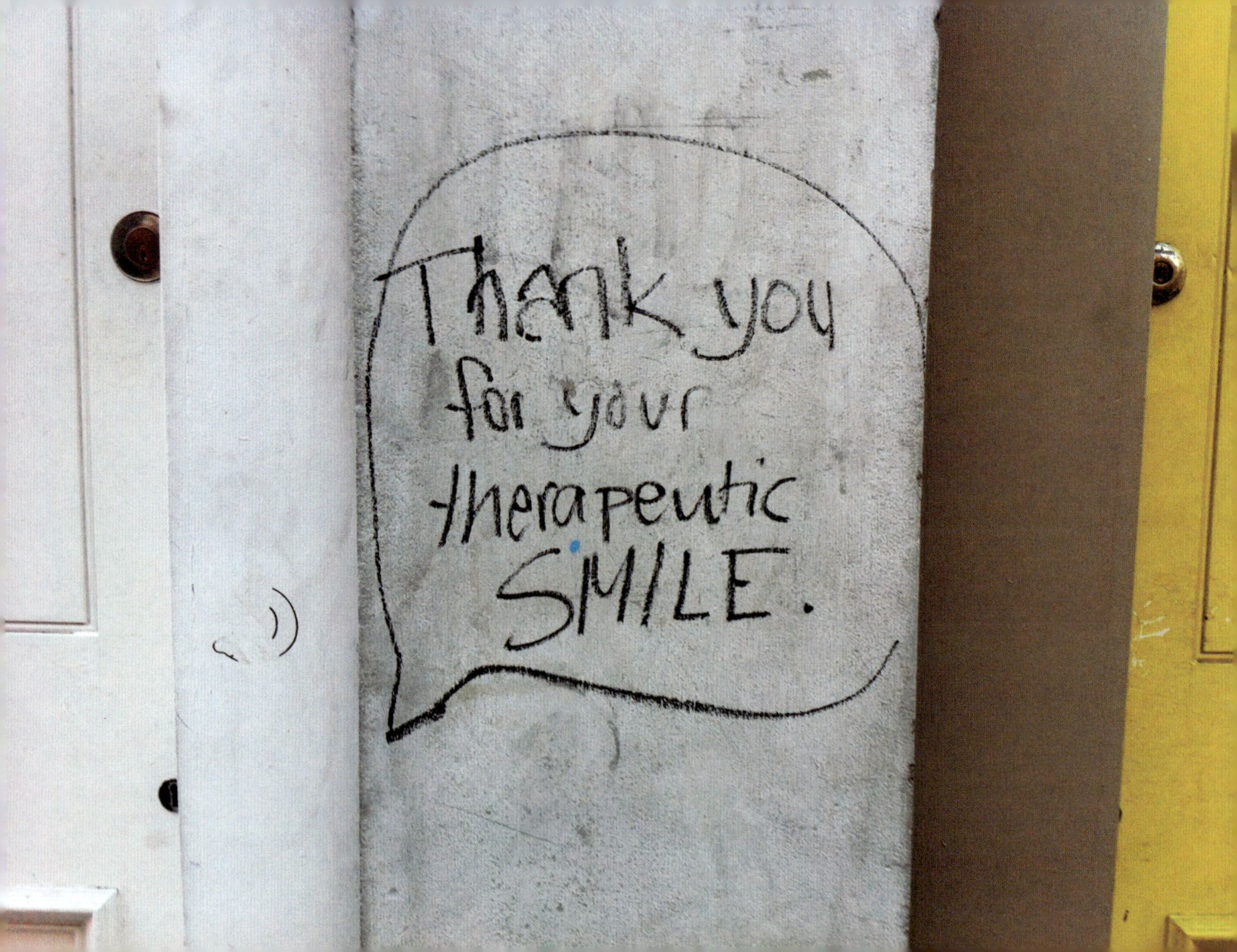

Thank you
for your
therapeutic
SMILE.

happy graffiti

street art with heart

jenny foulds

foreword by laura dockrill

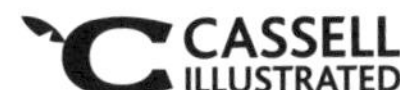

For Lee – my twin brain

An Hachette UK Company
www.hachette.co.uk

First published in Great Britain in 2013 by
Cassell, a division of Octopus Publishing Group Ltd
Endeavour House
189 Shaftesbury Avenue
London
WC2H 8JY
www.octopusbooks.co.uk

ISBN 978-1-84403-773-5

A CIP catalogue record for this book is available from the British Library.

Printed and bound in China

10 9 8 7 6 5 4 3 2 1

Publisher: Alison Starling
Editor: Pauline Bache
Art Director: Juliette Norsworthy
Design: Abigail Read and Grace Helmer
Production Controller: Sarah Kramer

The author and publisher have made every effort to contact the copyright holders of these images.
Frontispiece: **Unknown** Brick Lane, London
Title page tag: **Pac One**

Contents

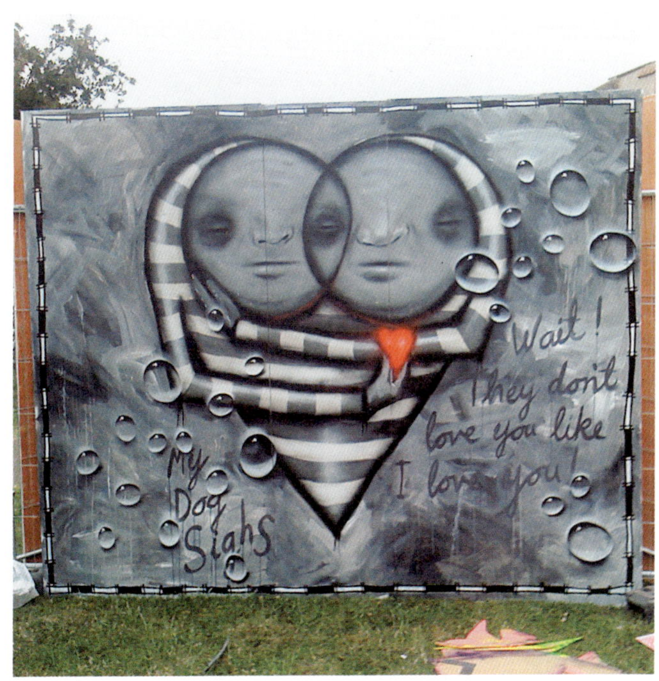

My Dog Sighs Upfest, Bristol ↑

Foreword by Laura Dockrill

Dear Reader,

I am writing this foreword immediately after turning the last page of Jenny's proof copy of this very book you are reading now, *Happy Graffiti*. It is grey and ugly outside and the clouds are being completely selfish and not letting the sunshine crack through, so I really needed a delight. I've just managed to pour myself a cup of tea before exploding my thoughts. Because that's what this book makes you want to do: A bit of exploding.

Just like graffiti – the activity and behaviour of it, the way it's produced, the way it makes somebody feel and the way it lasts (not very long, if at all) – this book is instant, spontaneous, direct and sharp to the heart. It's not just the image or material of the work itself but also the energy behind the images, the slogans and the mechanics behind conjuring such thought-out and often deeply constructive, complex sentences and ideas that are brief and to the point, just like their artists. Completely spinning the idea of what a 'graffer' is like on its head and banishing the stereotype of a hooded naughty boy keying the initials of his ex-girlfriend onto a phone box window, this stuff is a different business. This is poetry.

Happy Graffiti made me think of Balham station; horrendously packed and overcrowded with grumpy commuters every morning. The platform from a bird's eye view would look like a jam-packed, healthy corn on the cob. Across the road from the railway tracks are the backs of residential houses, quite nice ones (though obviously their views aren't ideal). In one of their windows there are no curtains, just a massive bit of wood balancing on the window sill facing outwards towards the platform and on it in oversized, bright pink, six-year-old handwriting reads:

'Hi Dad'

If that isn't going to cheer up a whole platform of grumpy commuters and remind them why they get up each morning (not to mention the proud Dad in question) then I don't know what will.

The first ever bit of interesting graffiti I remember seeing was scrawled on the door of a pub toilet, and it read:

'I like girls and I like boys and I don't have to make a choice'

And I remember thinking, 'Well you can't argue with that'. Lots of people had added to it, agreeing and commenting on the statement, and this was well before the days of intense YouTube banter, so I like to think of the good old-fashioned toilet door as a bit of a social network guru. It all started there.

Advertising is squashed in our faces but it has paid to be there. Nobody has snuck out in the middle of the night to create it, it probably hasn't ever changed somebody's mind about anything serious in fact.

Or take busking – it can be annoying, but it is an excellent way for new fresh talent to create a platform to showcase their music. *Happy Graffiti* is applying the same policies. In a city that can, at times, feel so concrete and bleak (I love London but it does, in places, seem like it was designed by a maths teacher), it's not surprising that some people want to splash some colour on the walls – it's our home, it should represent us. This is Art-busking, or 'Asking'. There you go, you can have that one Jenny.

To finish, I'm not condoning aimless, destructive 'tagging' or abuse that can be upsetting for homes and businesses. But pure, raw, beautiful, smart and poignant happy messages splattered over our streets seem like true music to my eyes. We shouldn't be pretending to be robots.

Jenny, good luck with this book, you naughty girl,

Laura x

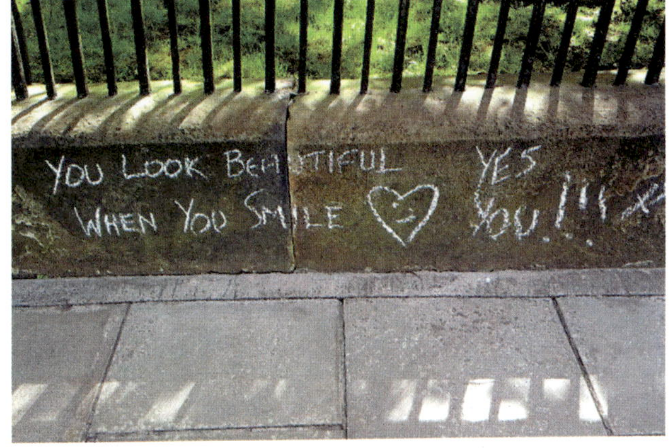

Unknown The Mound, Edinburgh ↑

Introduction

Oh hello you lot. I didn't see you there… Have you done something different with your hair?

Welcome to *Happy Graffiti*!

For those of you who don't know me, I'm Jenny, otherwise known as *HGHQ*. I keep the good ship nonsense that is *Happy Graffiti* ticking over with a little help from my lovely readers and the contributors to the website. Over the past year I have been collecting hundreds of photos of happy, silly or funny pieces of street art and graffiti and I've whittled them down to the collection that you'll see over the following technicolour pages. It's been such an amazing year, full of adventures in different countries, meeting some brilliant artists and even meeting a few of the *Happy Graffiti* followers on my travels.

So, 'Why happy graffiti?' I hear you say. Well, once upon a time I was at a party at my friend Stevie Star's house. As we chatted away beside the sink in his kitchen, something caught my eye outside. Stevie lived three stories up and his flat backed onto a creepy-looking lane, but someone had painted the word 'SMILE' on the wall at the back, five feet high, in white emulsion paint. Stevie explained that he was the culprit and he had done it the month previously. He hated doing dishes you see. He thought that seeing 'SMILE' whilst standing at the sink every day would make the task a happier one, and it did. This inspired me to keep my eyes open for positive graffiti, and in later years to take my camera wherever I went to capture expressions of happiness people had scribbled, painted and annotated on any surface they could get their paws on.

I started the *Happy Graffiti* website shortly after the London riots when the world was in the middle of an economic shit storm. People were miserable and just needed a bit of cheering up. I was walking through Shoreditch in London one afternoon when I happened upon a giant mural by an artist called ESPO that said, 'Let's Adore and Endure Each Other' (pages 16 and 17). I couldn't stop smiling and when I looked around everyone who was seeing it for the first time was smiling too. It got me thinking – graffiti gets a bad name, but it doesn't have to be all doom and gloom in a spray can. Wouldn't it be brilliant if positive graffiti started to outweigh the usual tags or negative graffiti that we see? What effect would that have on the people who walk past it every day? Could happy graffiti change our attitudes or even our moods? If you could make ten, one hundred, one thousand, even ten thousand people smile in a day just from a simple bit of positive paint on a wall, shouldn't you then take that opportunity? LET'S START A HAPPY GRAFFITI REVOLUTION!

What started off as a tiny Facebook page has grown arms and legs and turned into a lovely community of like-minded, happy souls across all aspects of social media. The website is growing too, with hits every day from all over the world. I also receive pictures of international happy graffiti every week. What's interesting about these is that, no matter where you are in the world, positive graffiti and street art have the same messages and the same themes. This happy movement transcends culture or language.

In my quest for happy graffiti, three things have become apparent…

1. The transient nature of graffiti and street art: If you're not quick, it's gone. On my prowls around Brick Lane, I only leave a few weeks in between each visit because the area changes so rapidly.

2. The wide-ranging definition of happy graffiti: Positive, funny, uplifting and sometimes a tiny bit rude! Anything that puts a smile on someone's chops as they walk past. It can be a joke, a declaration of love, a silly picture or an upbeat, life-affirming and thought-provoking message of hope.

3. The many different mediums in which happy messages are written: Whether it's a beautifully designed giant mural, a paste-up stuck to a wall by a well-established and talented artist, a scribble on a toilet wall, a messily sprayed scrawl on a brick wall by an anonymous passer-by – each message is as valid and as important as the other.

So… Whilst ambling through this collection of photos, please take a moment to think about why the messages were written. Why did someone write that on that cubicle door, or spray that on that brick wall? What led them there? It's important to remember too that, for the purpose of the little *Happy Graffiti* book, the everyday spreaders of the happy stuff are just as important as the wonderfully talented and well-established artists. That said, I don't want to take away from the graffiti writers and street artists who spend so much time designing and planning these works of tiny genius. This book wouldn't be possible without their sheer talent and colourful brains, and anyone who can cheer up our grey cities with these colourful words and images should be championed! If the artists are the revolutionaries then the everyday scribblers are the vigilantes. This book is about celebrating them all.

I hope this little corner of happy things inspires you to keep an eye out for the messages left behind by these cheerful souls. Above all else, I hope this book makes you smile, and if it does that then the revolution is definitely well and truly underway.

Jenny x
Head of Happy Things at *Happy Graffiti*

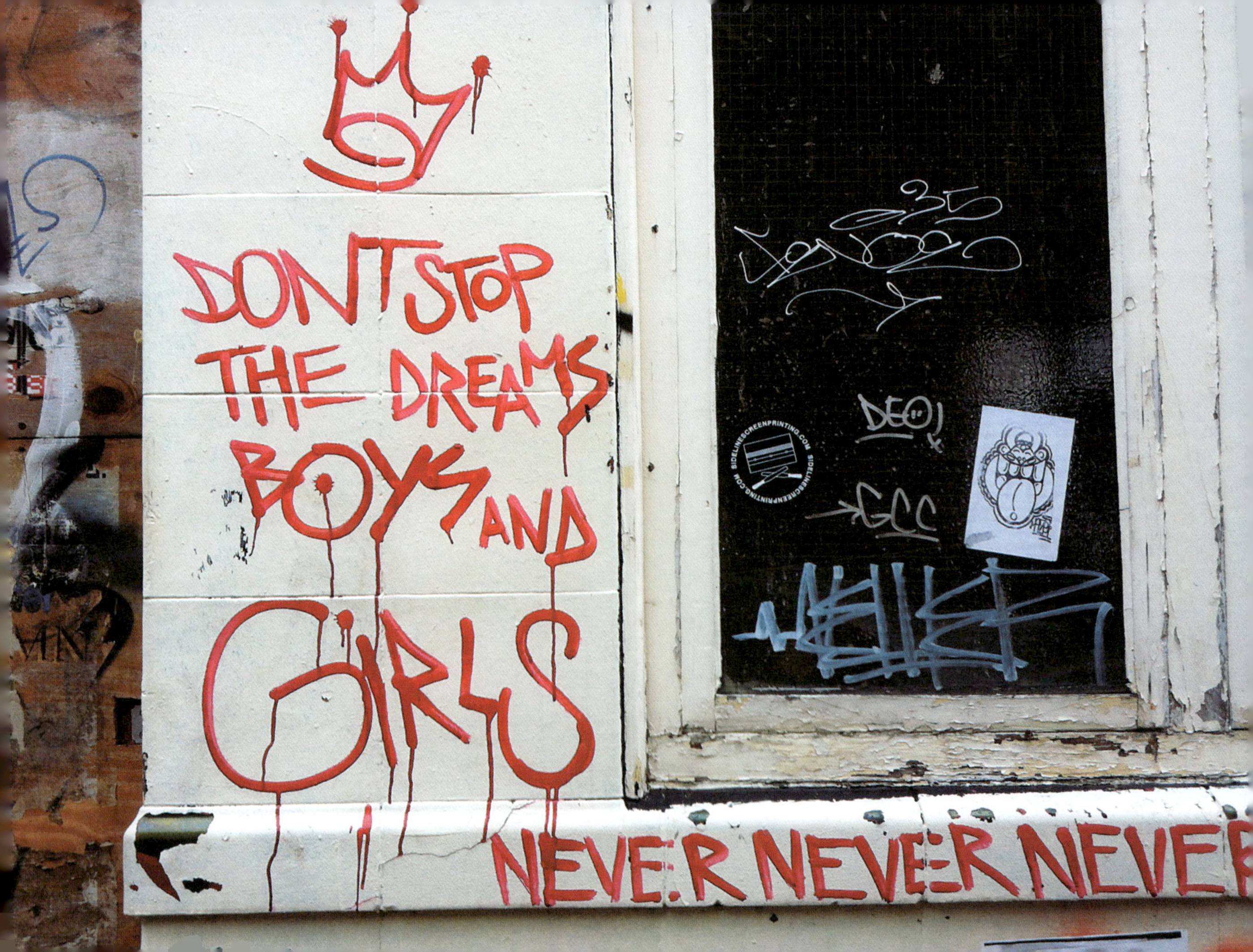
DONT STOP
THE DREAMS
BOYS AND
GIRLS
NEVE:R NEVE:R NEVE
DEO
GCC
SIDELINESCREENPRINTING.COM

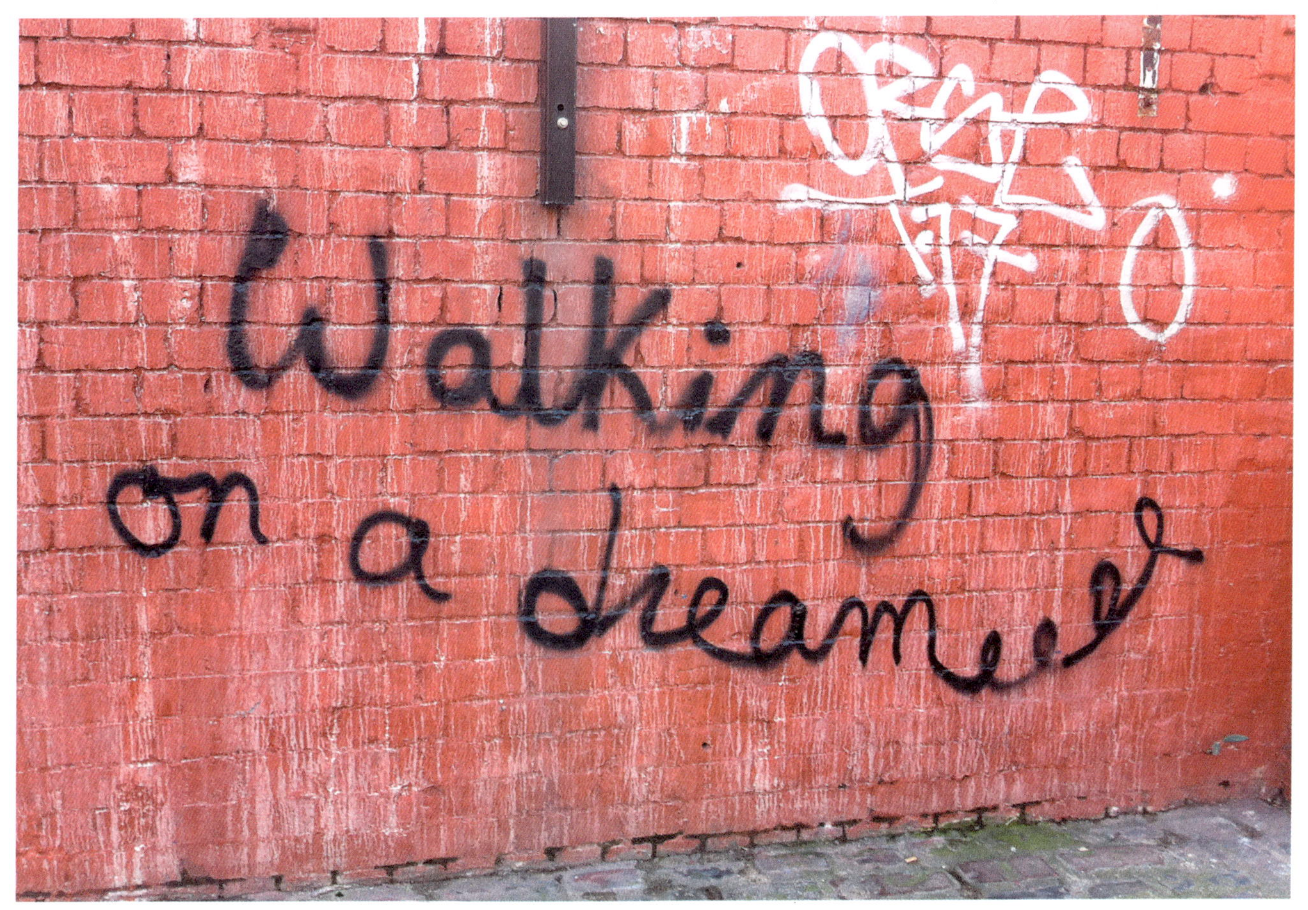

Unknown Brick Lane, London ← and **Unknown** Shoreditch, London ↑

Unknown Shoreditch, London ← and **Camille Walala** Hackney, London →

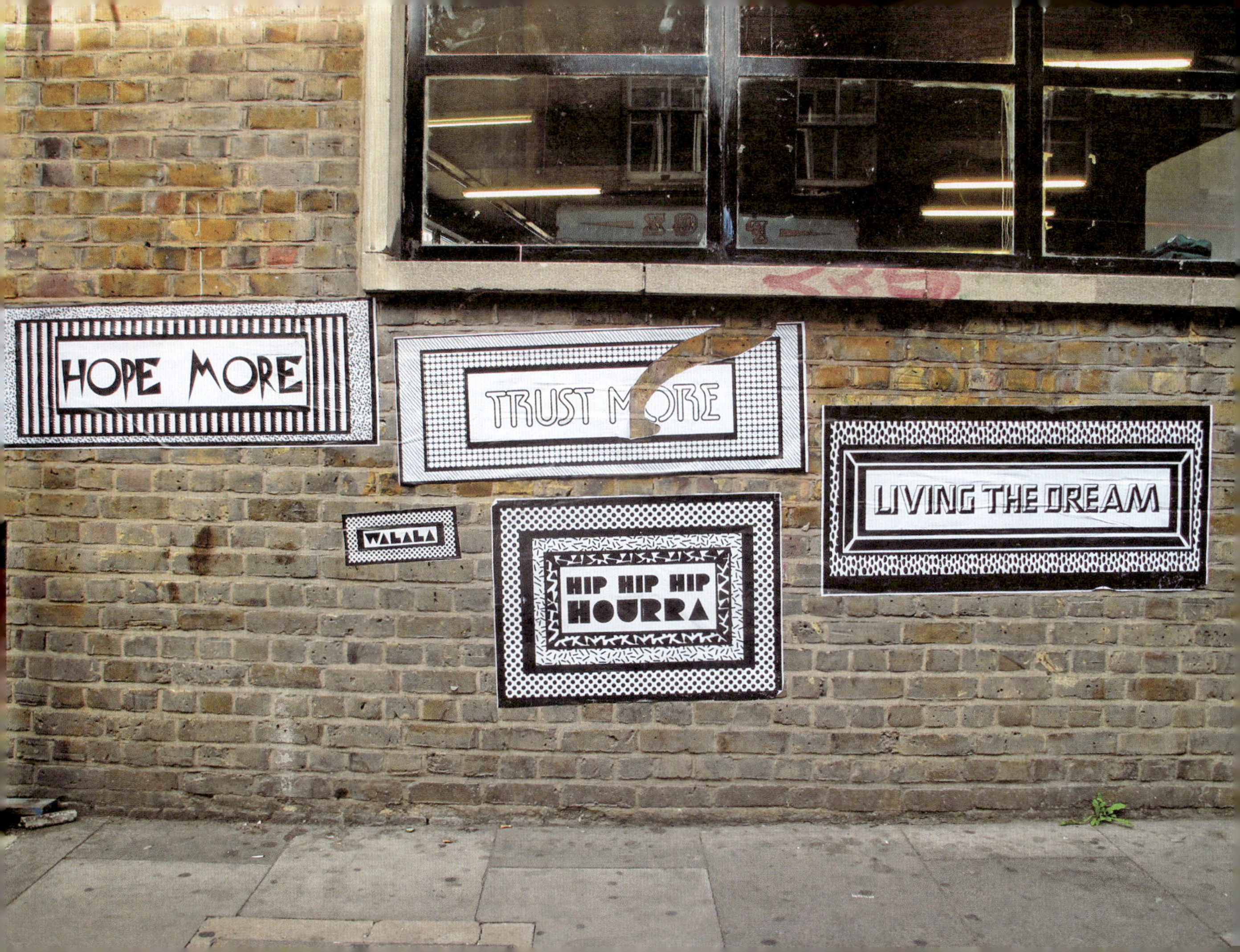
HOPE MORE
TRUST MORE
LIVING THE DREAM
WALALA
HIP HIP HIP
HOURRA

Ben Eine

Eine is one of London's most prolific and original street artists. Regular visitors to East London will be familiar with the giant letters and words that adorn his preferred canvases: the walls and shutters of many businesses. This is Eine's speciality. From single letters to complex and wry combinations, his alphabet can be found throughout London. The huge individual letters on shop shutters are in a style Eine has made his own.

Originality, a distinctive style and a clear profile set his letters apart from all others.

Ben Eine Aldgate, London →

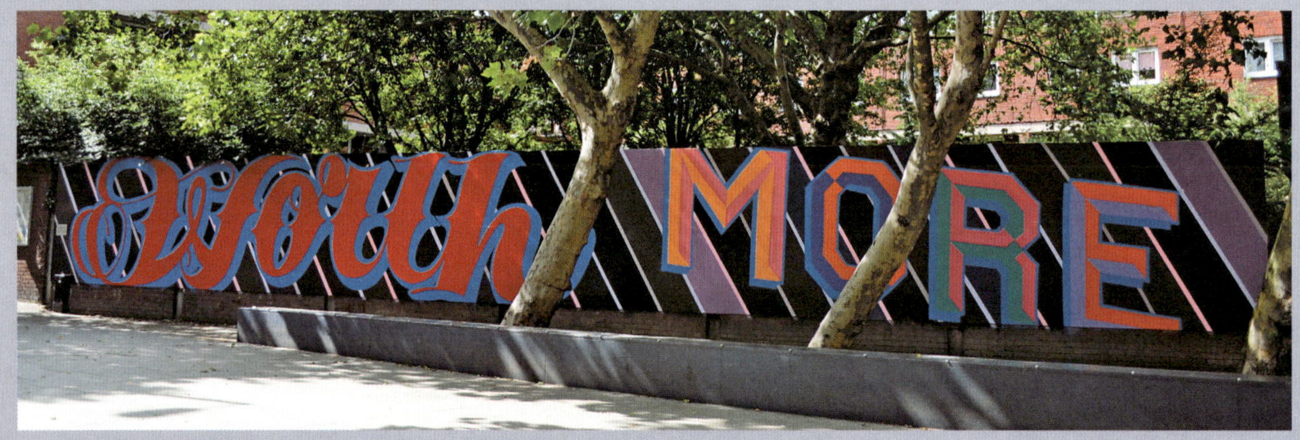

Ben Eine Old Street, London ↑

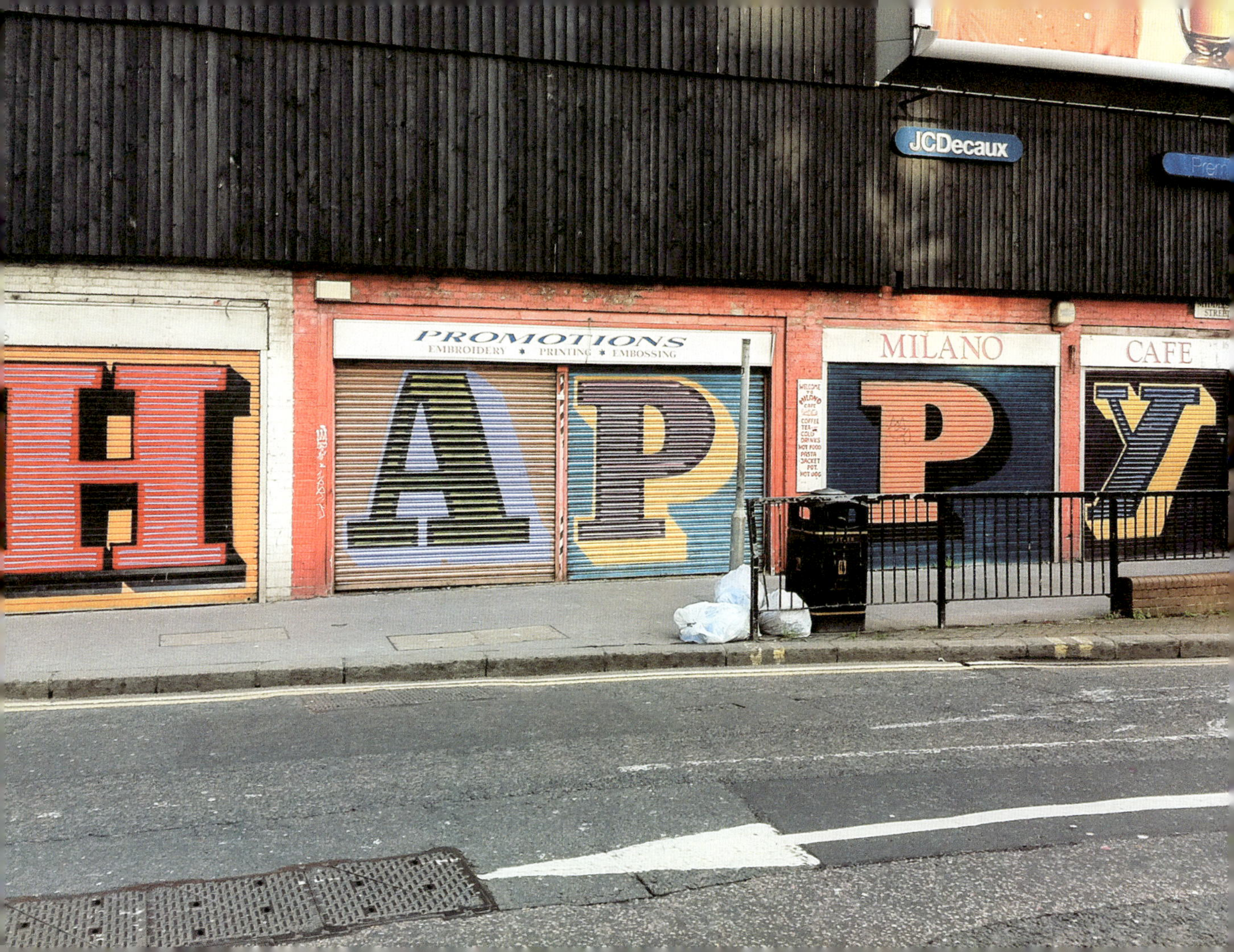
JCDecaux
PROMOTIONS
EMBROIDERY ✱ PRINTING ✱ EMBOSSING
MILANO
CAFE
H
A
P
P
Y

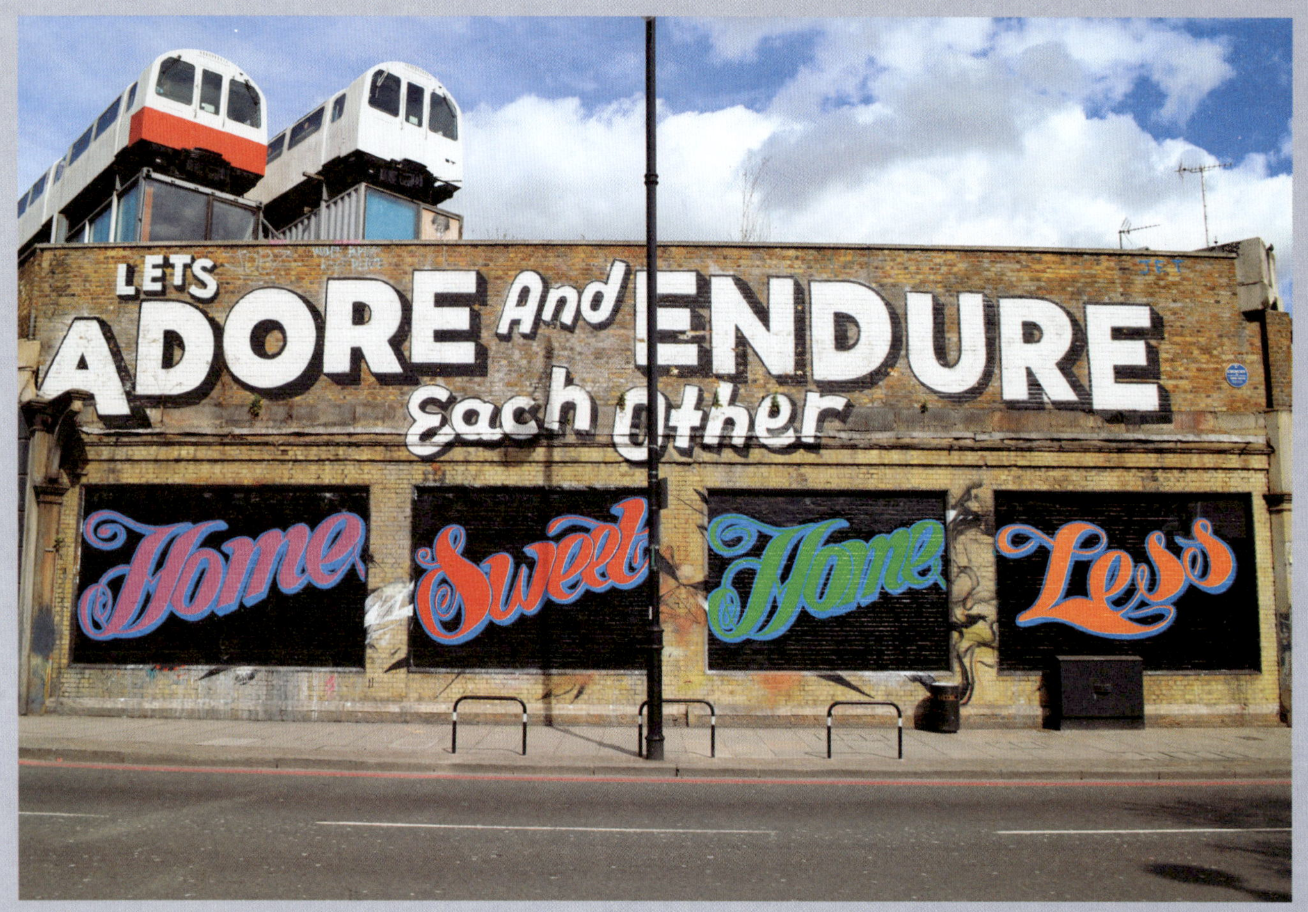

 Ben Eine/ESPO Shoreditch, London ↑

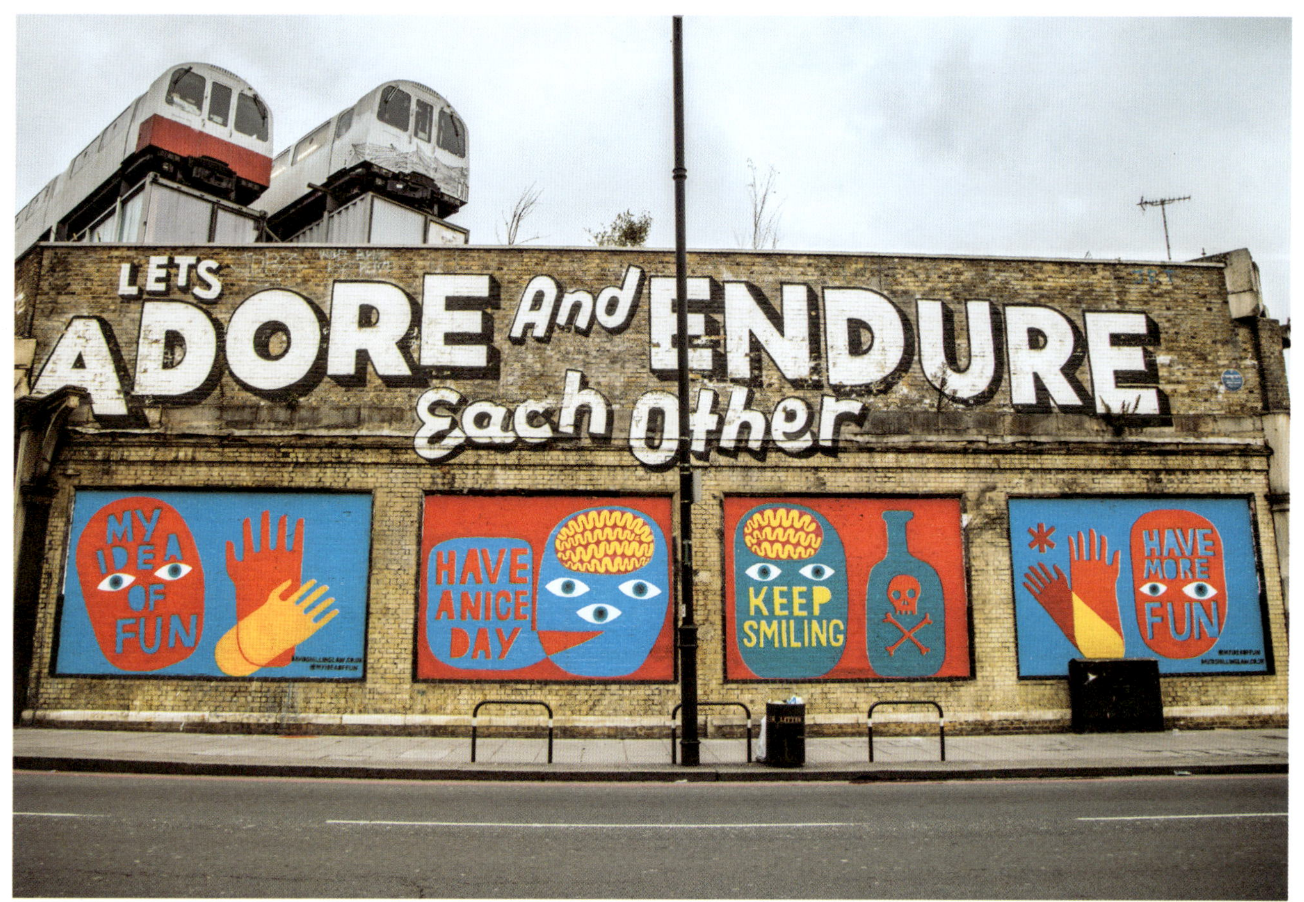

David Shillinglaw/ESPO Shoreditch, London ↑

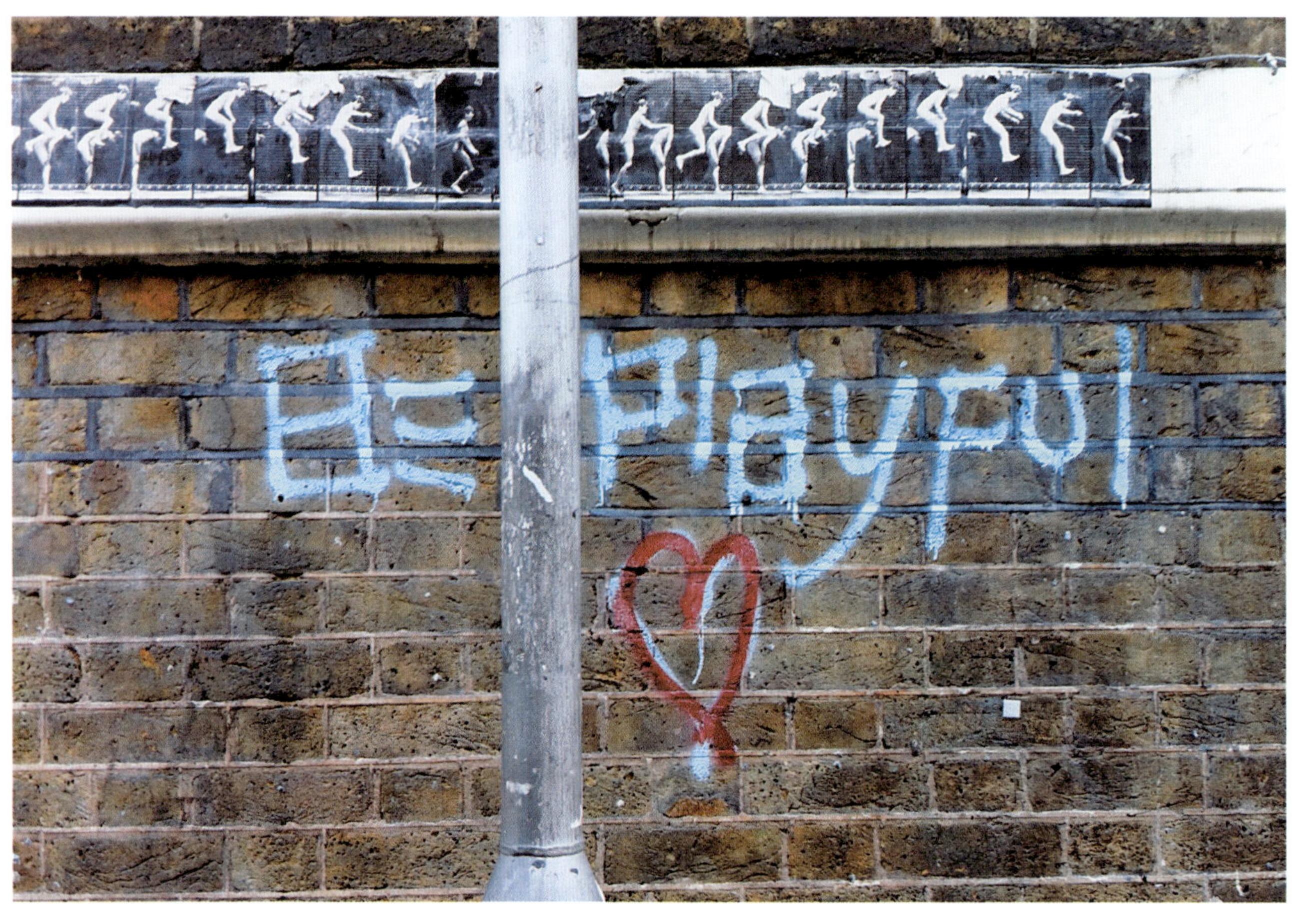

 Unknown Brick Lane, London ↑

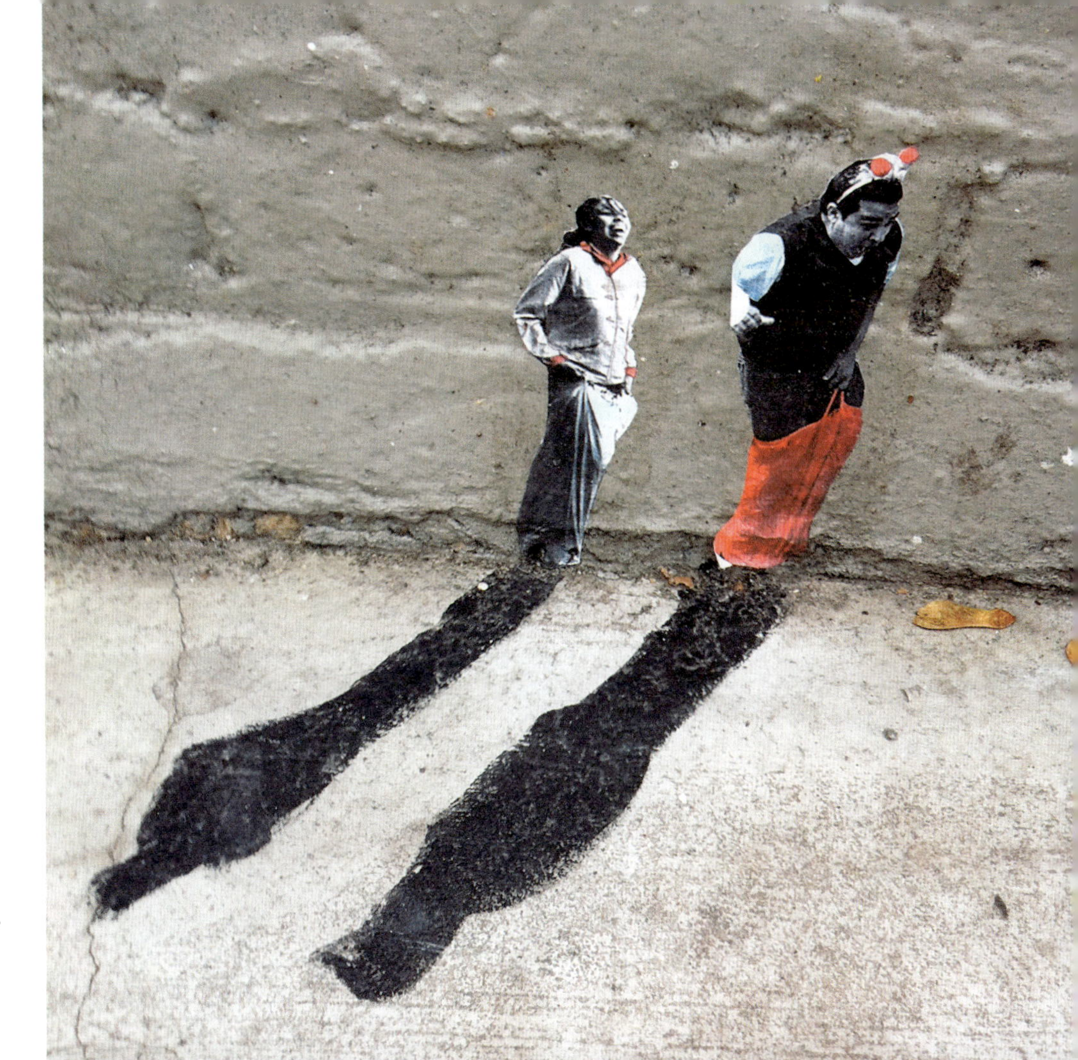

Pablo Delgado Shoreditch, London →

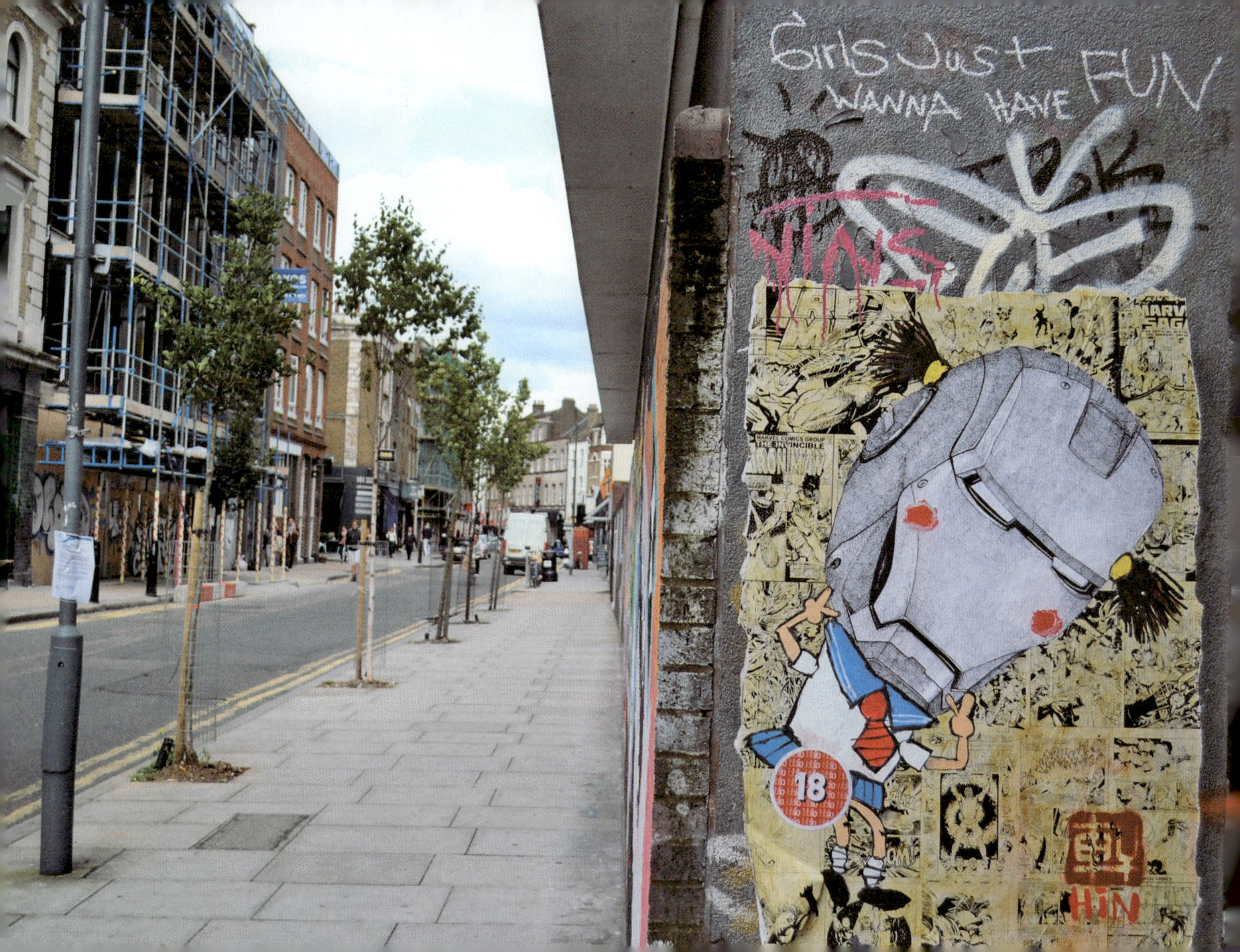
Girls Just
WANNA HAVE FUN
18
HIN

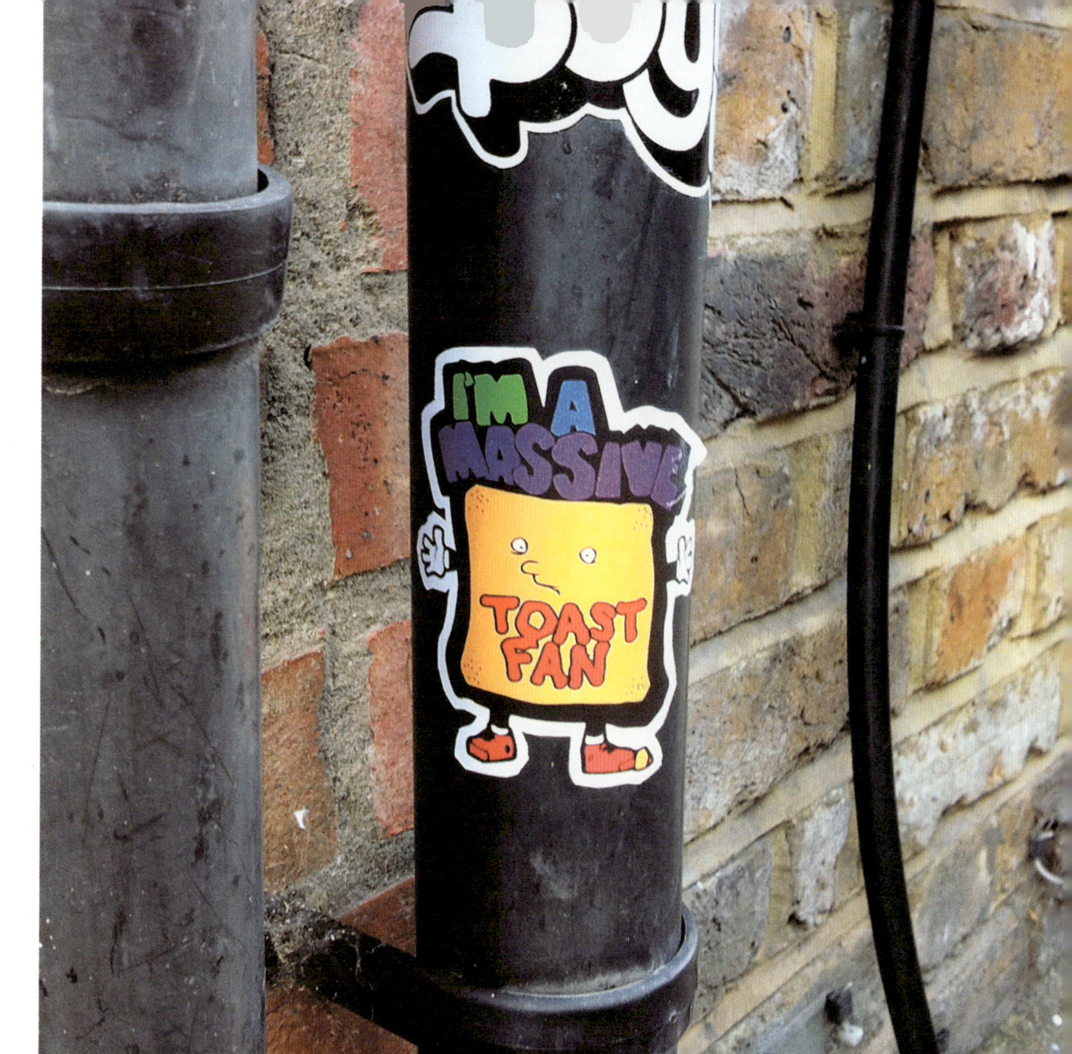

Hin Shoreditch, London ←
and **Unknown** Shoreditch, London →

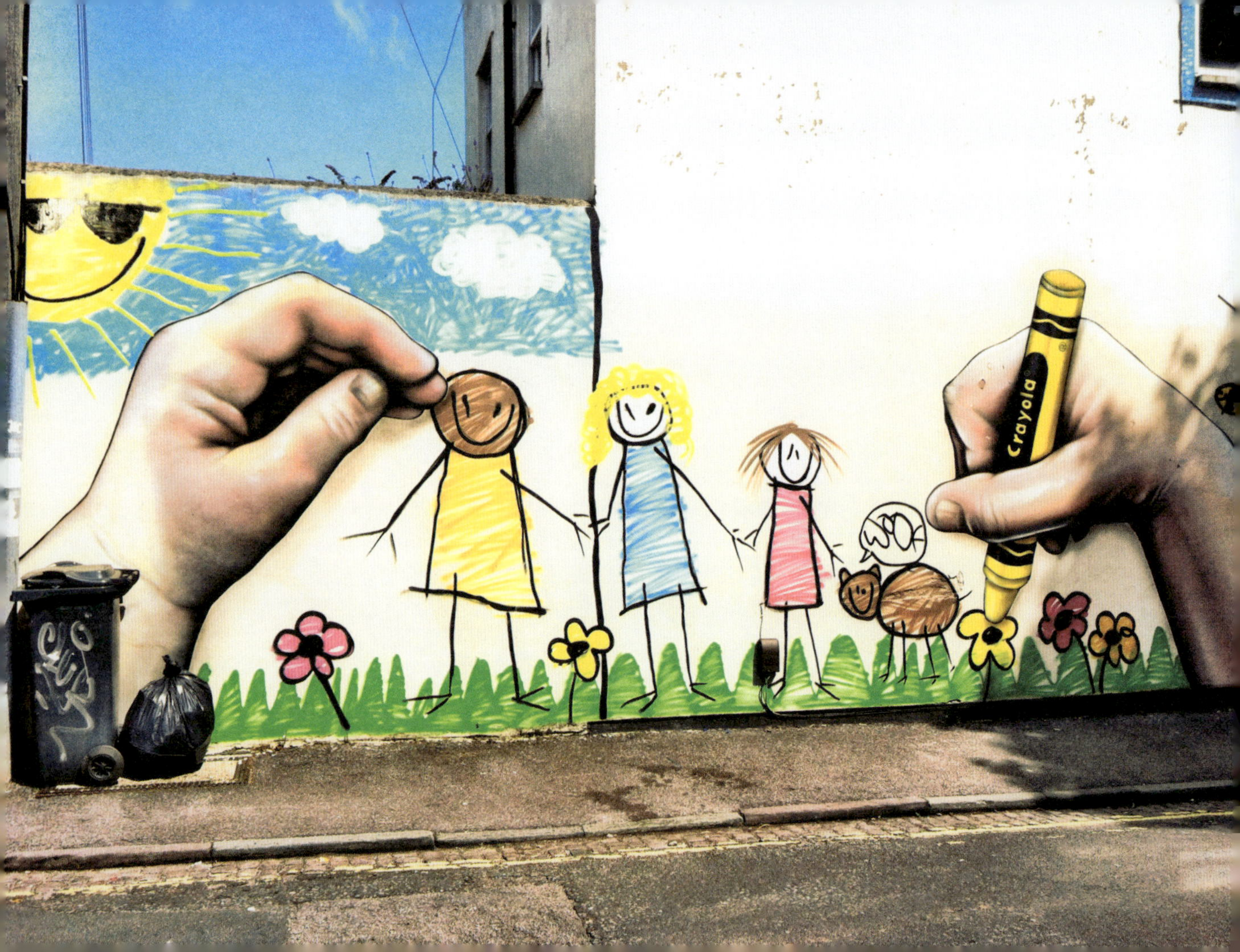
WOOF
Crayola

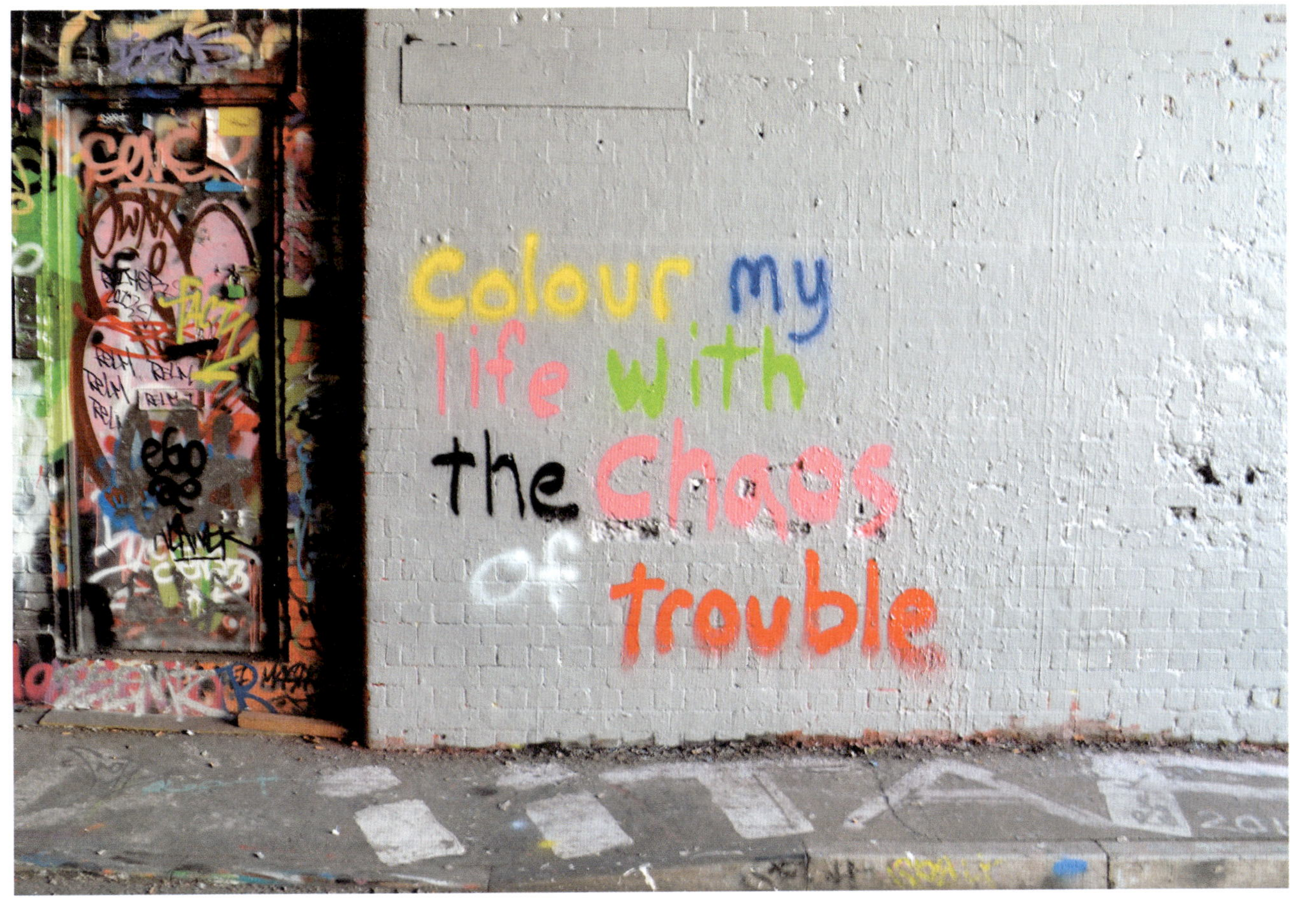

Dones Montpelier, Bristol ← and **The Girl Done Good** Leake Street Tunnel, London ↑

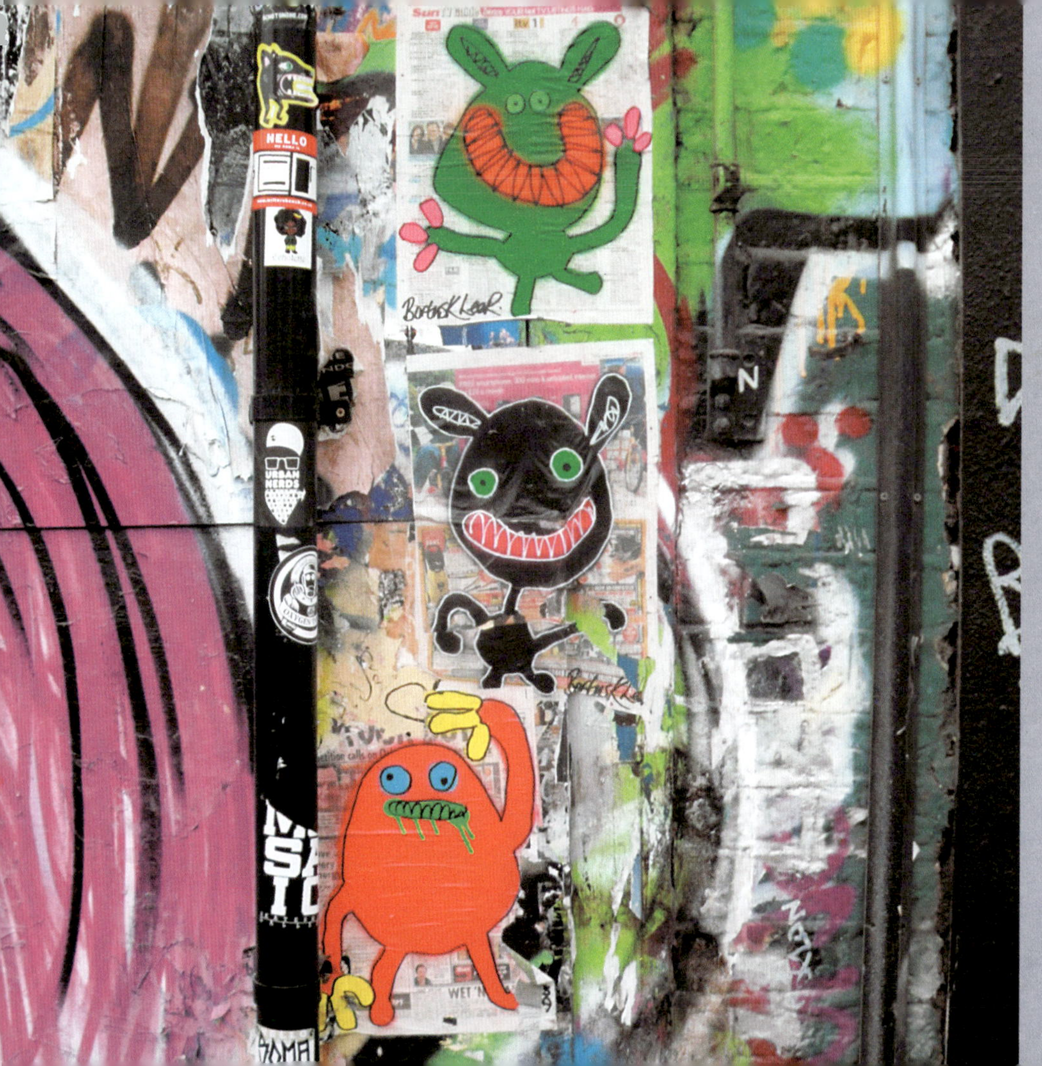

Bortusk Leer

The fruit of a forbidden love between a one-legged trapeze artist and a retired communist party official turned dancing-ferret-trainer, Leer's early years are shrouded in mystery (some say he came from a nuclear bunker, others claim the circus). But what *is* known is that by his teens he could be found joyfully daubing walls around the globe with his fantastical childlike characters and psychedelic vermin. 'Art Comedy' was born and Leer never looked back (especially when being chased by the secret-secret police with pictures of big-headed monsters streaming out behind him).

His mission statement is simply to cheer you up a bit and put a smile on your face.

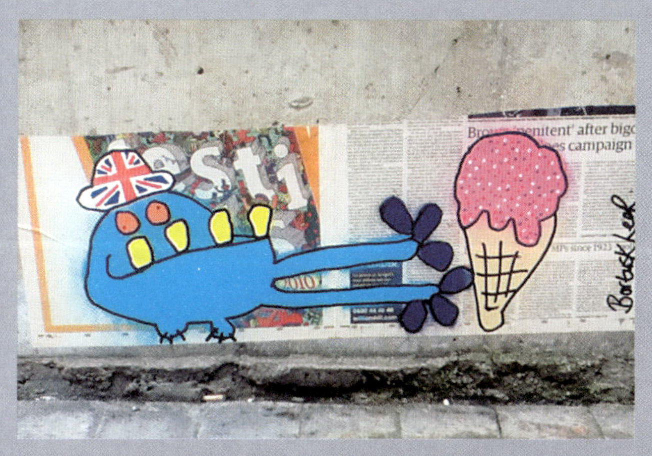

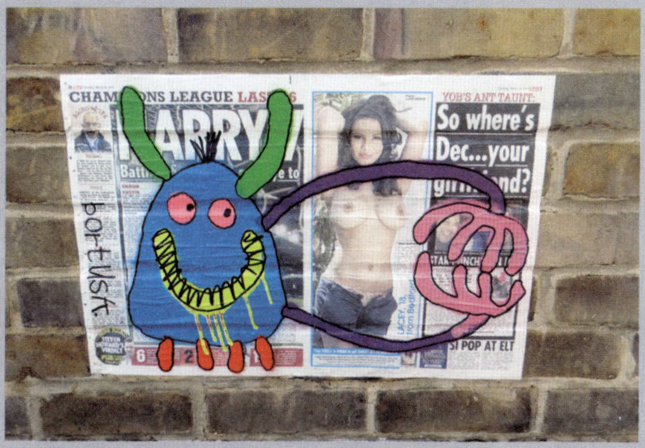

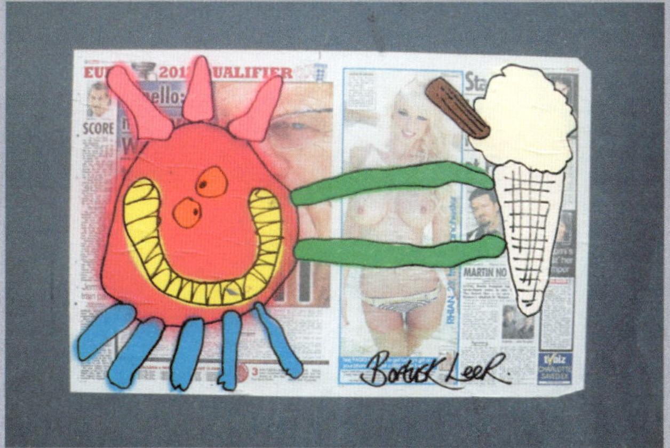

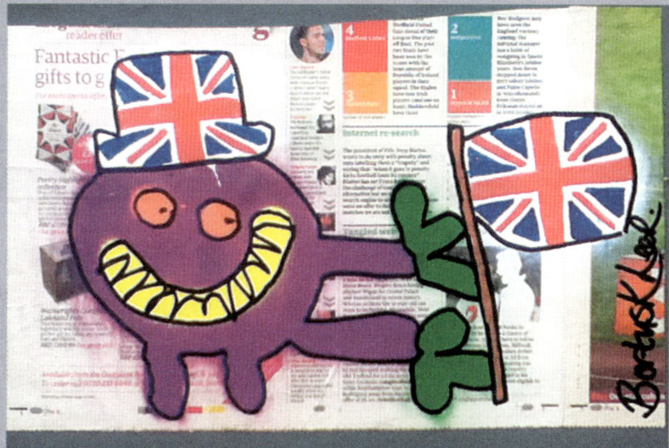

Bortusk Leer Hackney, London ← and Hackney, London (top right) and Shoreditch, London ↑

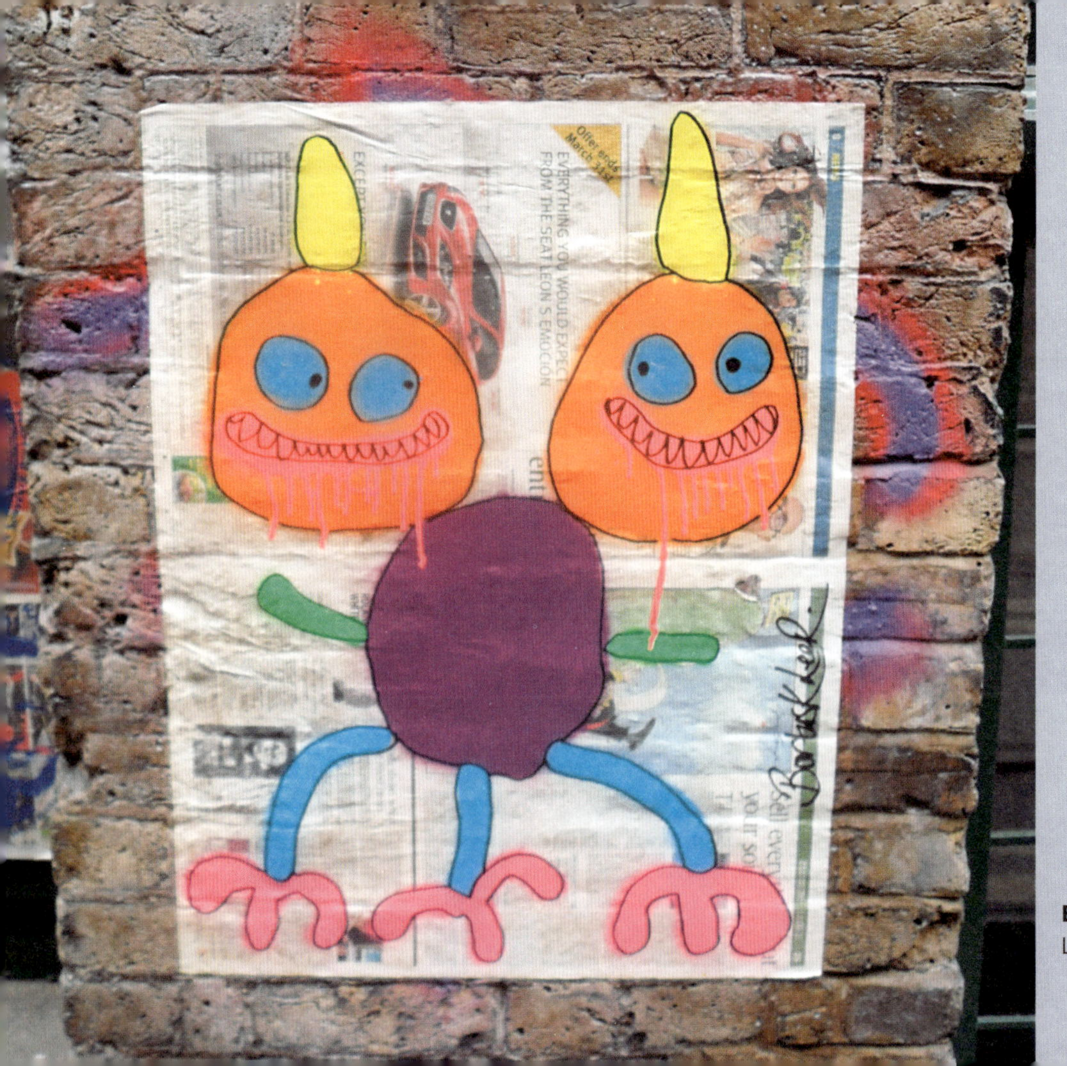

Bortusk Leer Hackney, London ←

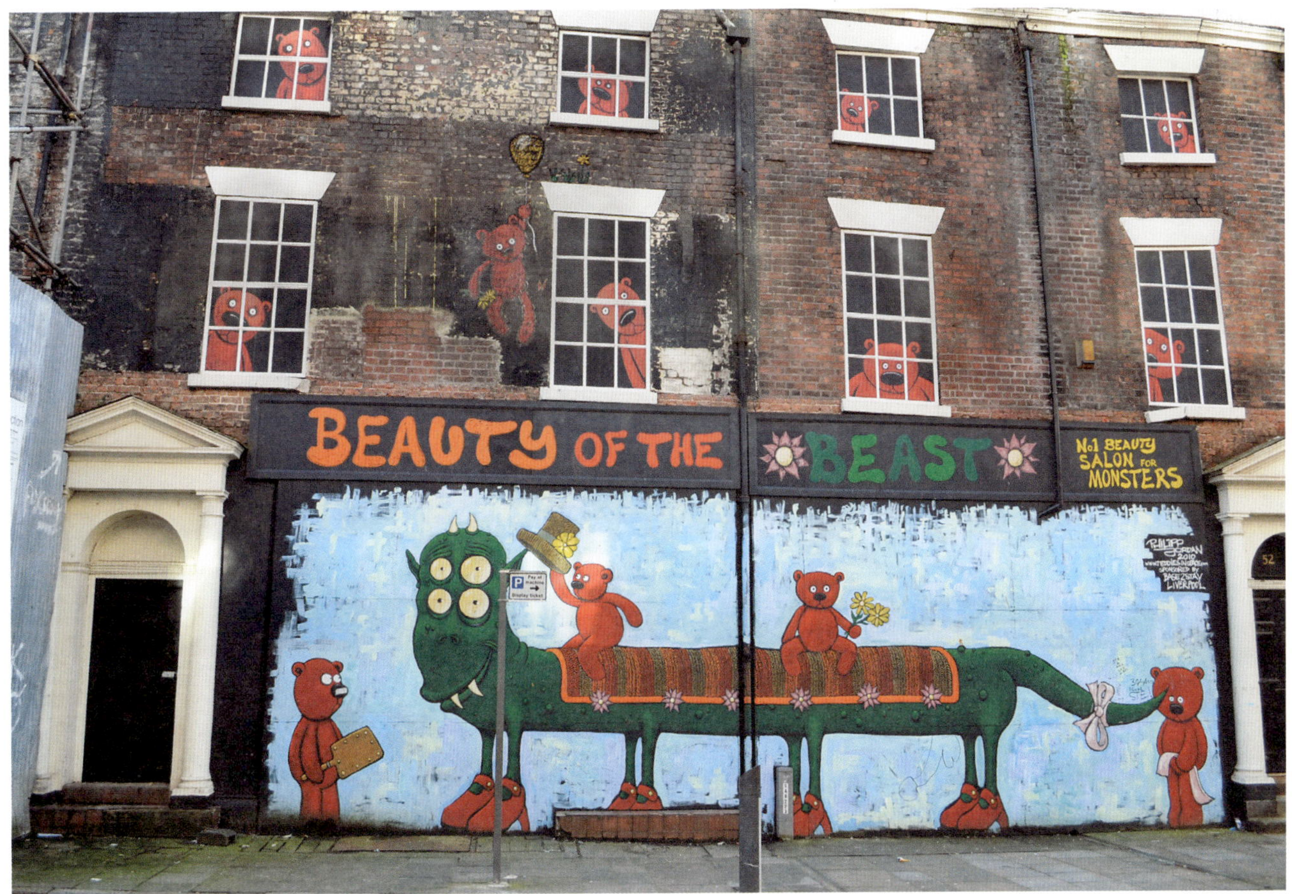

Philipp Jordan Seel Street, Liverpool ↑

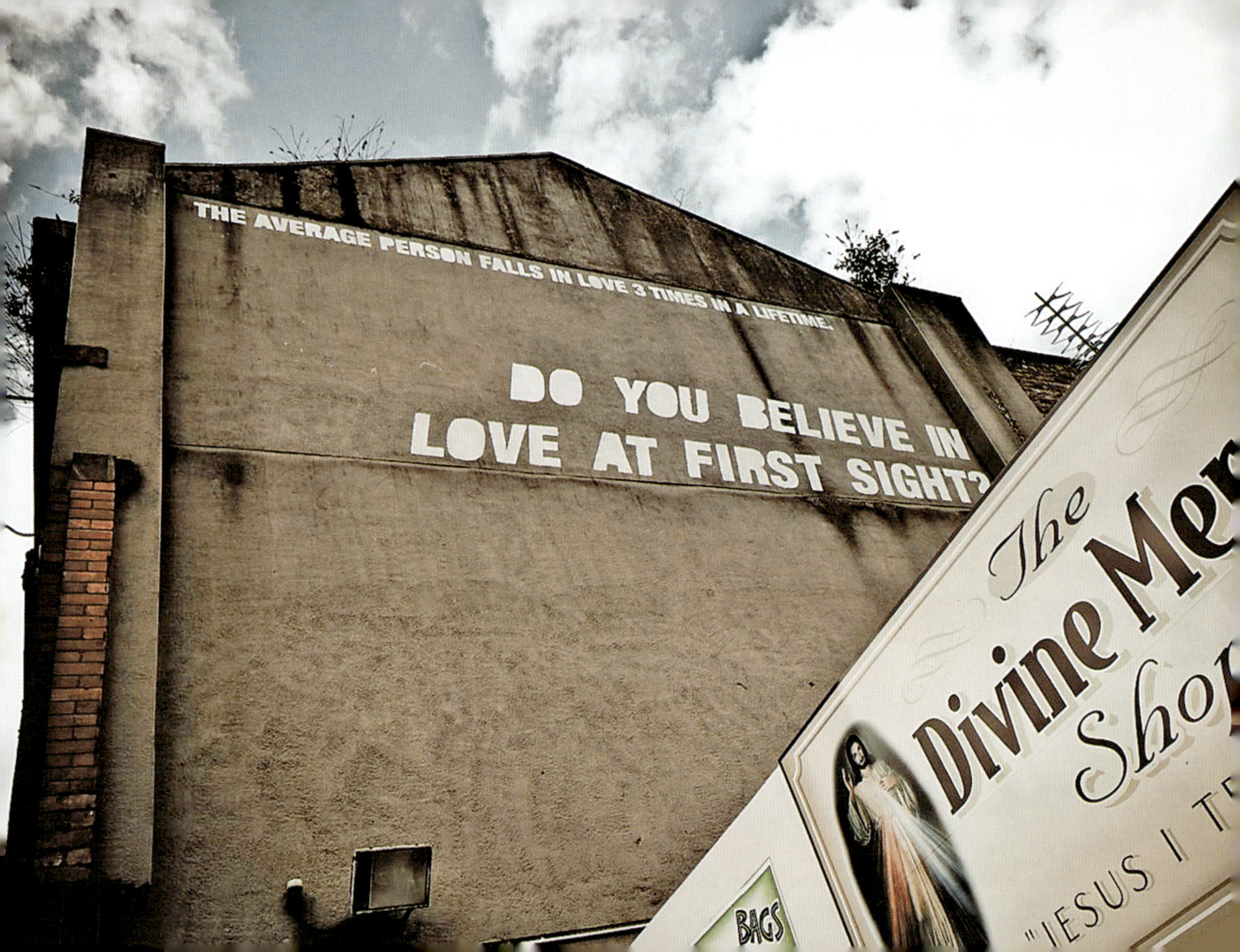
THE AVERAGE PERSON FALLS IN LOVE 3 TIMES IN A LIFETIME.
DO YOU BELIEVE IN LOVE AT FIRST SIGHT?
The
Divine
BAGS

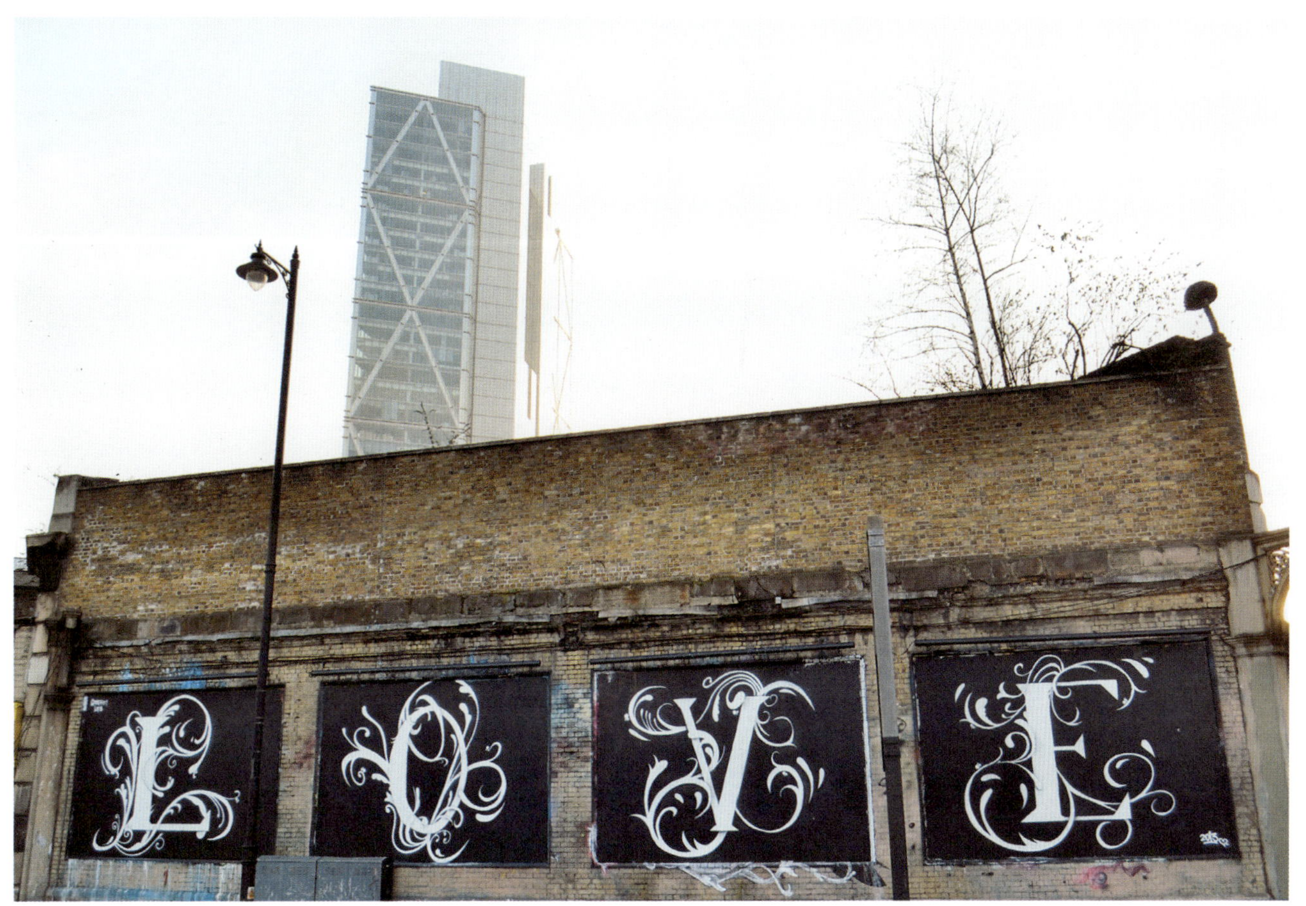

Visible Virals London Road, Liverpool ← and **Graffiti Life** Shoreditch, London ↑

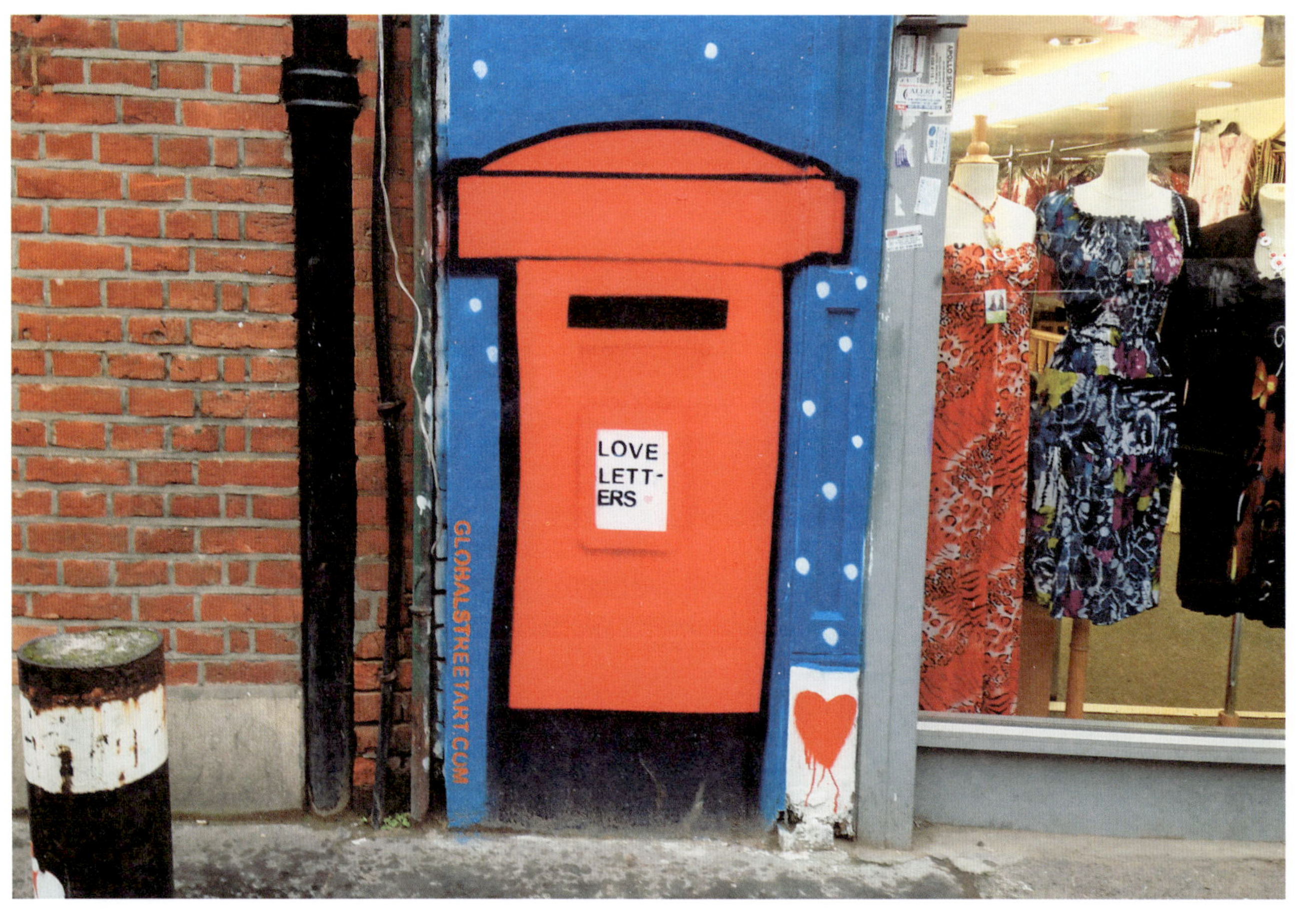

 Hunto Shoreditch, London ↑ and **Levingos** Euston station, London →

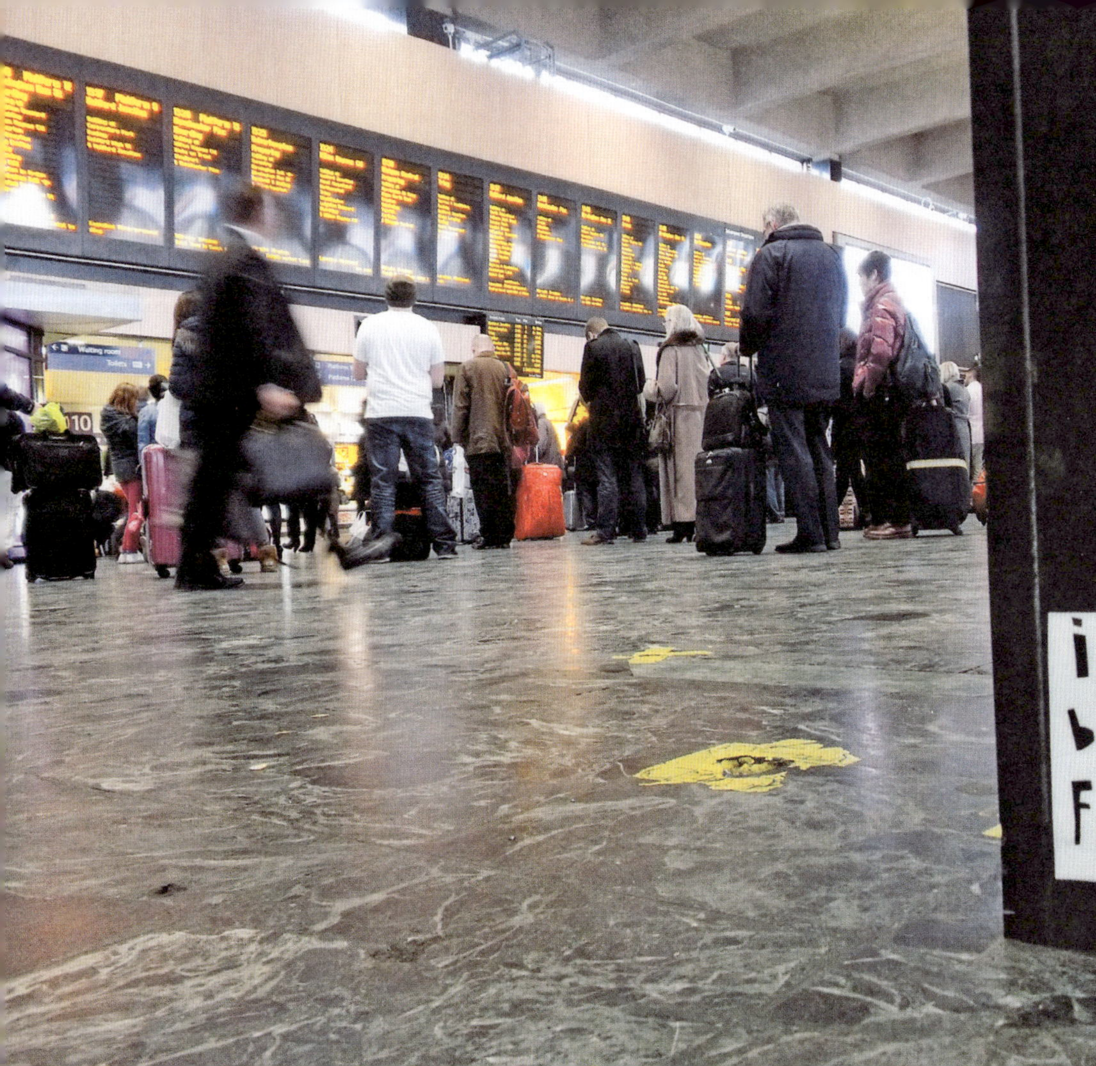
i felt
butter-
flieS

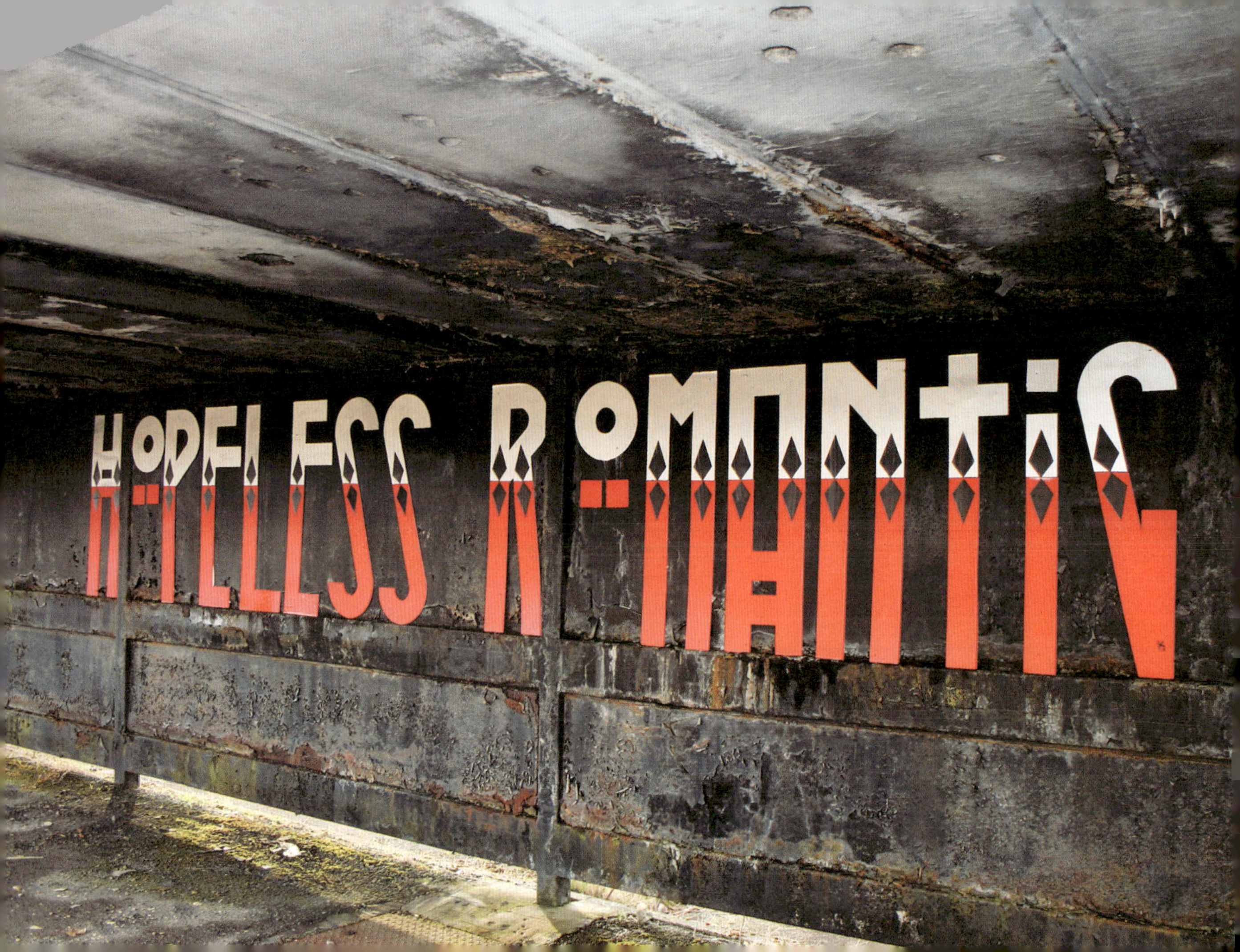
HOPELESS ROMANTIC

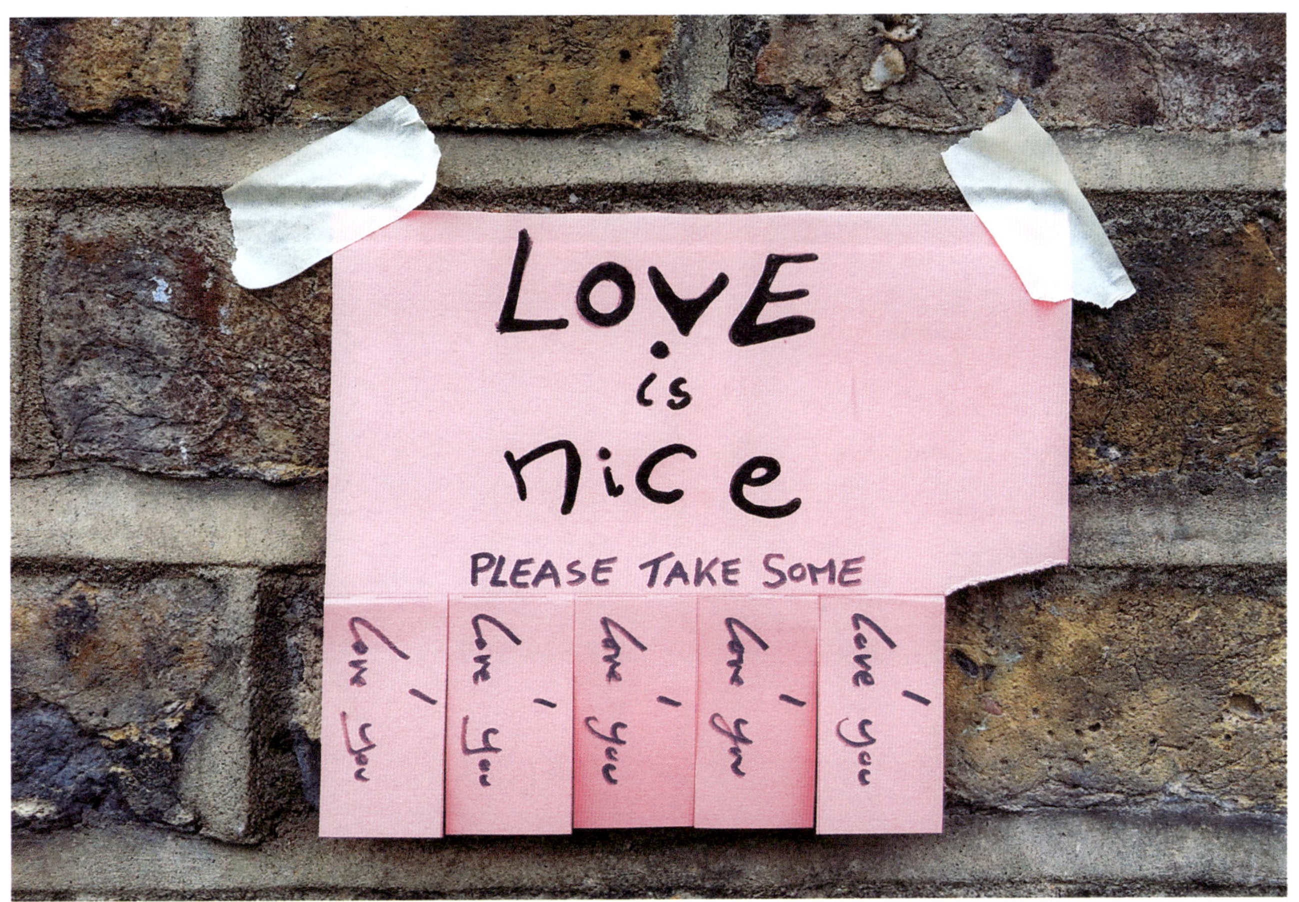

Throne Glasgow ← and **Martina O'Shea** Hackney Wick, London ↑

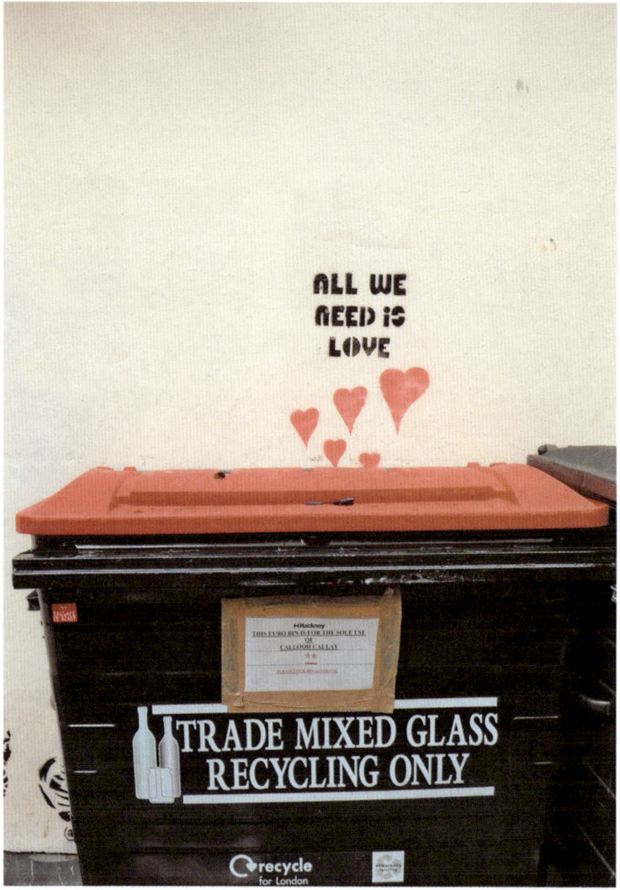

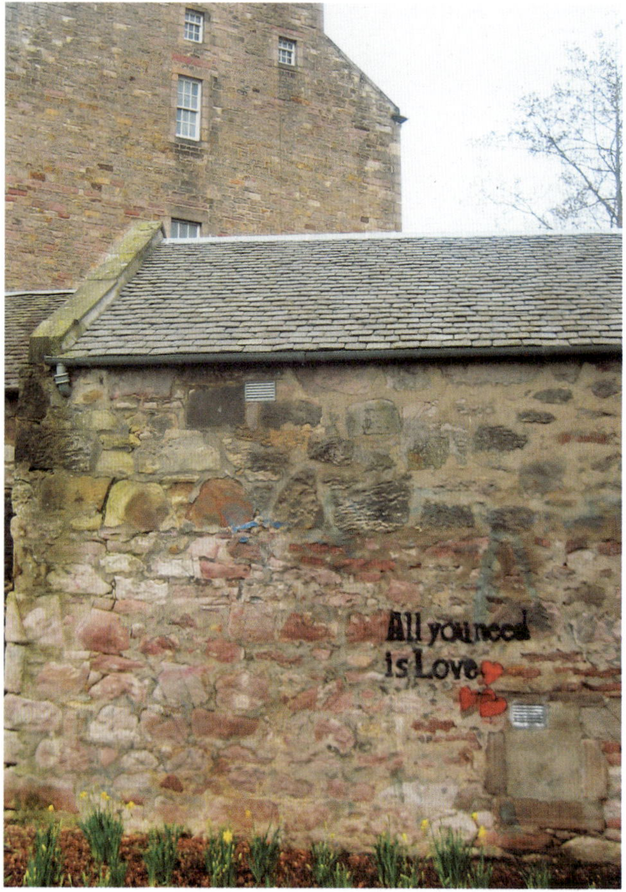

Unknown Shoreditch, London, **Unknown** The Meadows, Edinburgh ↑ and **Unknown** Hackney Wick, London →

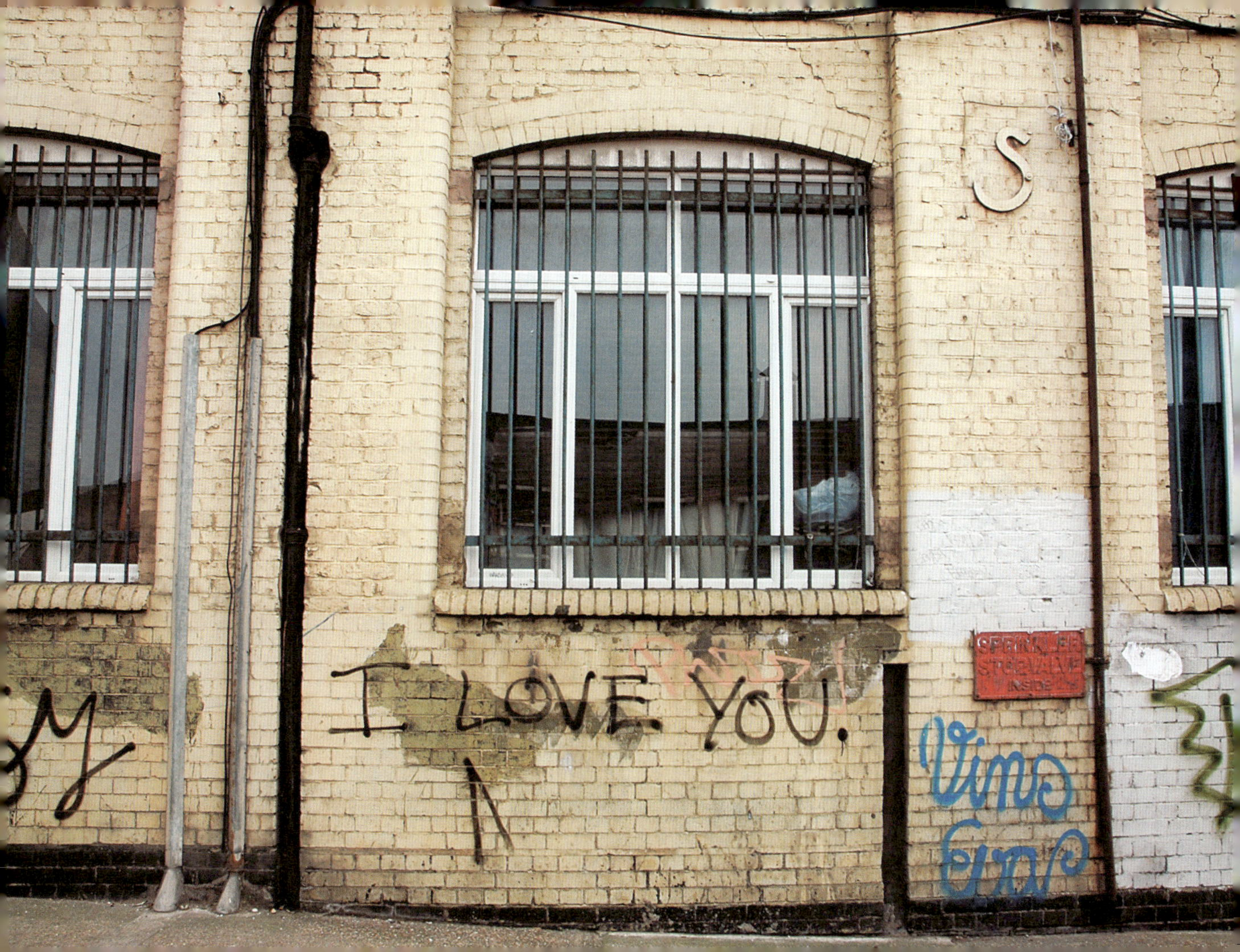

I LOVE YOU.
SPRINKLER
INSIDE

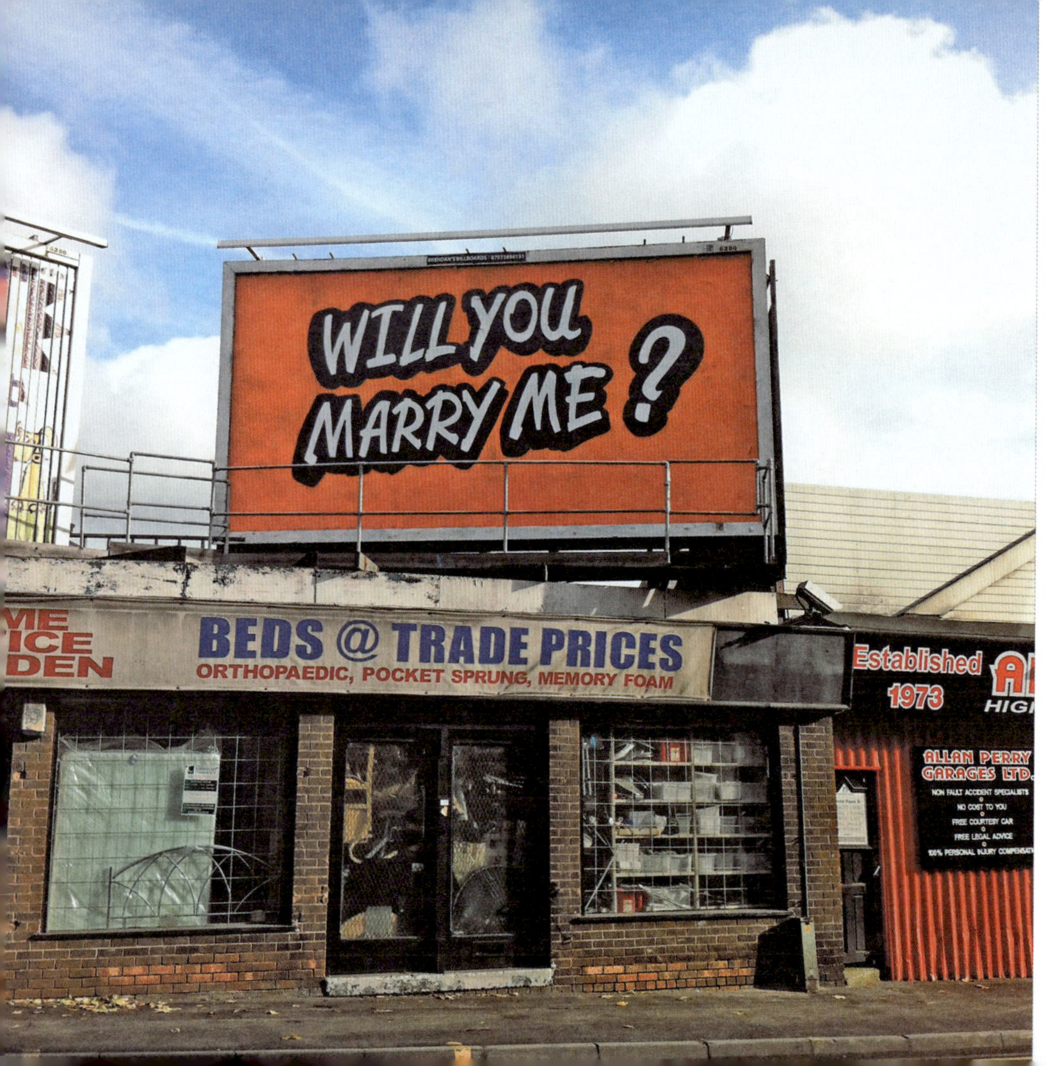

Kid30 Huntingdon Street, Nottingham ← and **Unknown** Victoria Park, London →

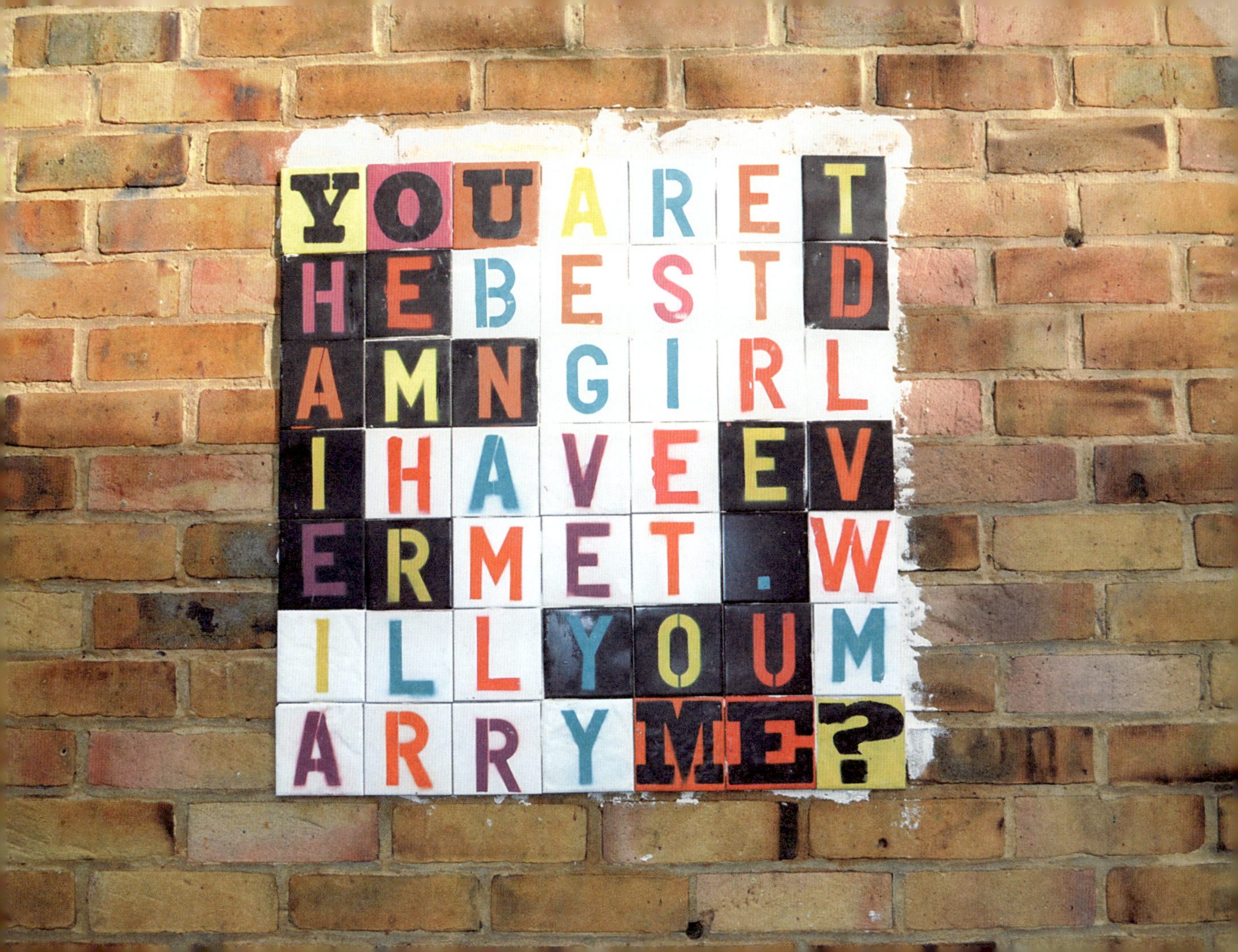
YOUARET
HEBESTD
AMNGIRL
IHAVEEV
ERMET.W
ILLYOUM
ARRYME?

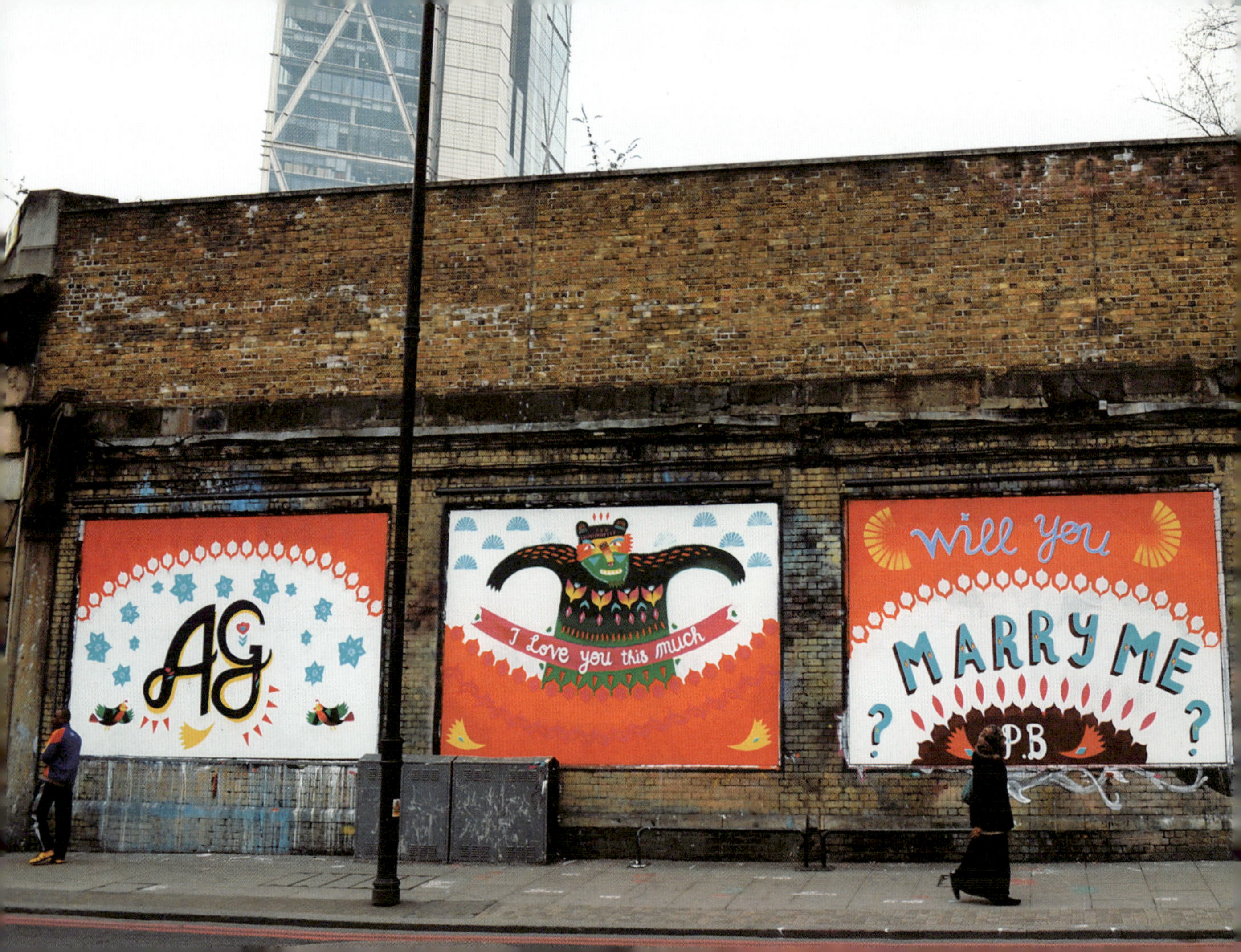
AG
I Love you this much
will you
MARRY ME
?
P.B
?

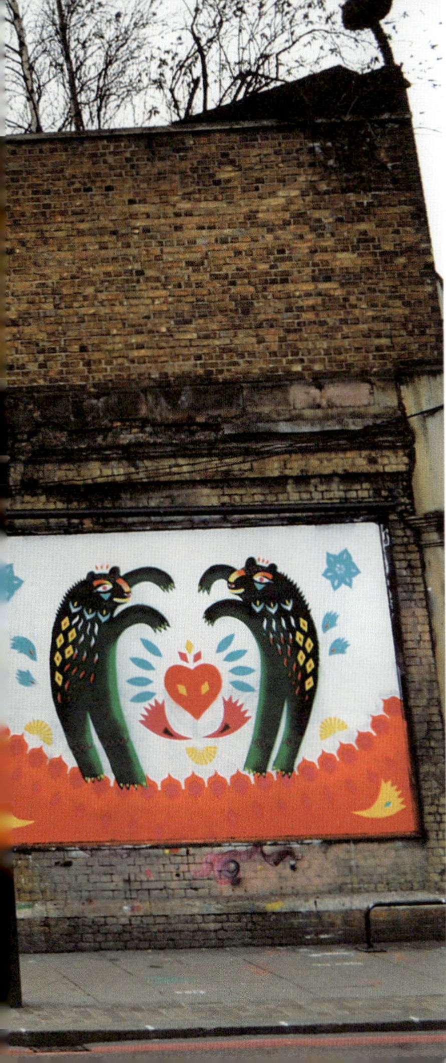

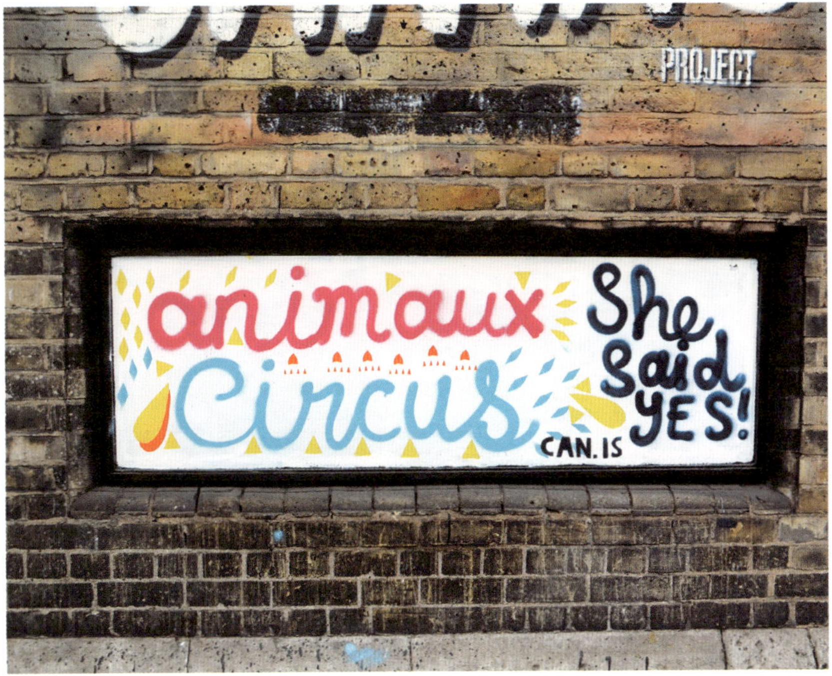

Animaux Circus Shoreditch, London ← and Shoreditch, London ↑

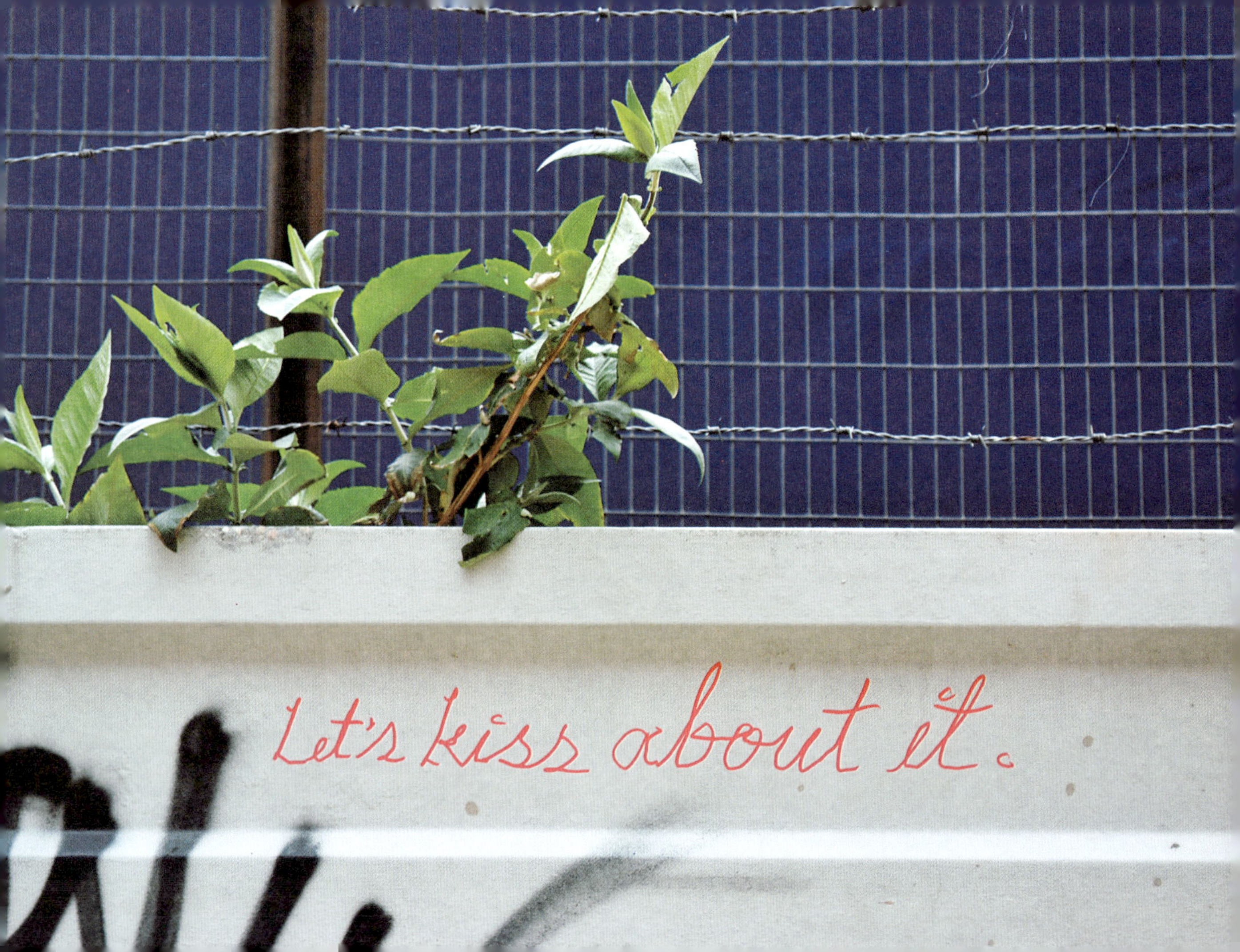
Let's kiss about it.

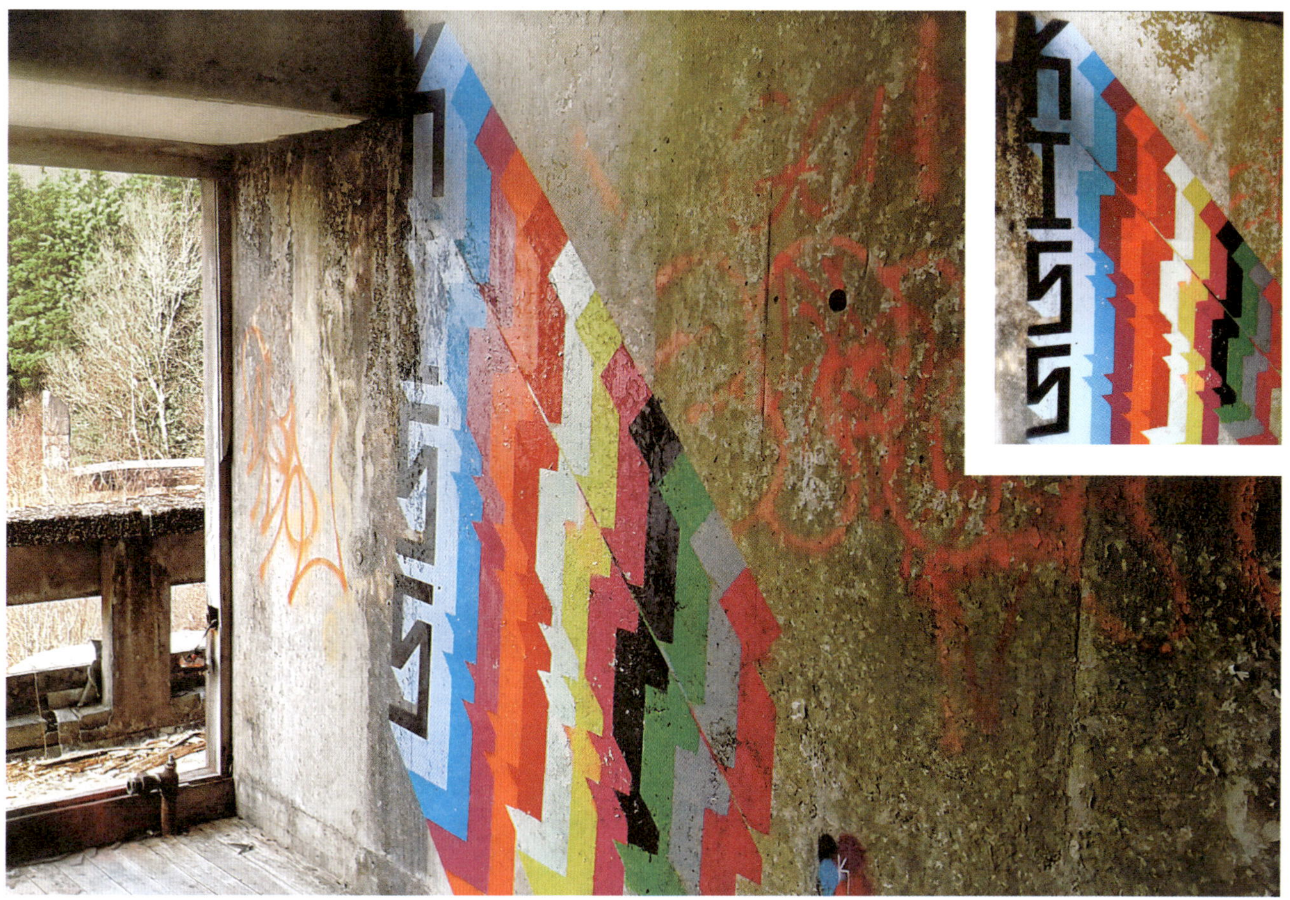

Unknown Shoreditch, London ← and **Throne** Glasgow ↑

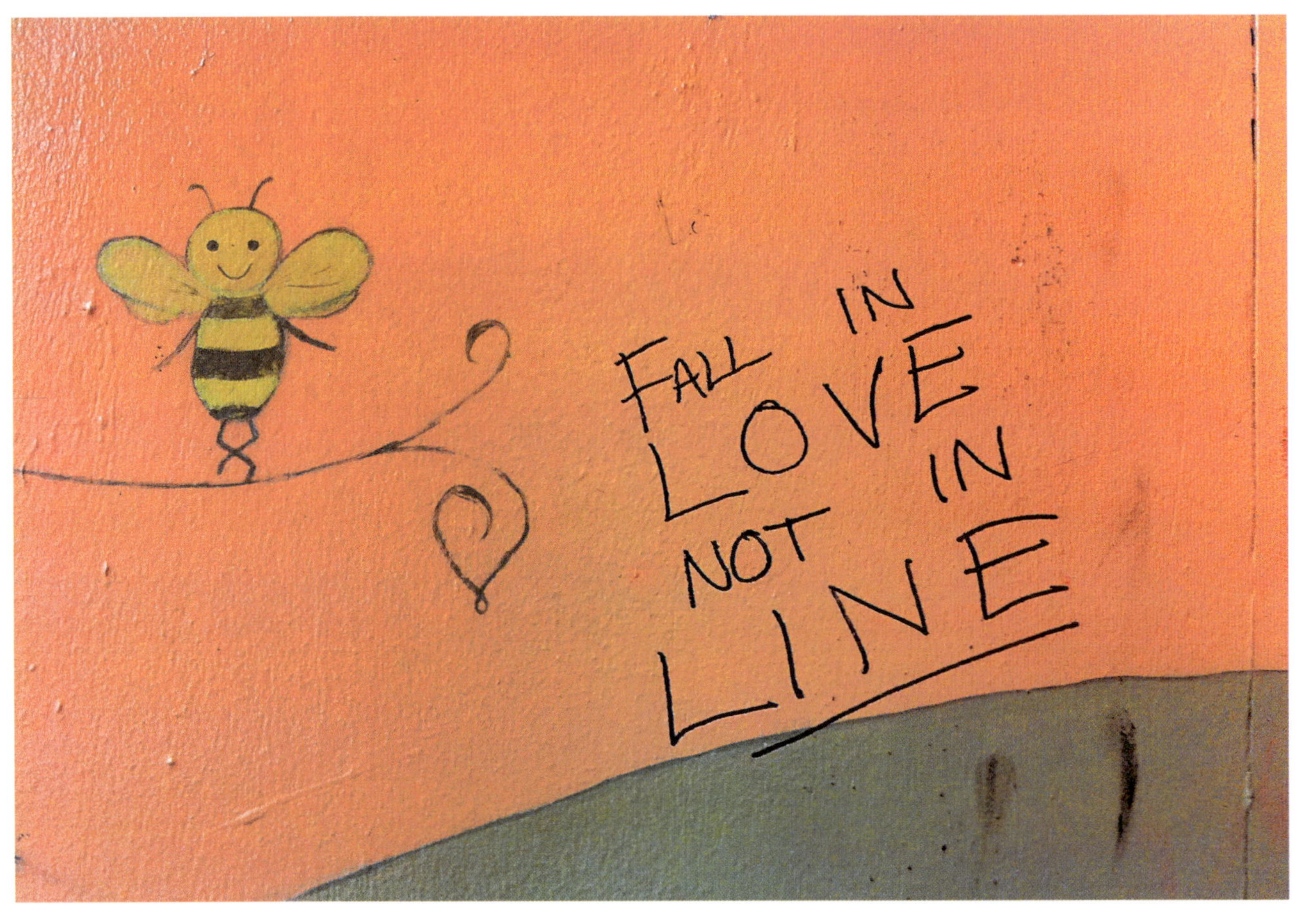

 Unknown Brick Lane, London ↑

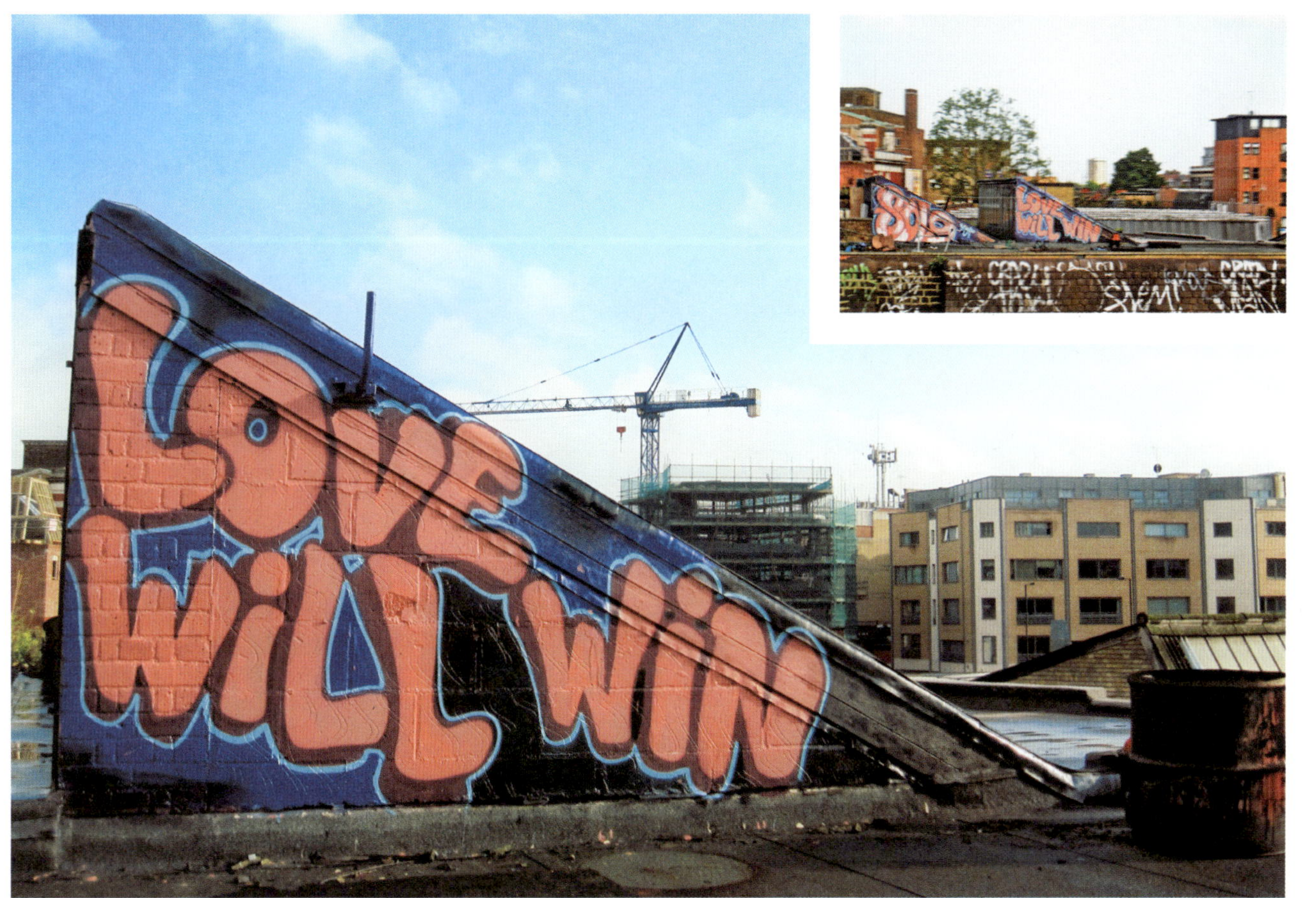

Solo One London Fields, London ↑

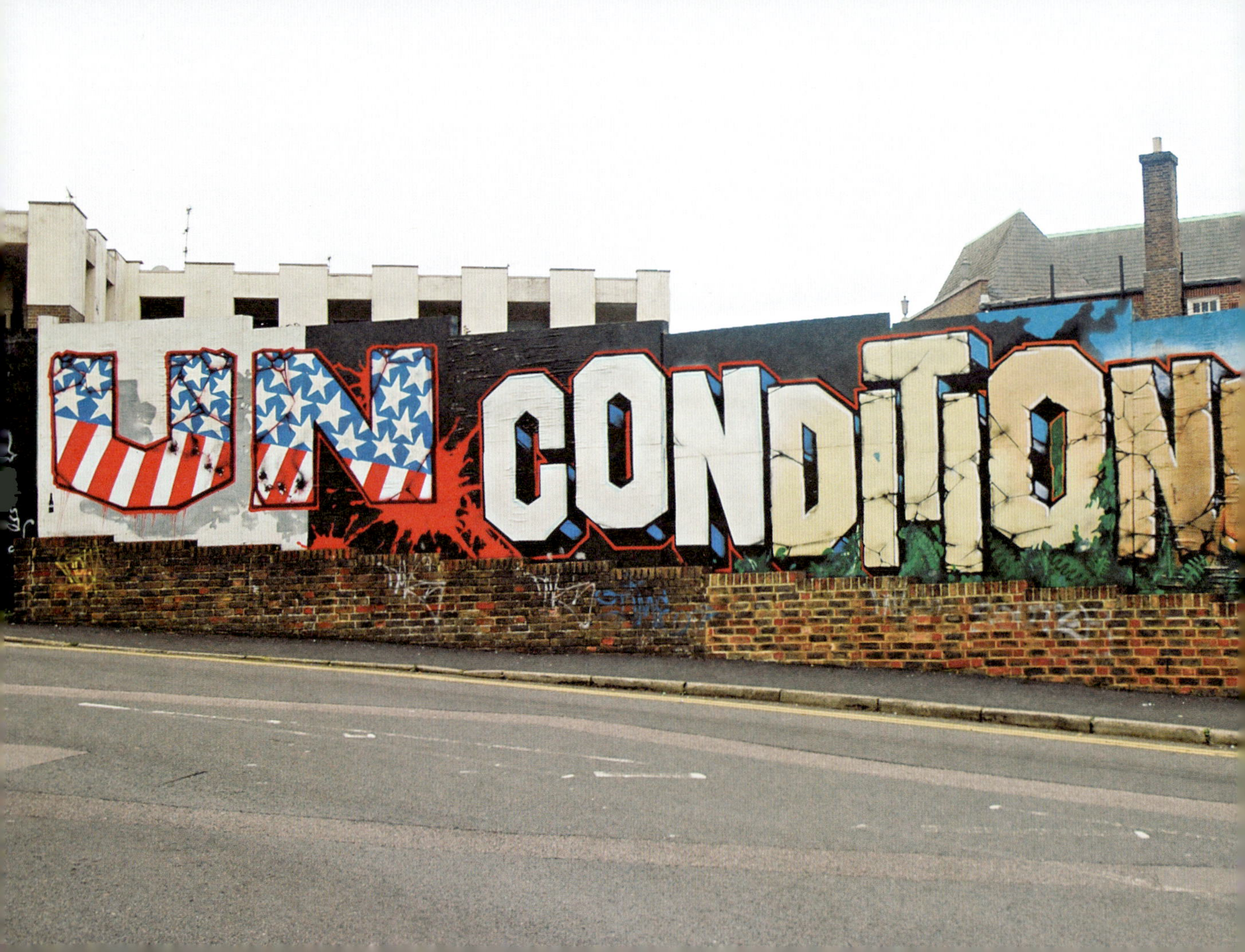
UNCONDITION

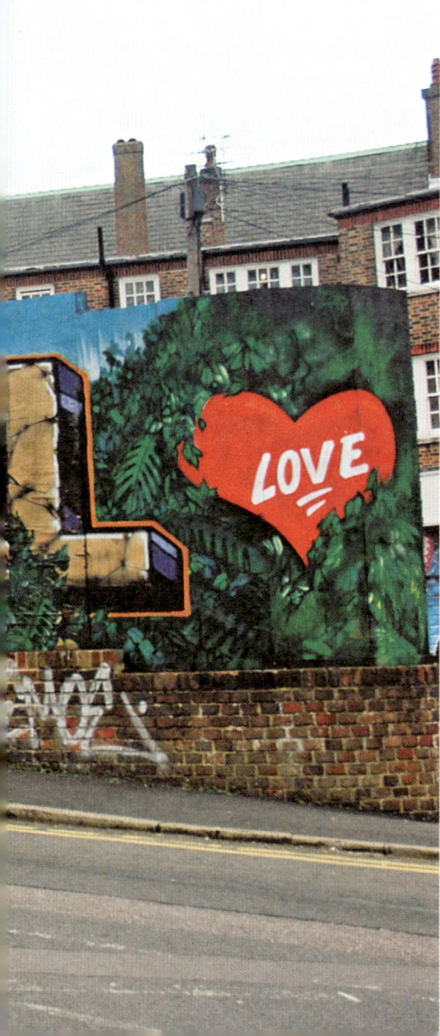

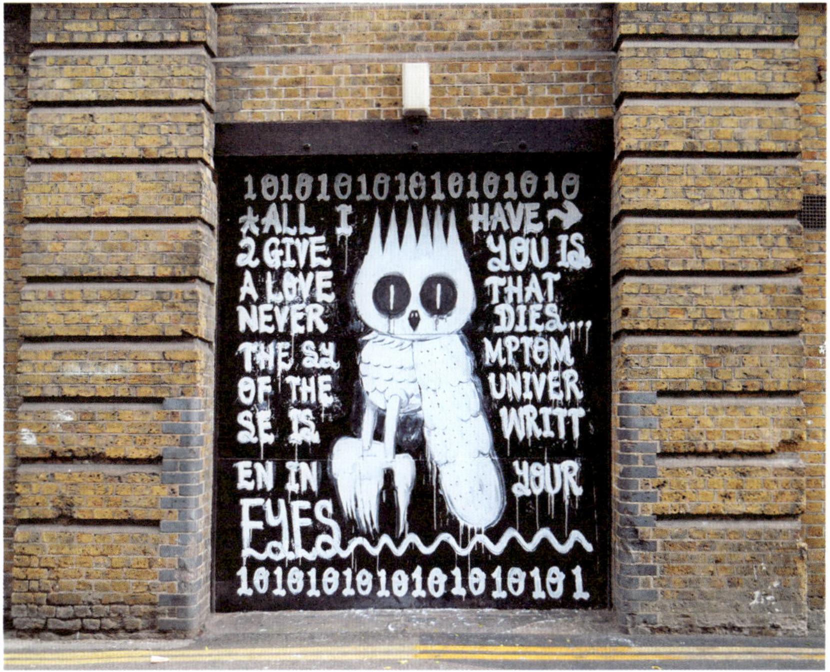

Unknown Elder Place, Brighton ← and **Dscreet** Shoreditch, London ↑

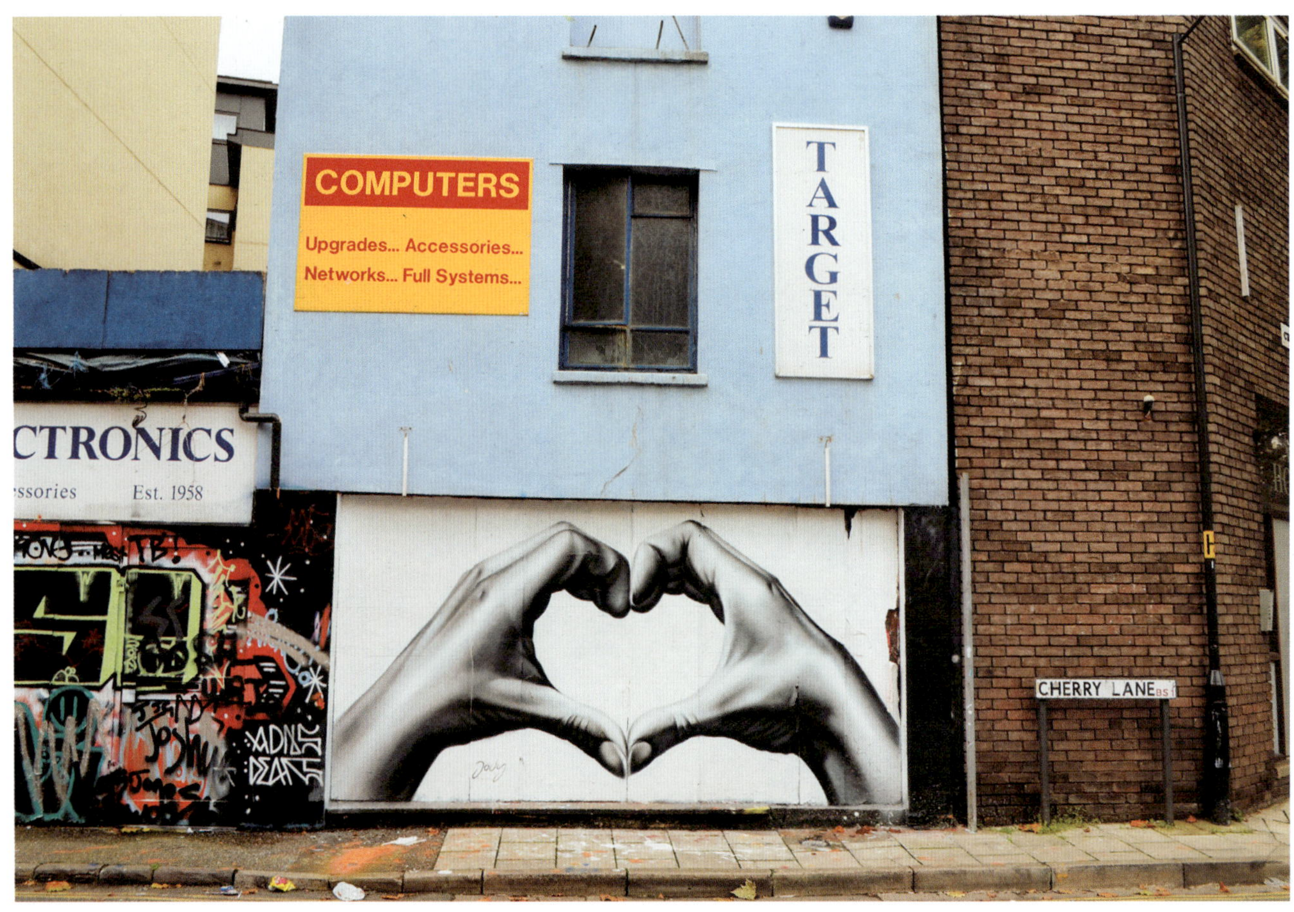

 Jody Stokes Croft, Bristol ↑ and **Unknown** Hackney Road, London →

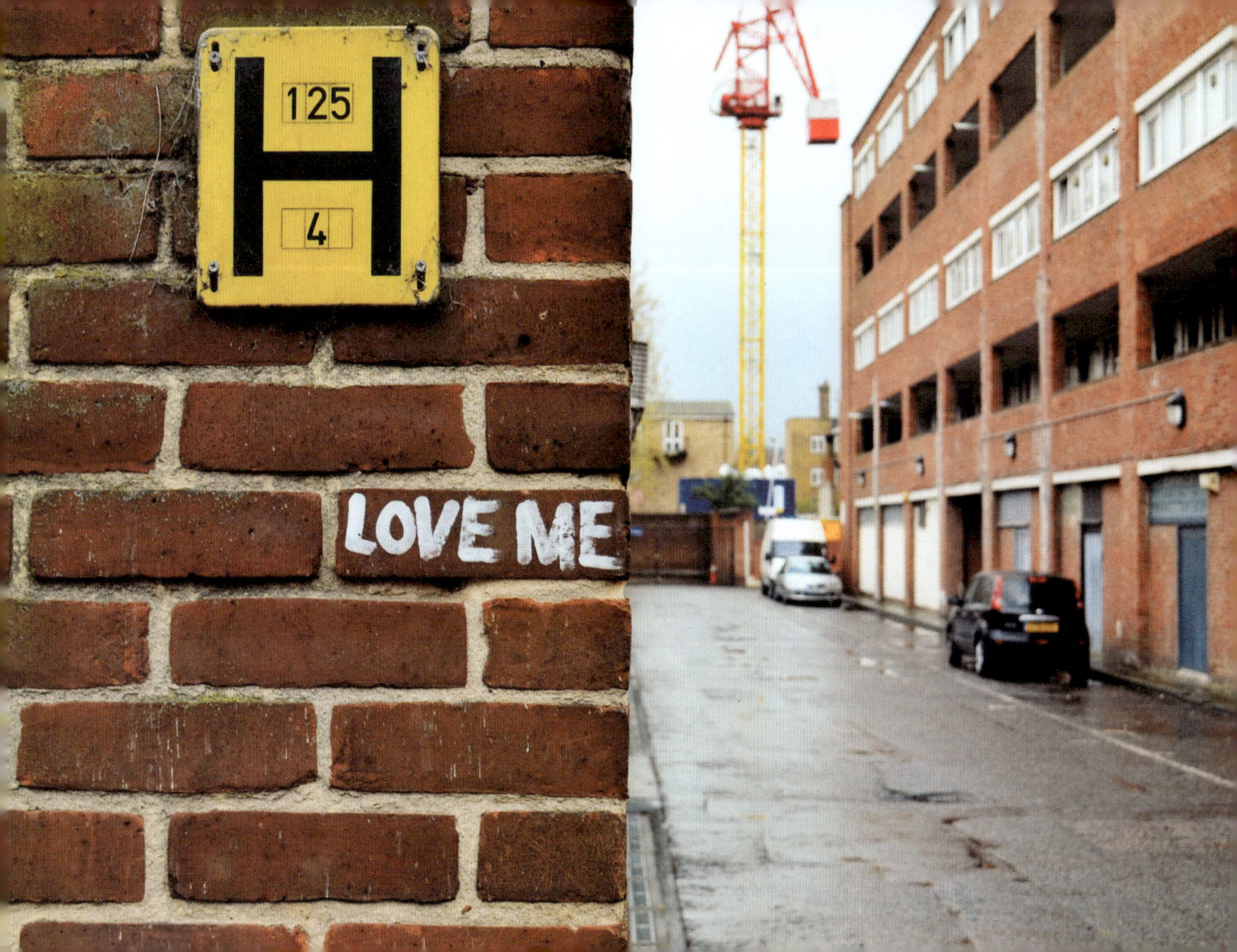
H
125
4
LOVE ME

Morley

Morley specializes in bold, typographic posters which he wheatpastes within the urban landscape. Blending humour, hope and his unique perspective on life, Morley's aim is to act as a friendly voice amongst the cacophony of billboard messages and corporate slogans.

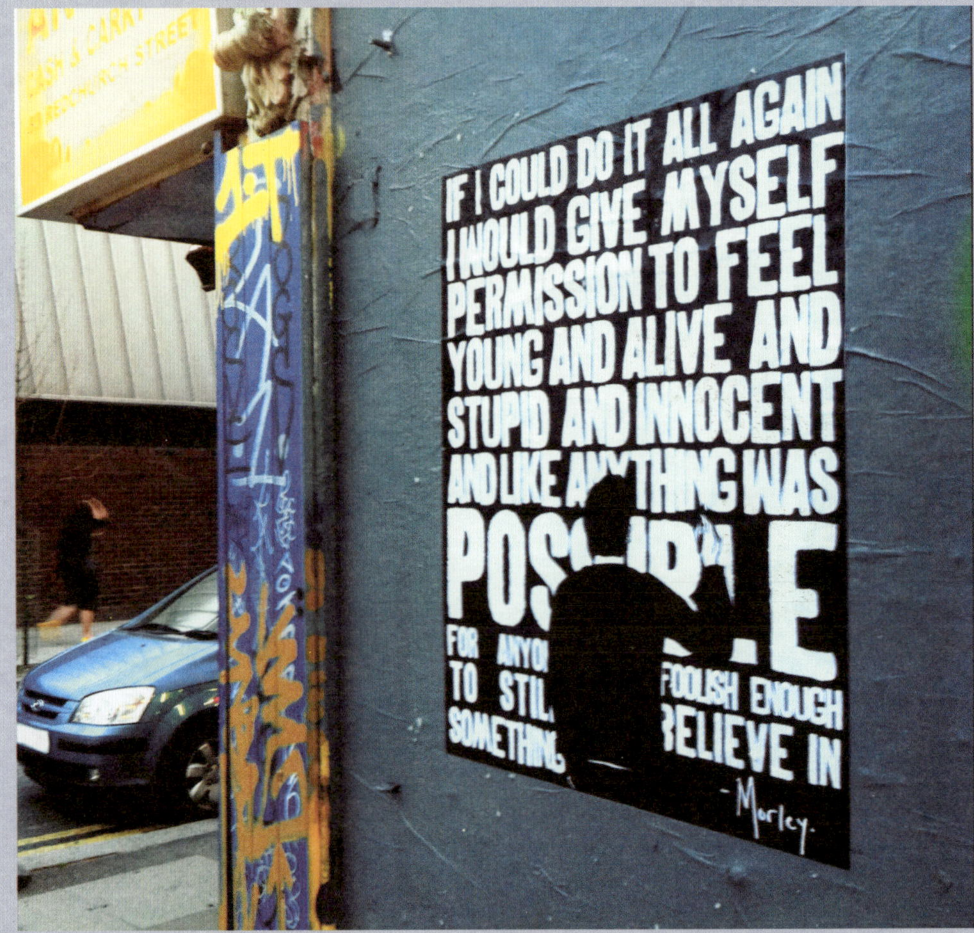

Morley Hackney, London and Shoreditch, London →

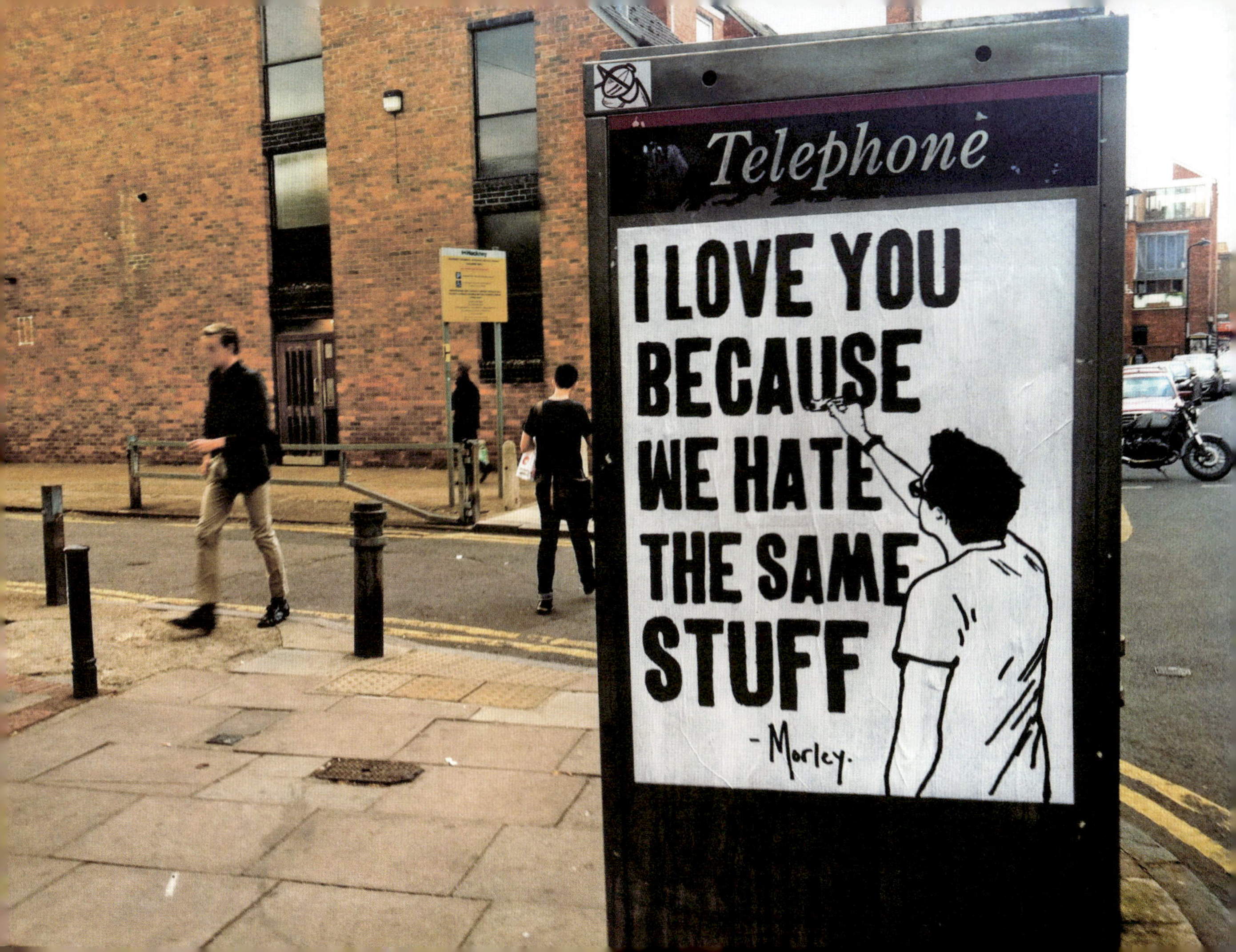
Telephone
I LOVE YOU
BECAUSE
WE HATE
THE SAME
STUFF
- Morley.

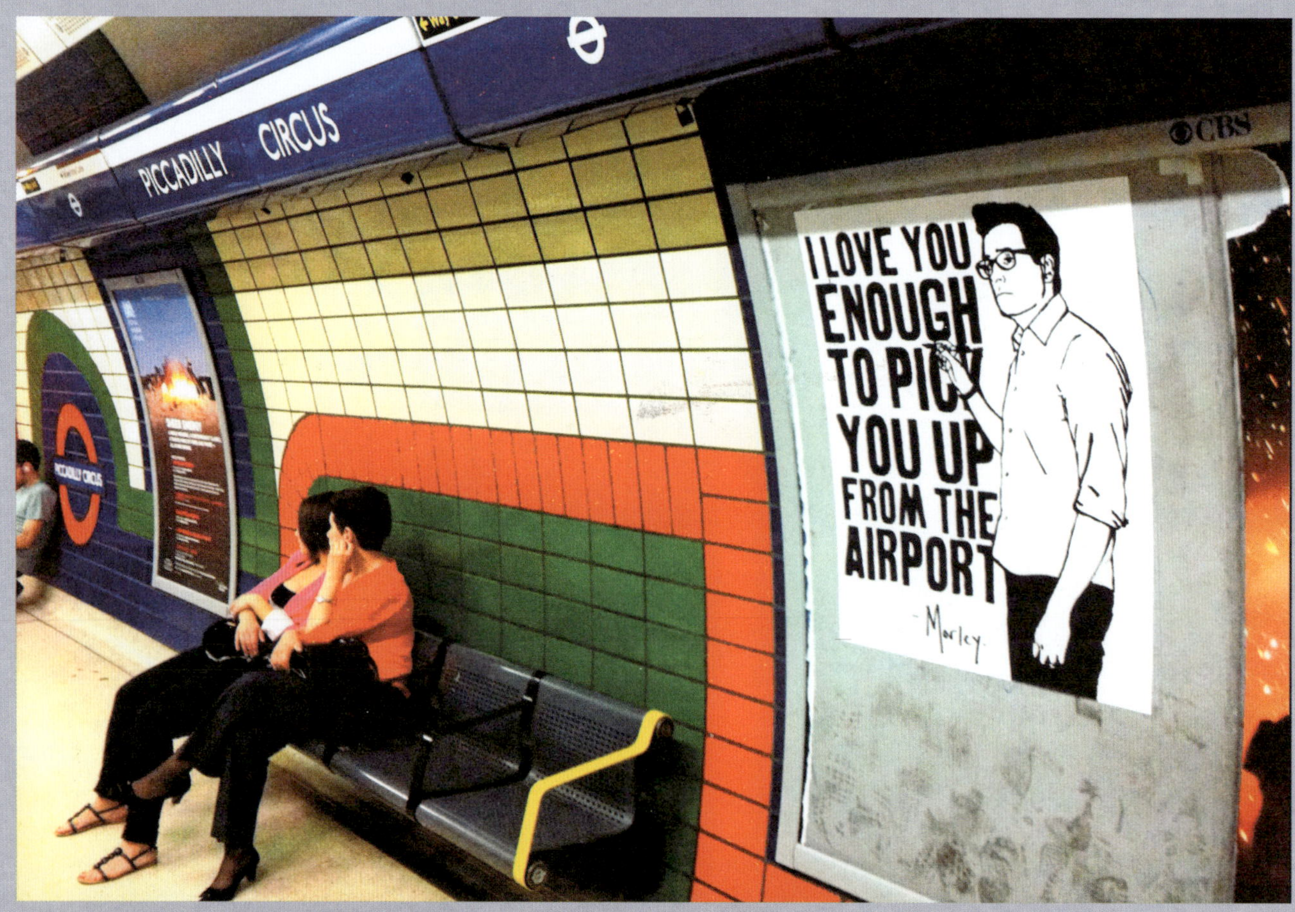

 Morley Piccadilly Circus station, London ↑ and Shoreditch, London →

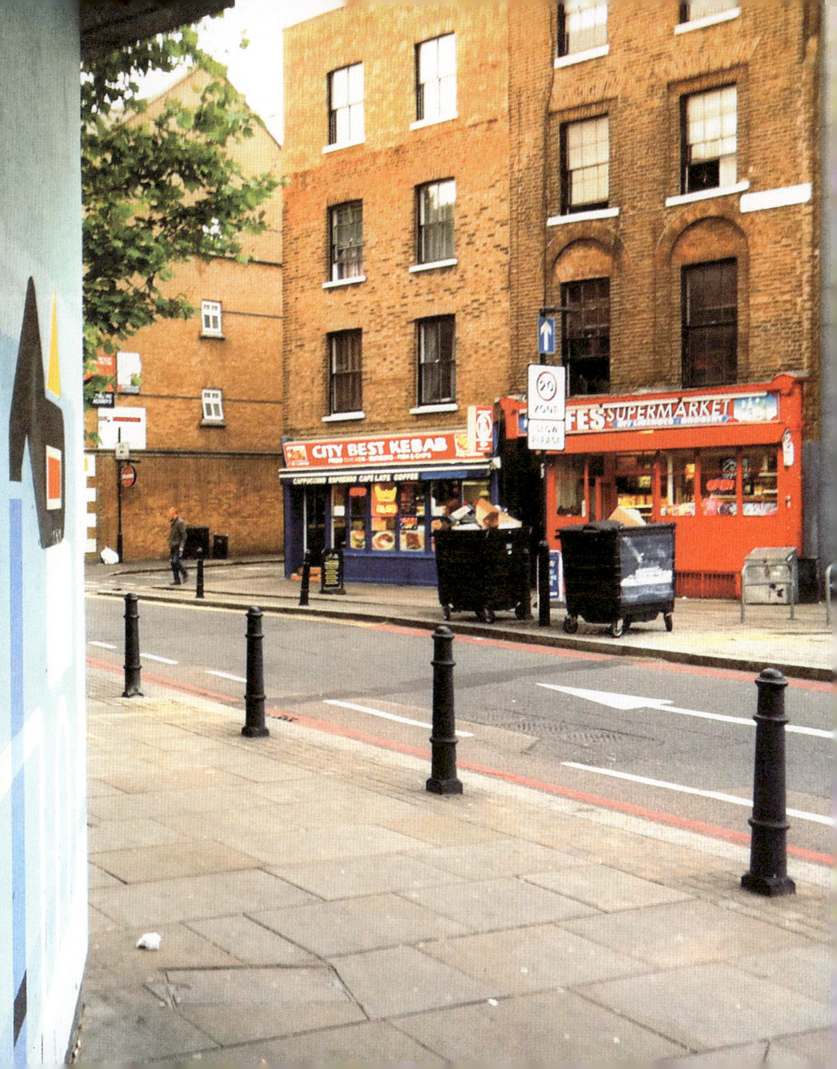
LET'S FALL IN LOVE
LIKE BOTH
OUR
PARENTS
AREN'T
DIVORCED
- Morley.
CITY BEST KEBAB
SUPERMARKET

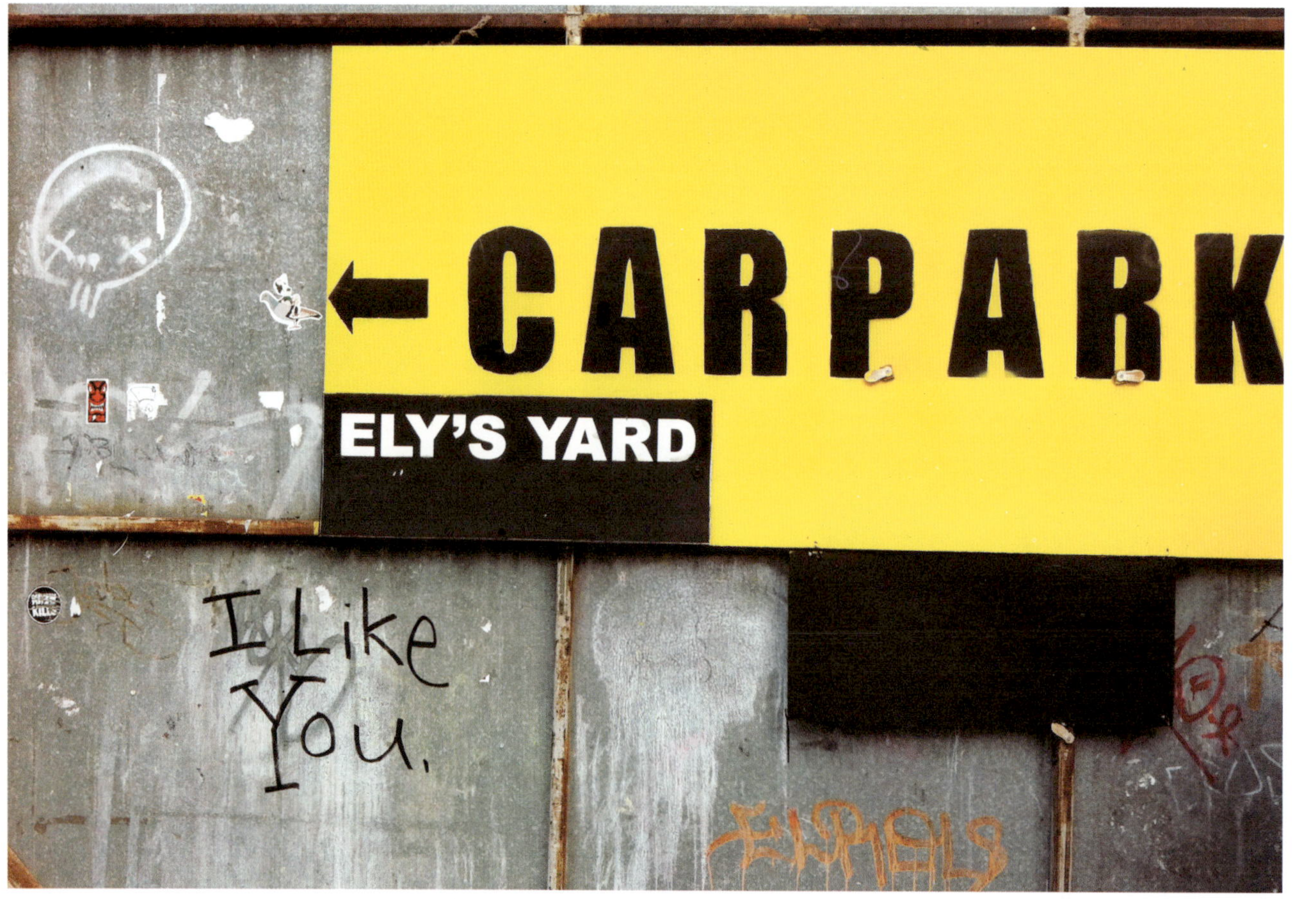

 Unknown Brick Lane, London ↑ and **Solo One** London →

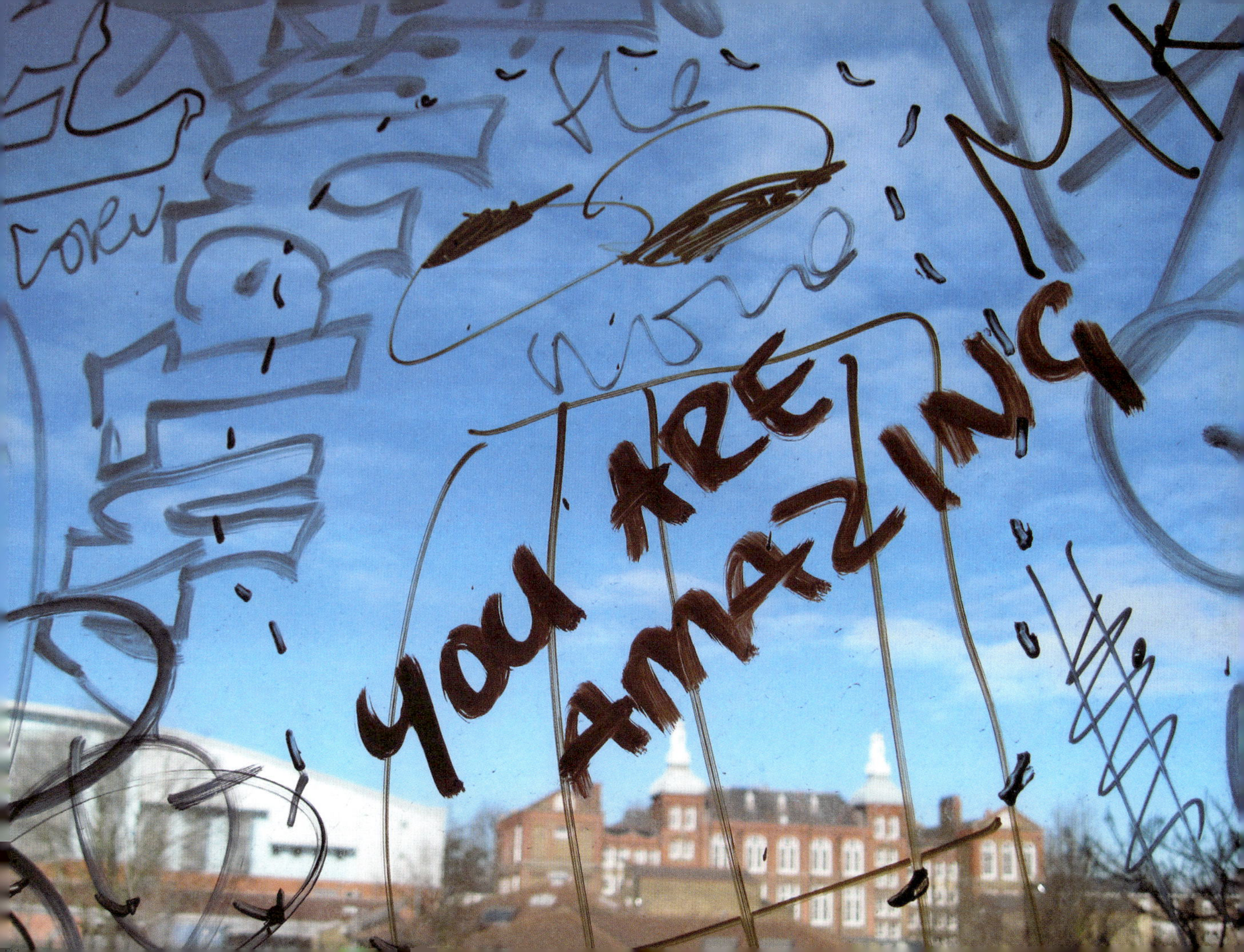
YOU ARE
AMAZING

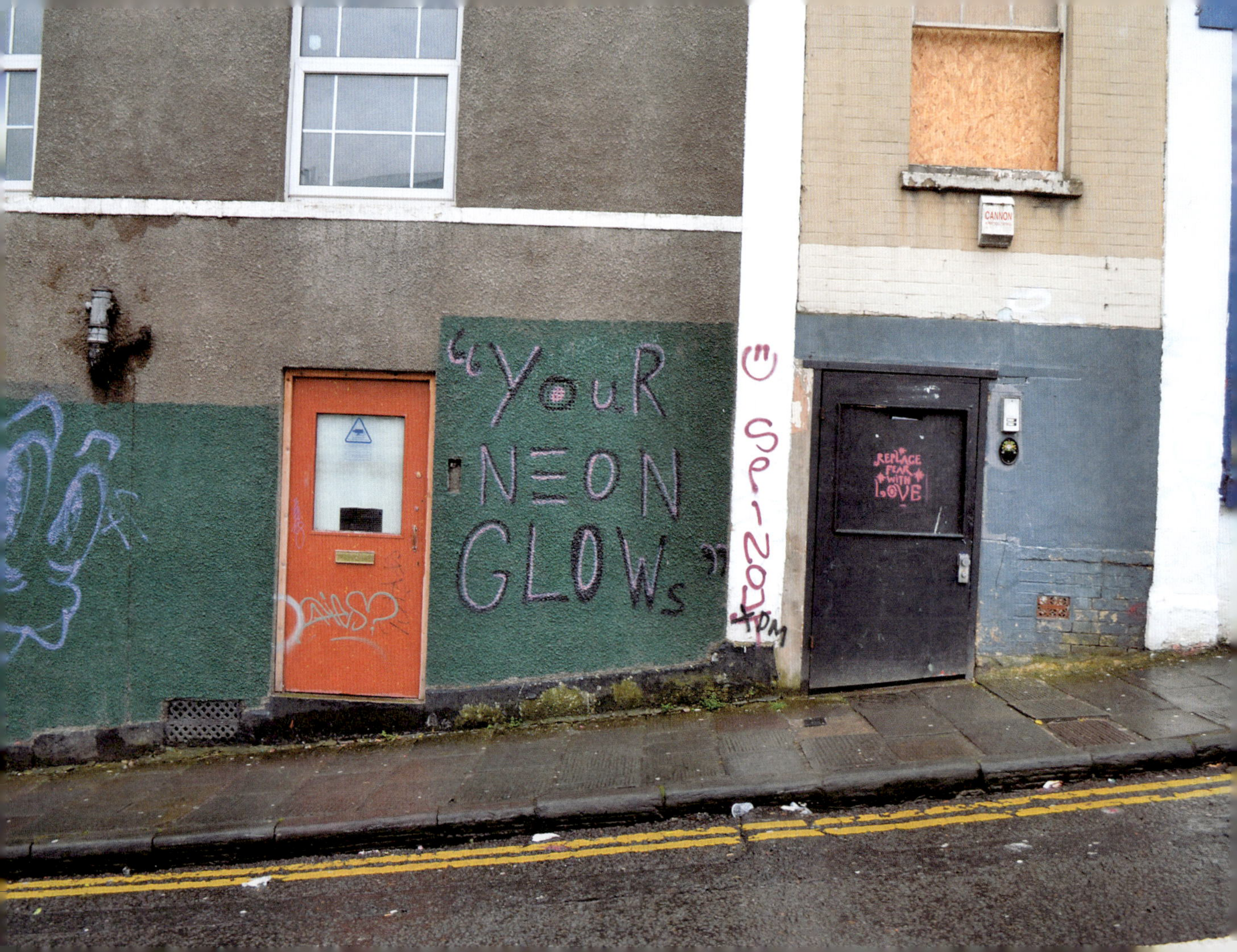

CANNON
"YOUR NEON GLOWS"
REPLACE FEAR WITH LOVE

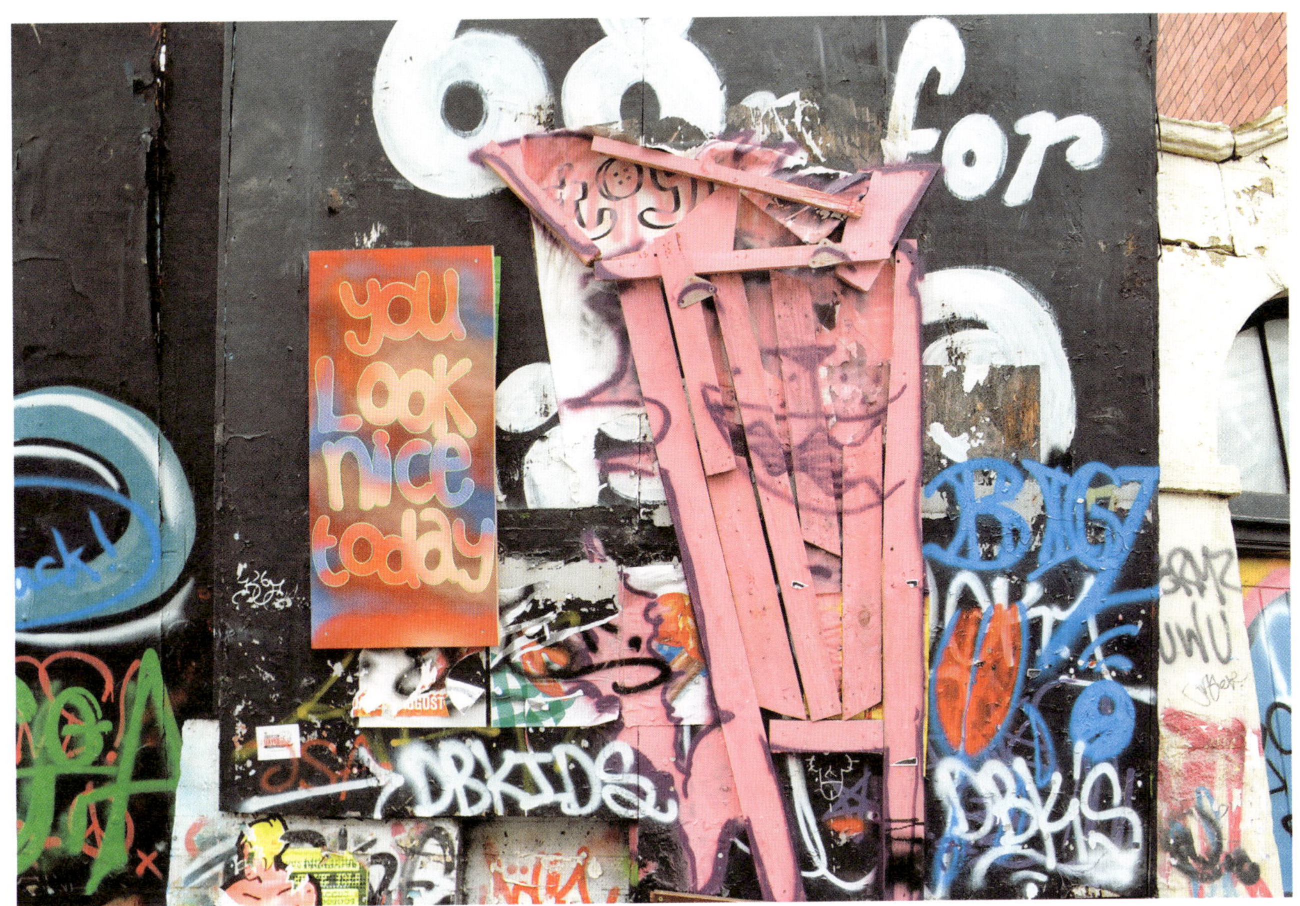

Unknown Stokes Croft, Bristol ← and **Unknown** Stokes Croft, Bristol ↑

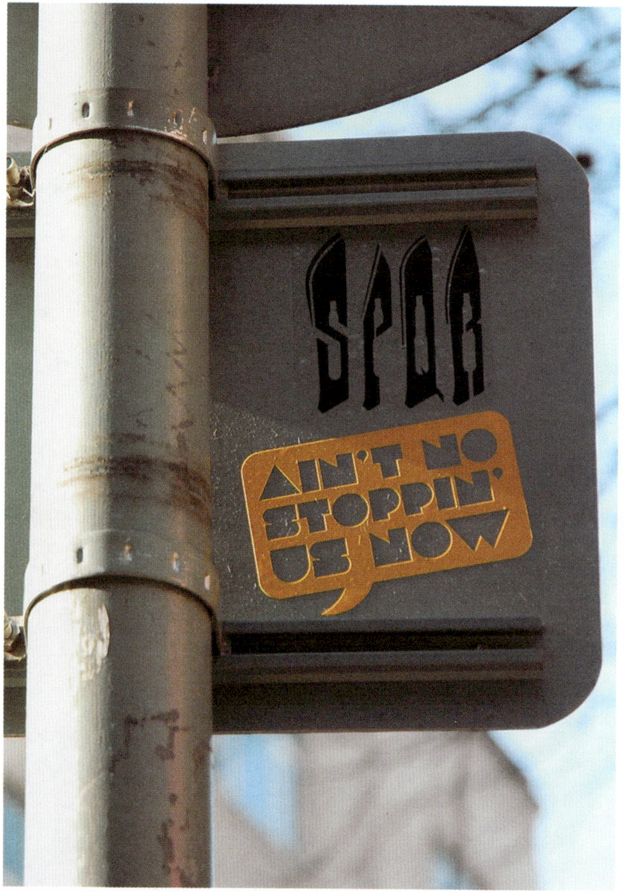

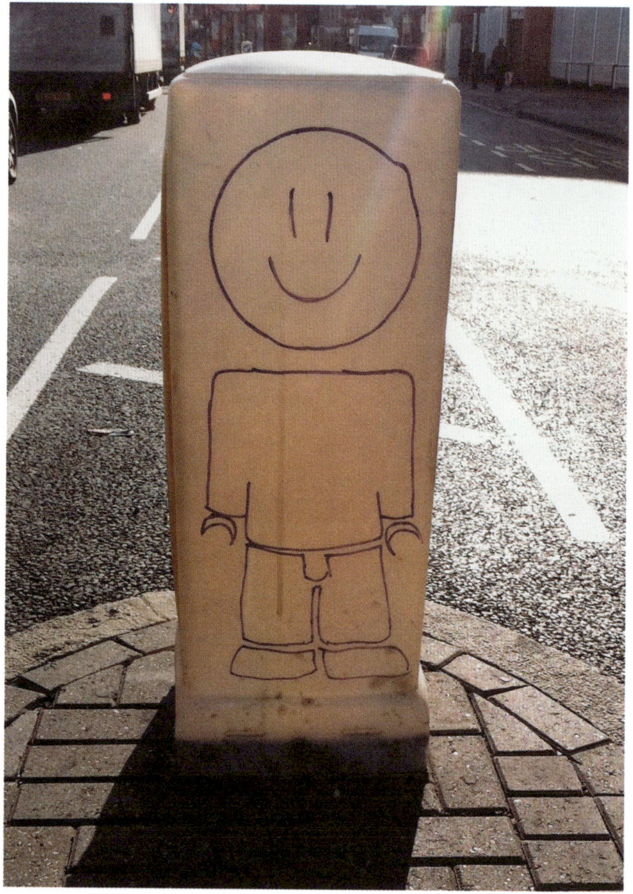

Unknown Nelson Street, Bristol, **Unknown** Shoreditch, London ↑

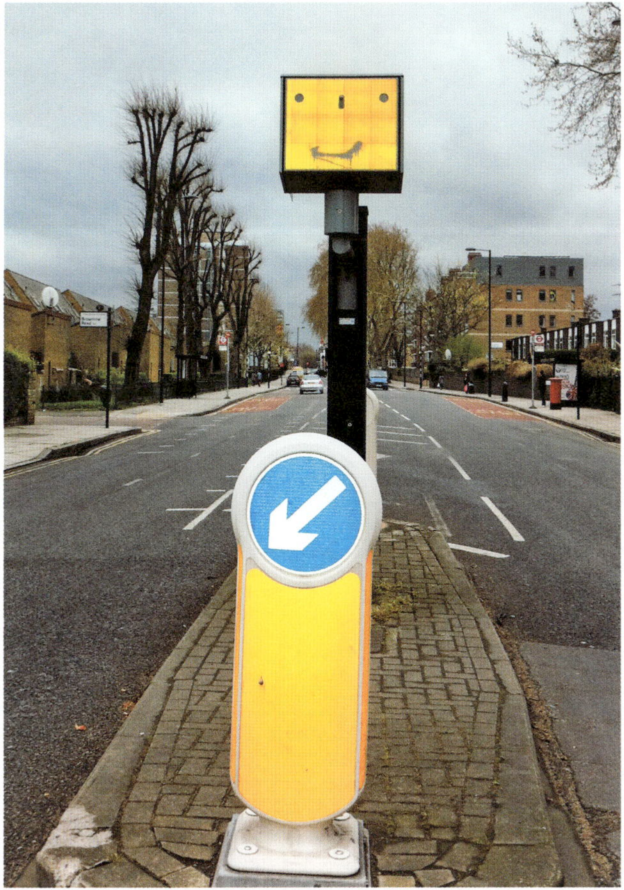

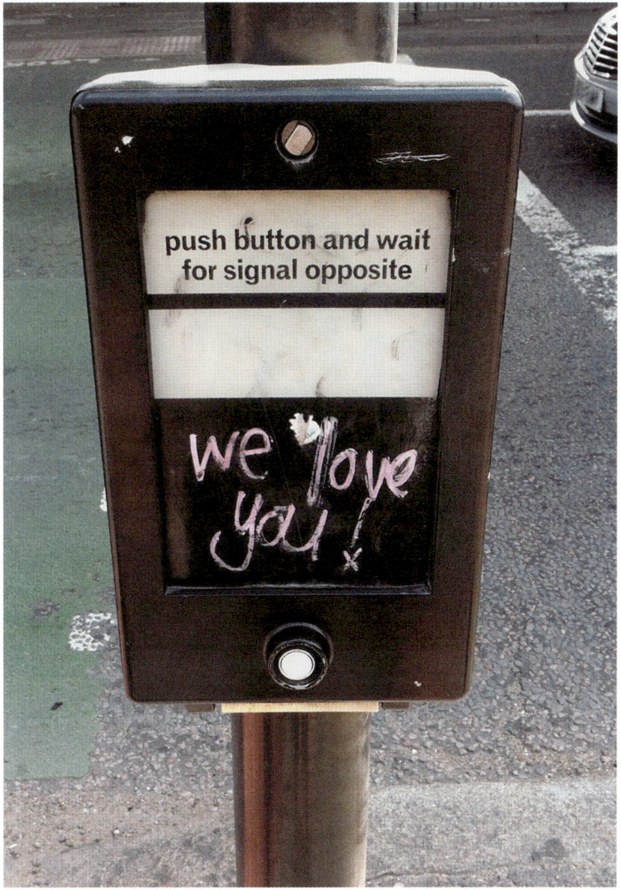

Unknown Dalston, London, **Unknown** Brentford, London ↑

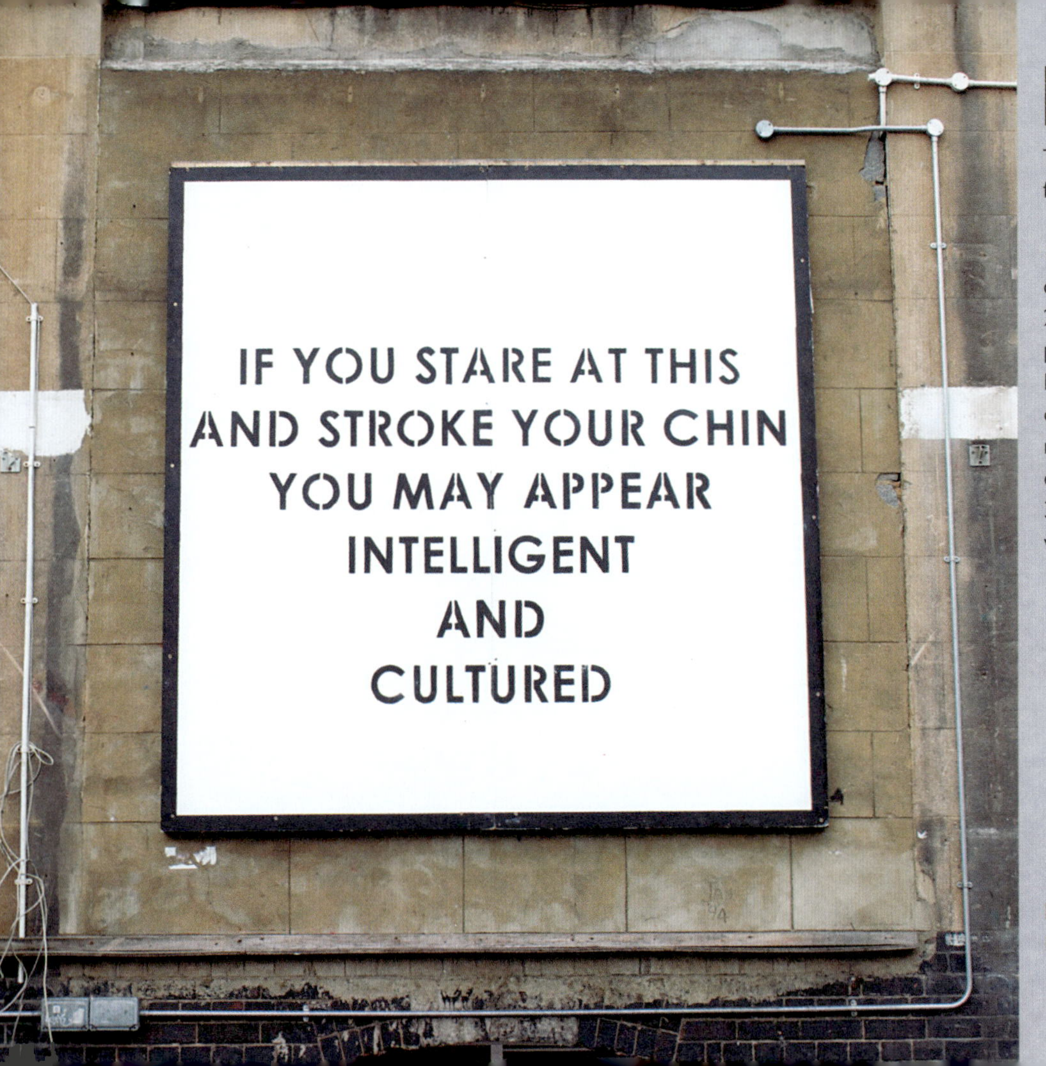

Mobstr

The Mobstr calls himself so for 3 reasons:

1. He owned a pet lobster called mobster.
2. Like real mobsters he partakes in illegal business. His illegal activity is painting on walls without permission, not being part of an organized crime gang.
3. The third reason is to do with mirrors.

Mobstr Brick Lane, London ←

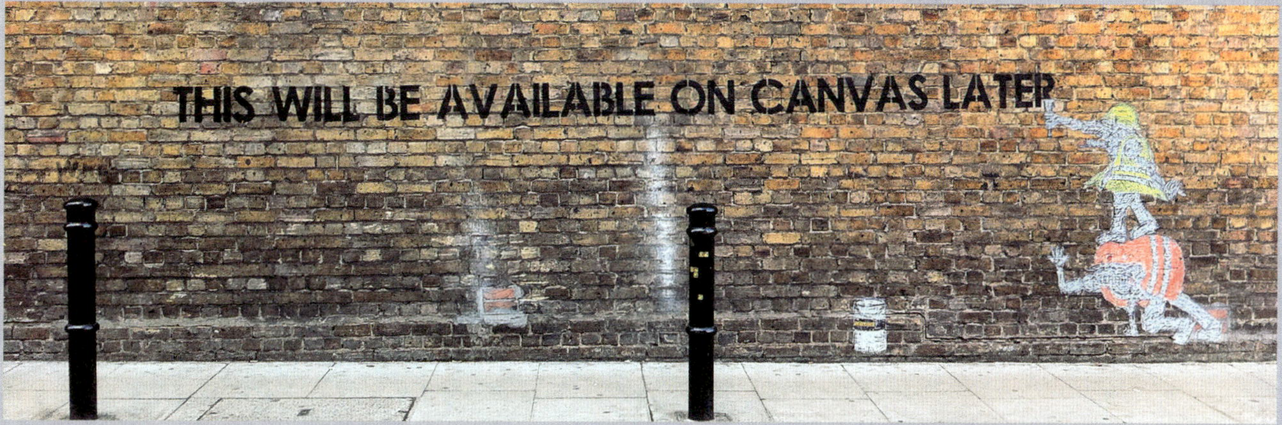

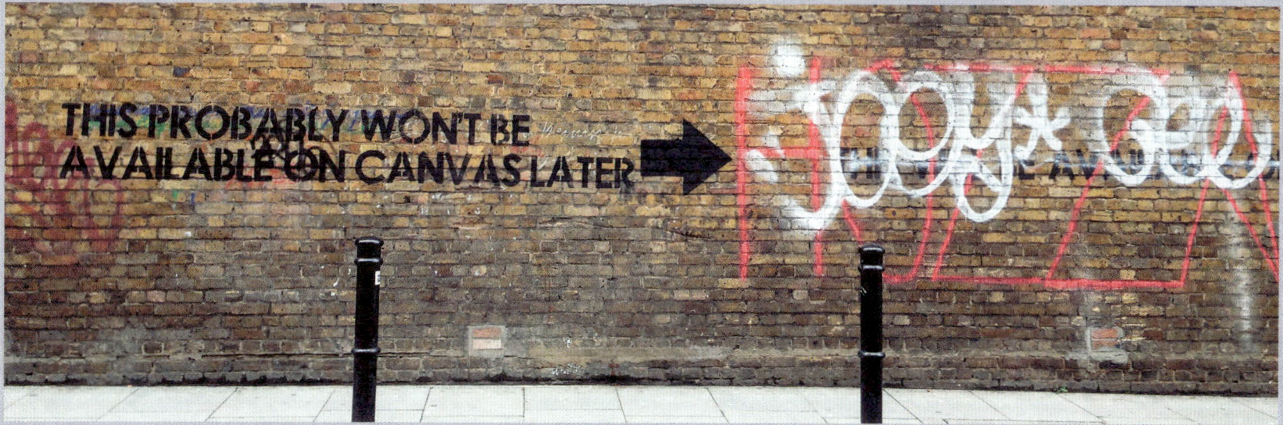

Mobstr Brick Lane, London ↑

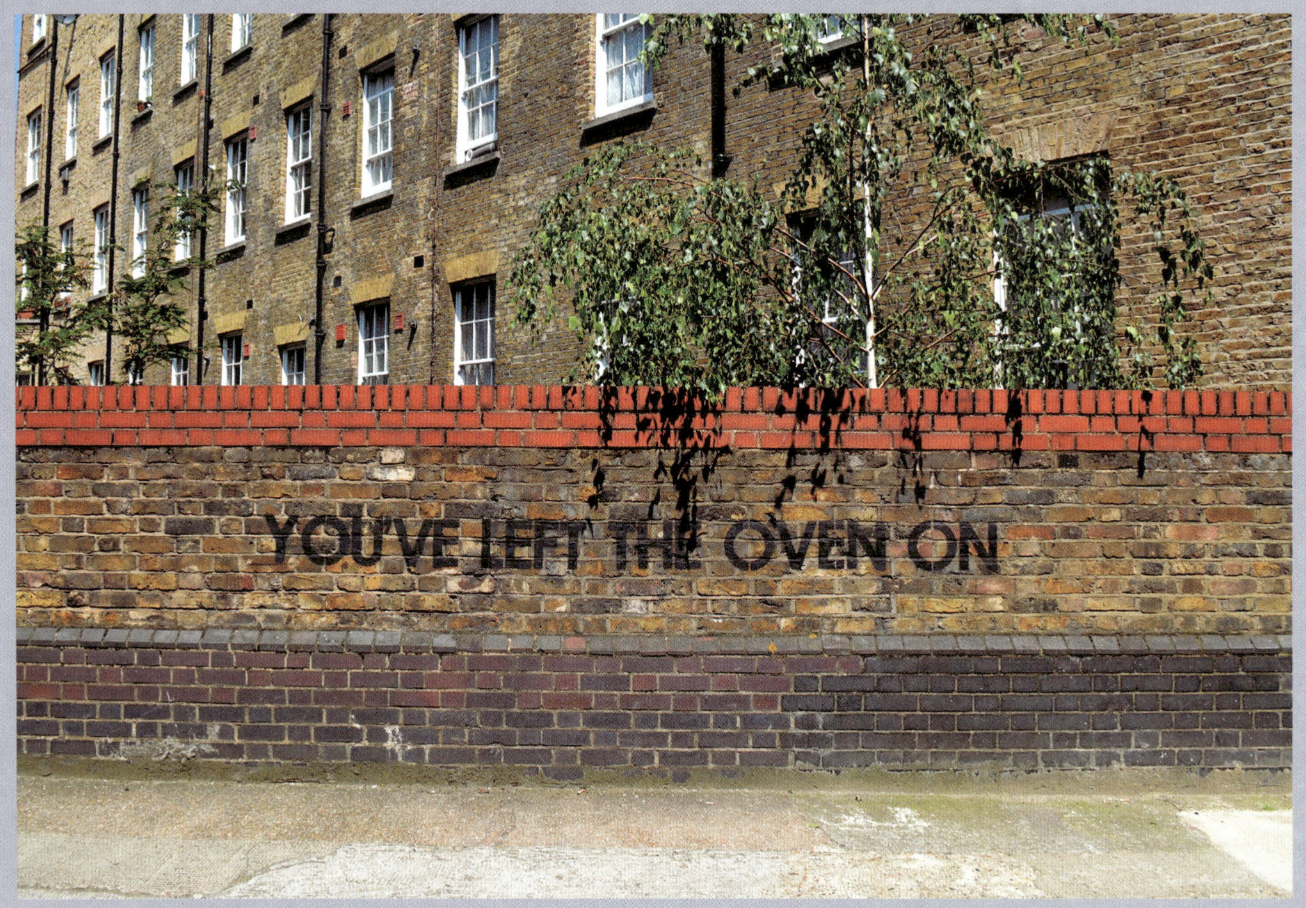

 Mobstr Spitalfields, London ↑

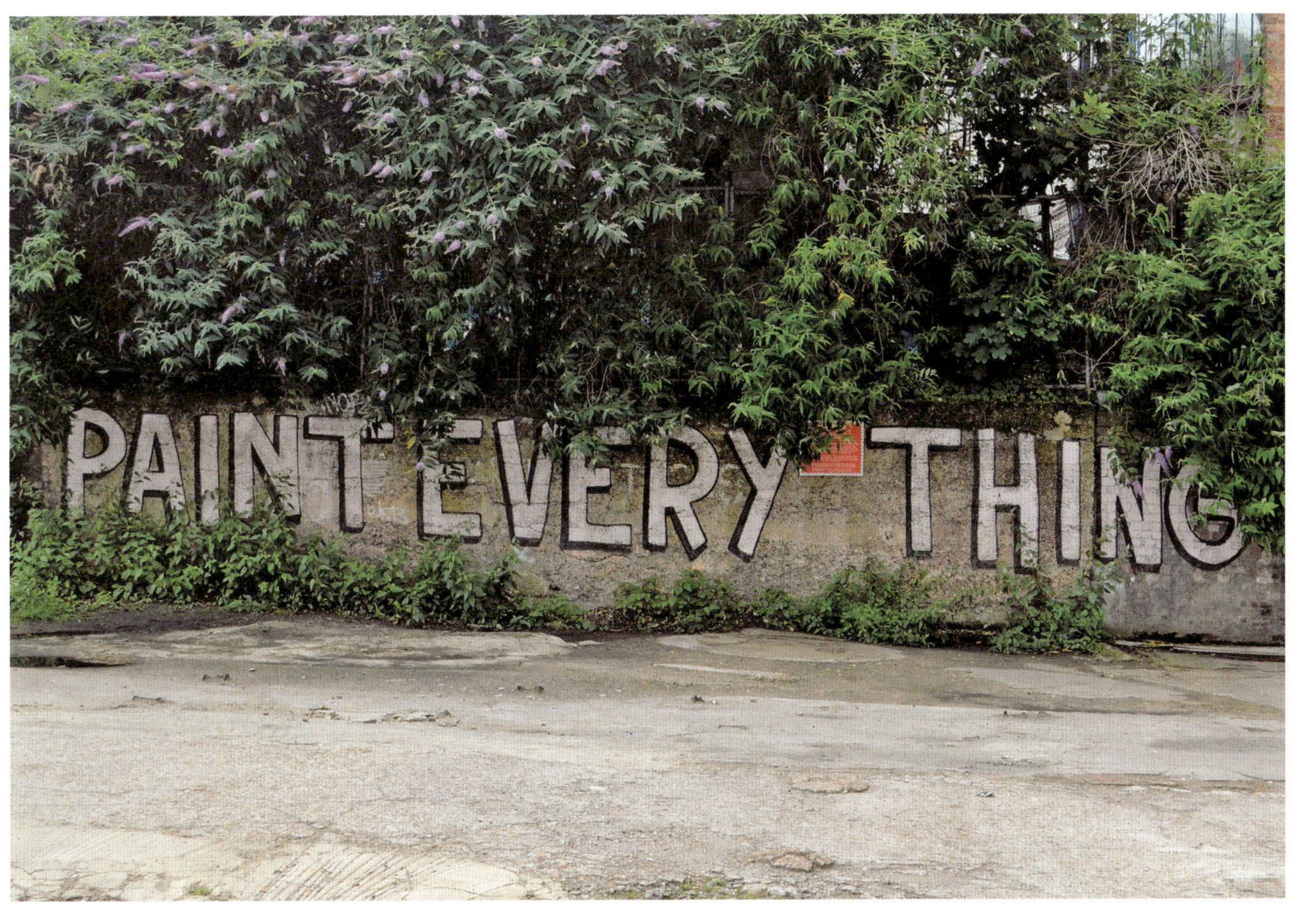

Unknown Dalston, London ↑

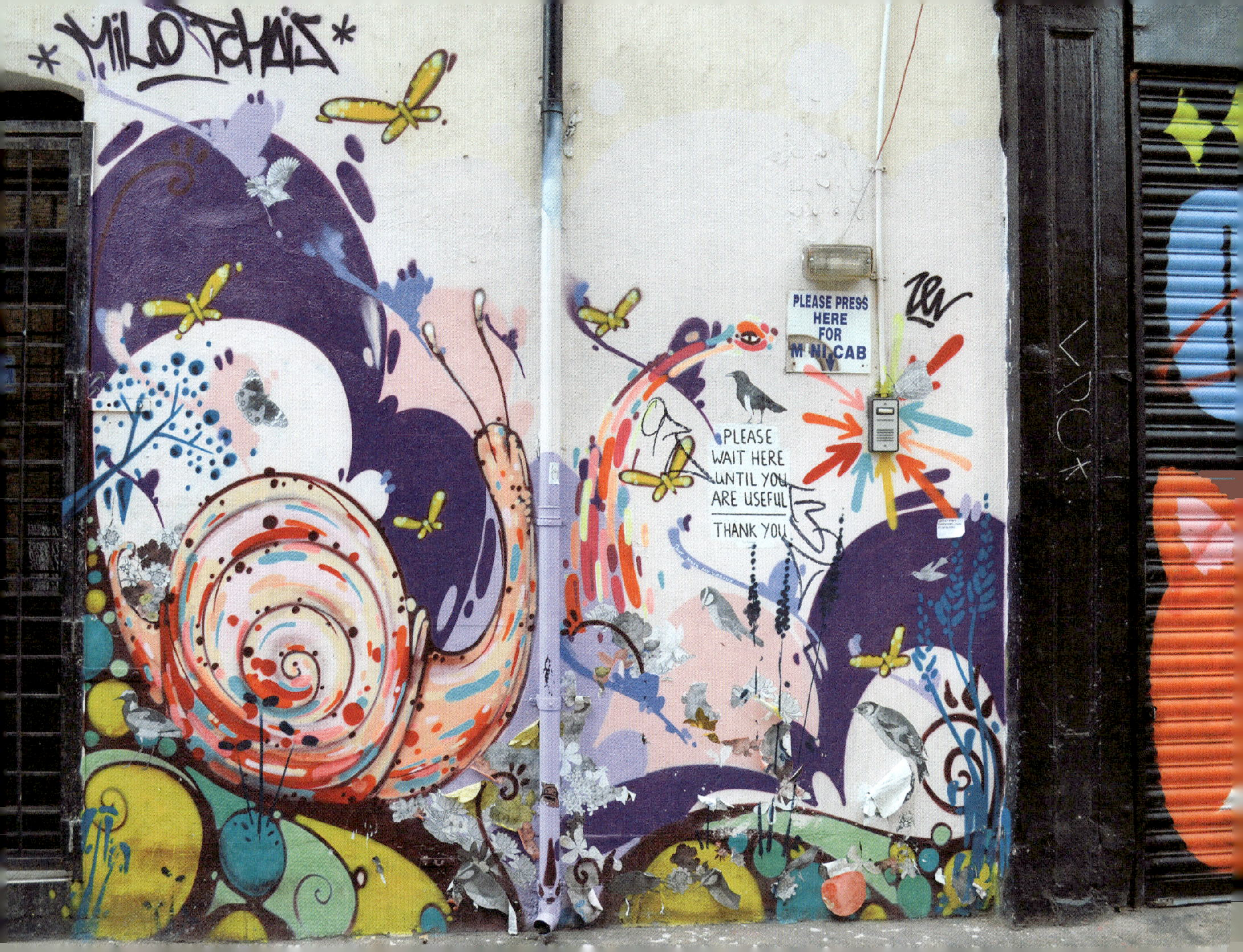
PLEASE PRESS HERE FOR M NI CAB
PLEASE WAIT HERE UNTIL YOU ARE USEFUL
THANK YOU

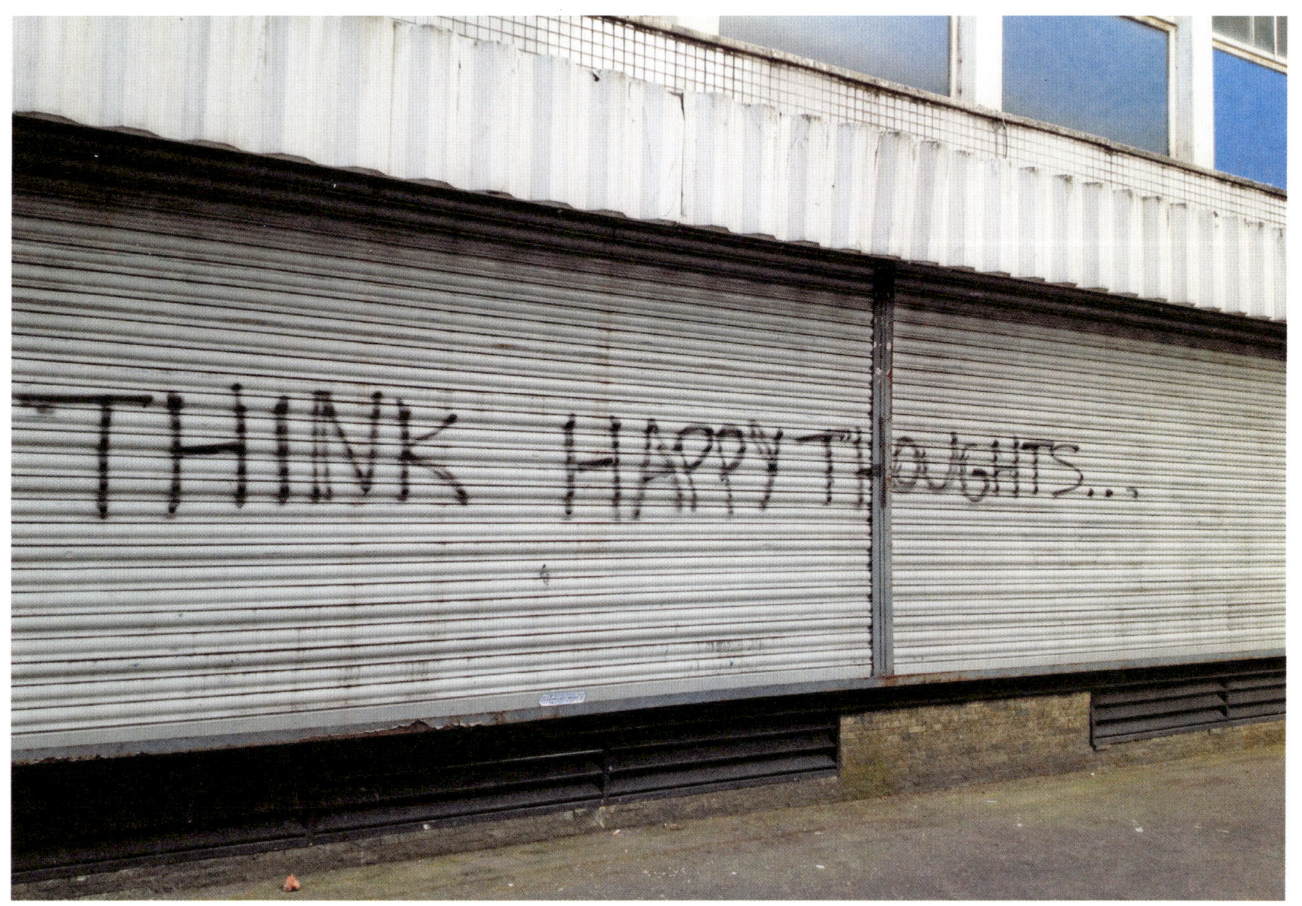

Ian Stevenson/Milo Tchais Shoreditch, London ← and **Unknown** Port Street, Manchester ↑

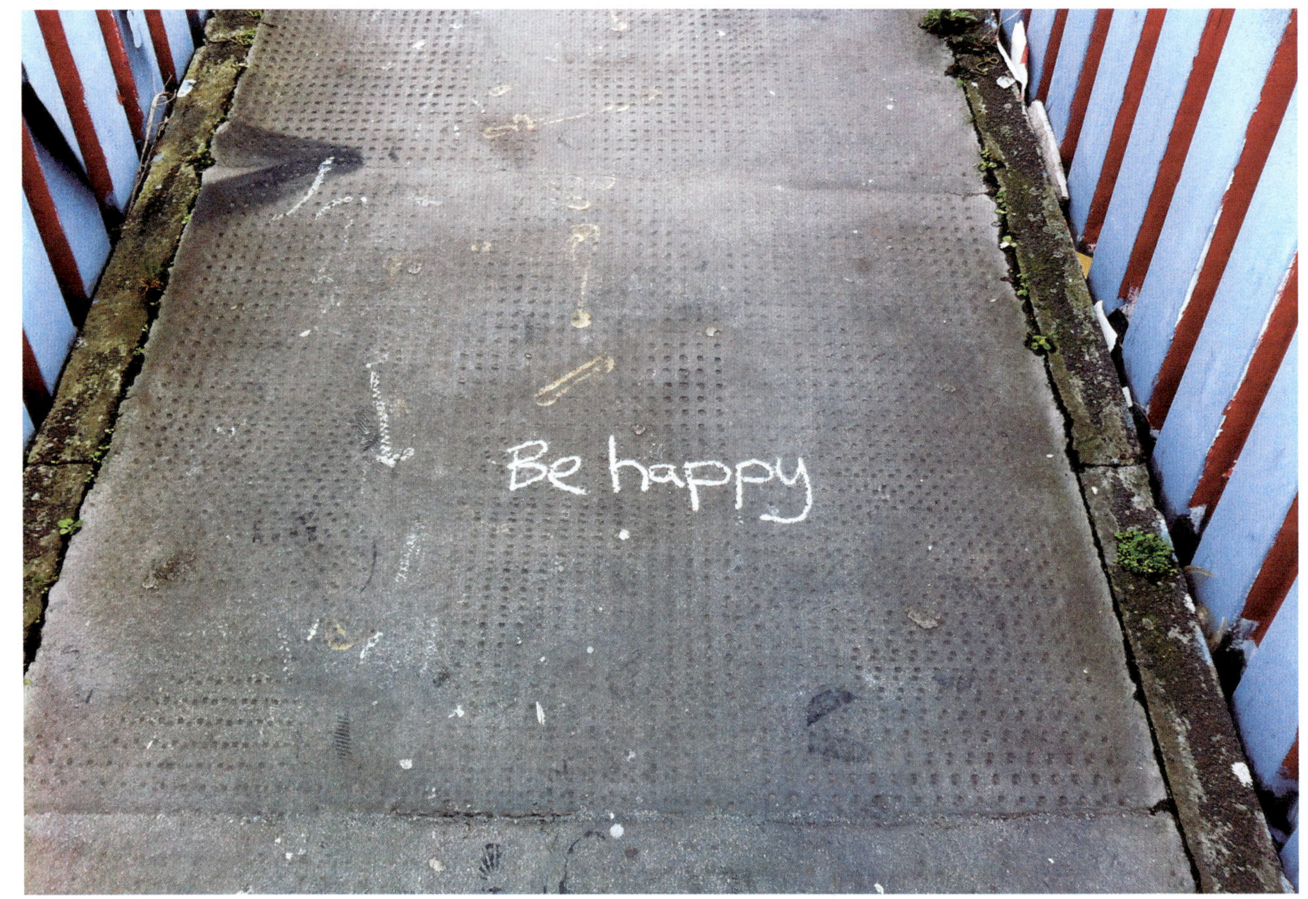

 Unknown Shoreditch, London ↑

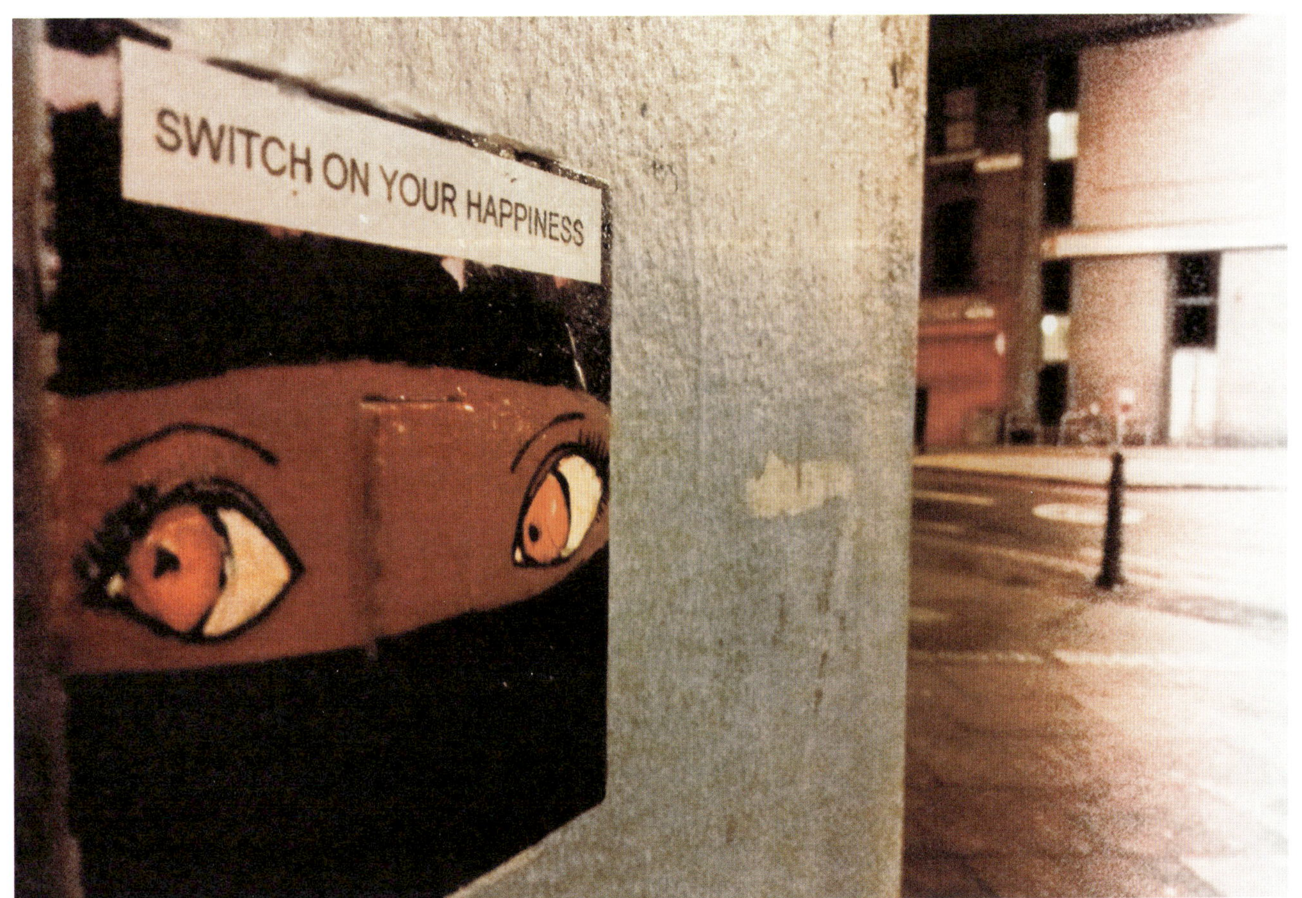

Sophia Fox Hackney, London ↑

Binty Bint

Binty Bint is a UK-based artist known for her young, bright and vibrant street art pieces. Recognized by its candy colours and chicken characters, her playful art is gracing the grey walls of the world with a refreshing, vibrant energy.

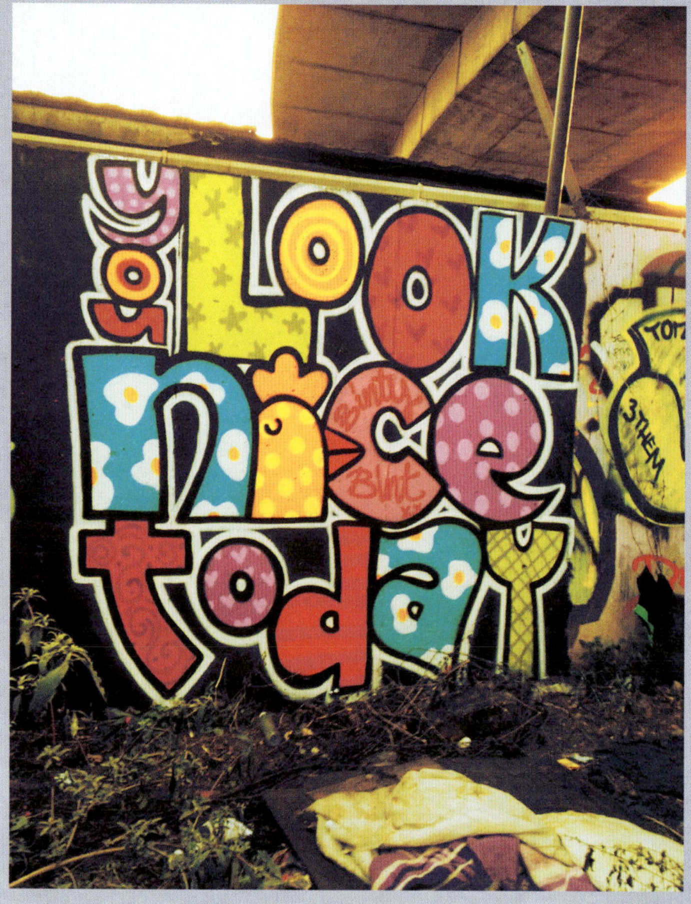

Binty Bint Latimer Road, London ↑

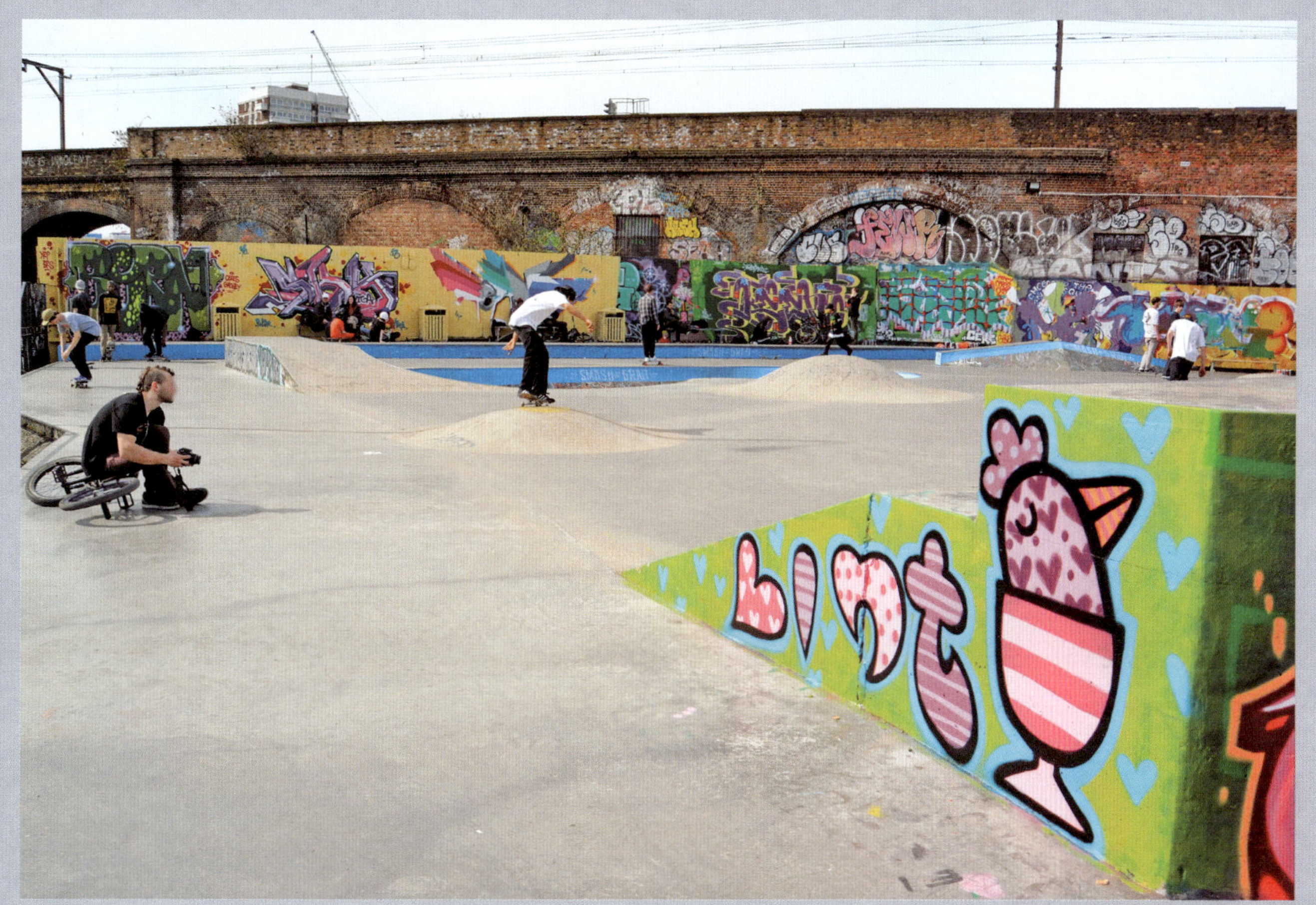

Binty Bint Mile End, London ↑

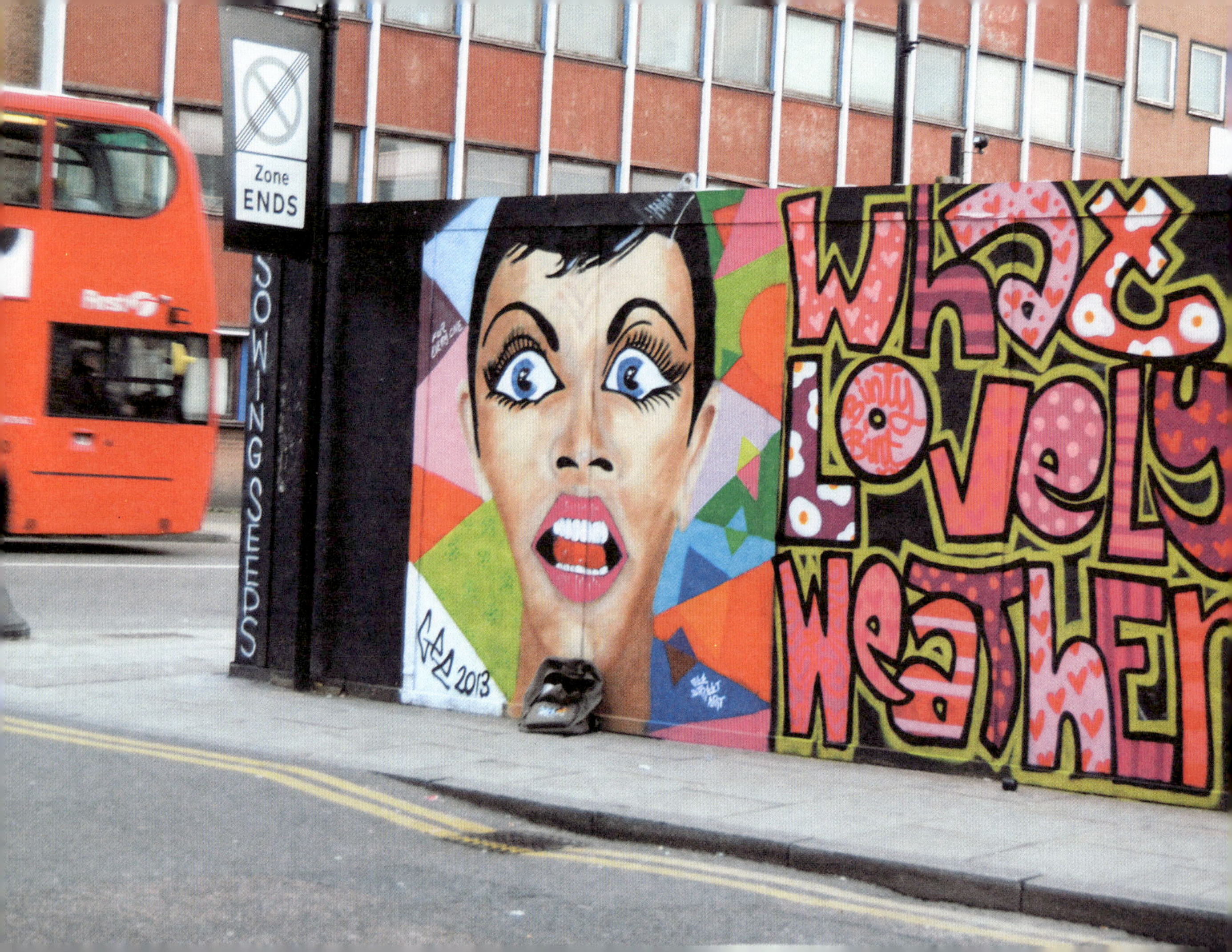
Zone
ENDS
SOWING SEEDS
What Lovely Weather
GEZ 2013

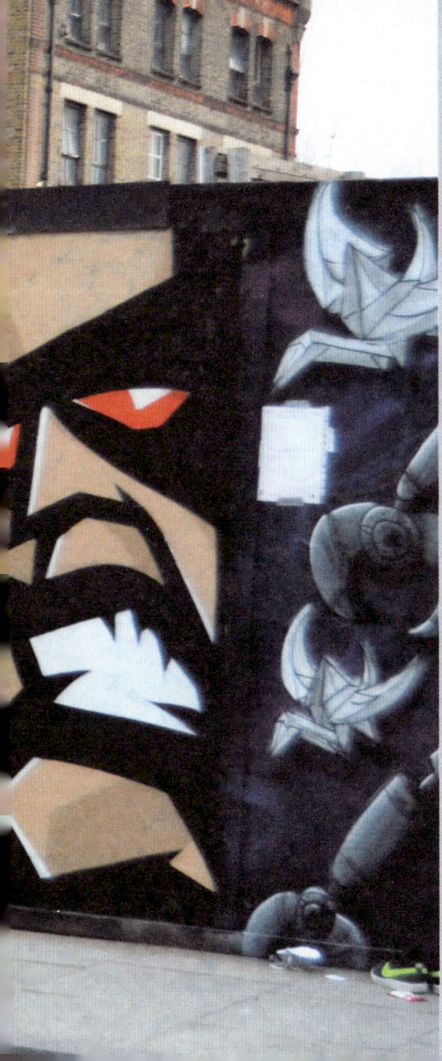

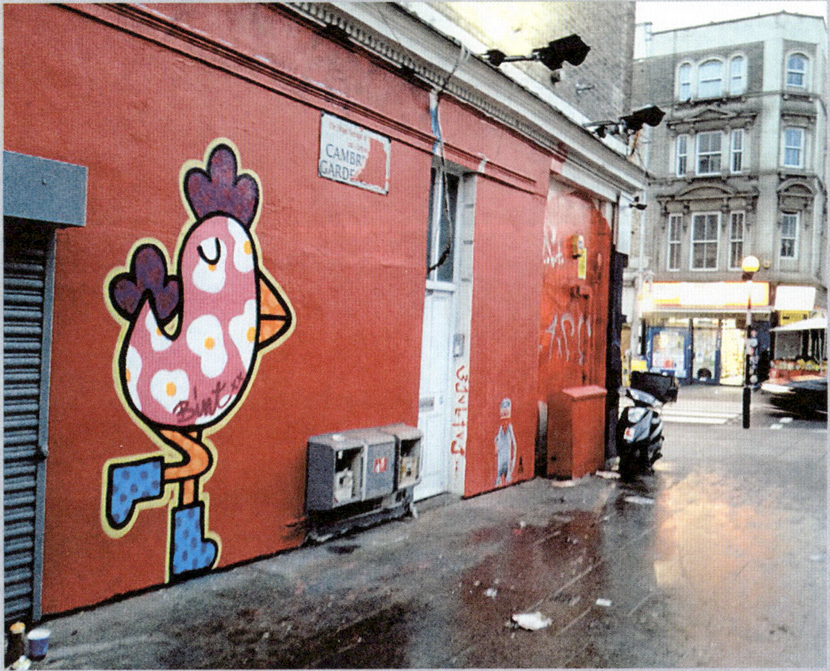

Binty Bint Hackney Road, London ← and Ladbroke Grove, London ↑

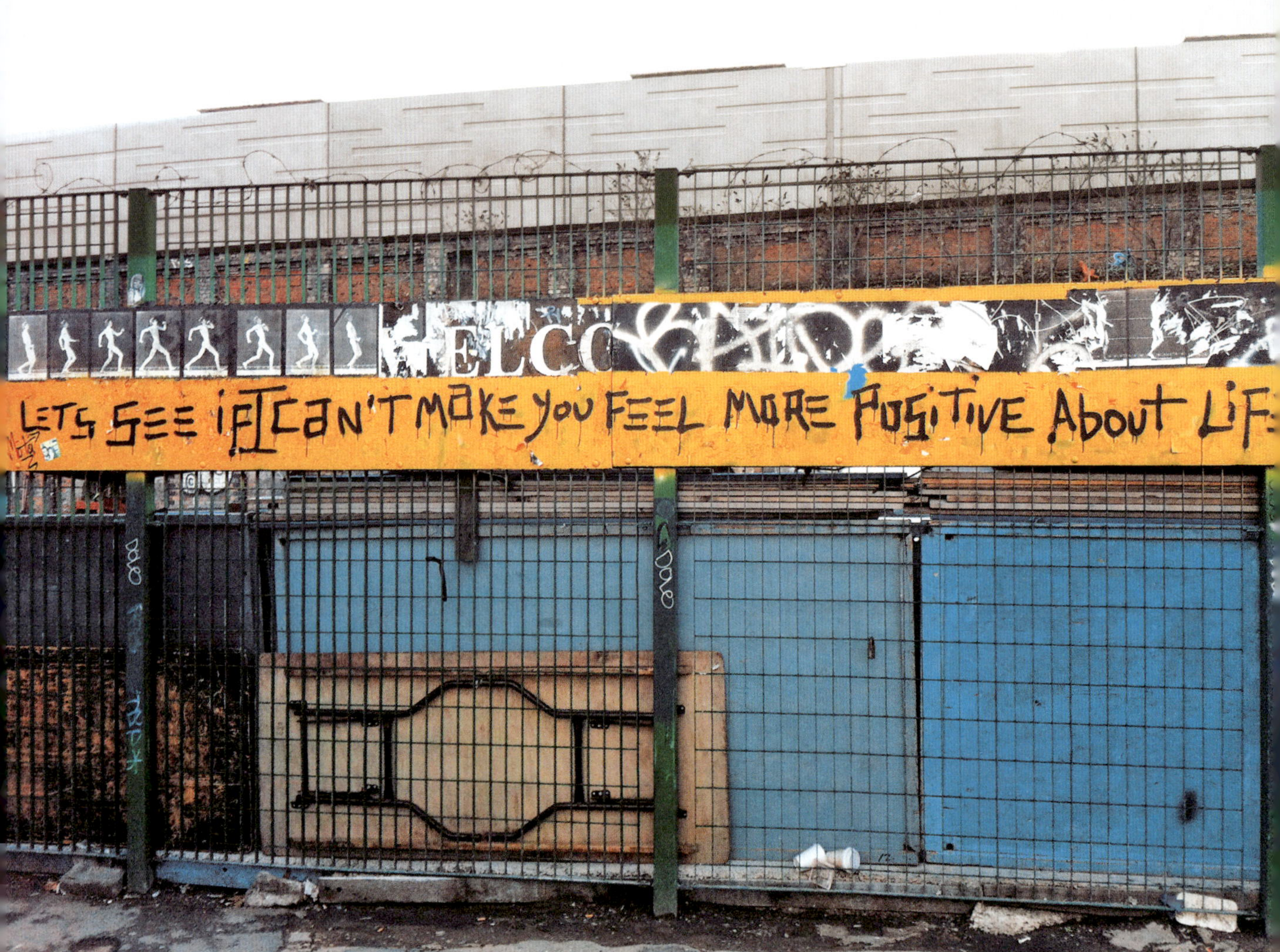
ELCO
LETS SEE IF I CAN'T MAKE YOU FEEL MORE POSITIVE About LIF

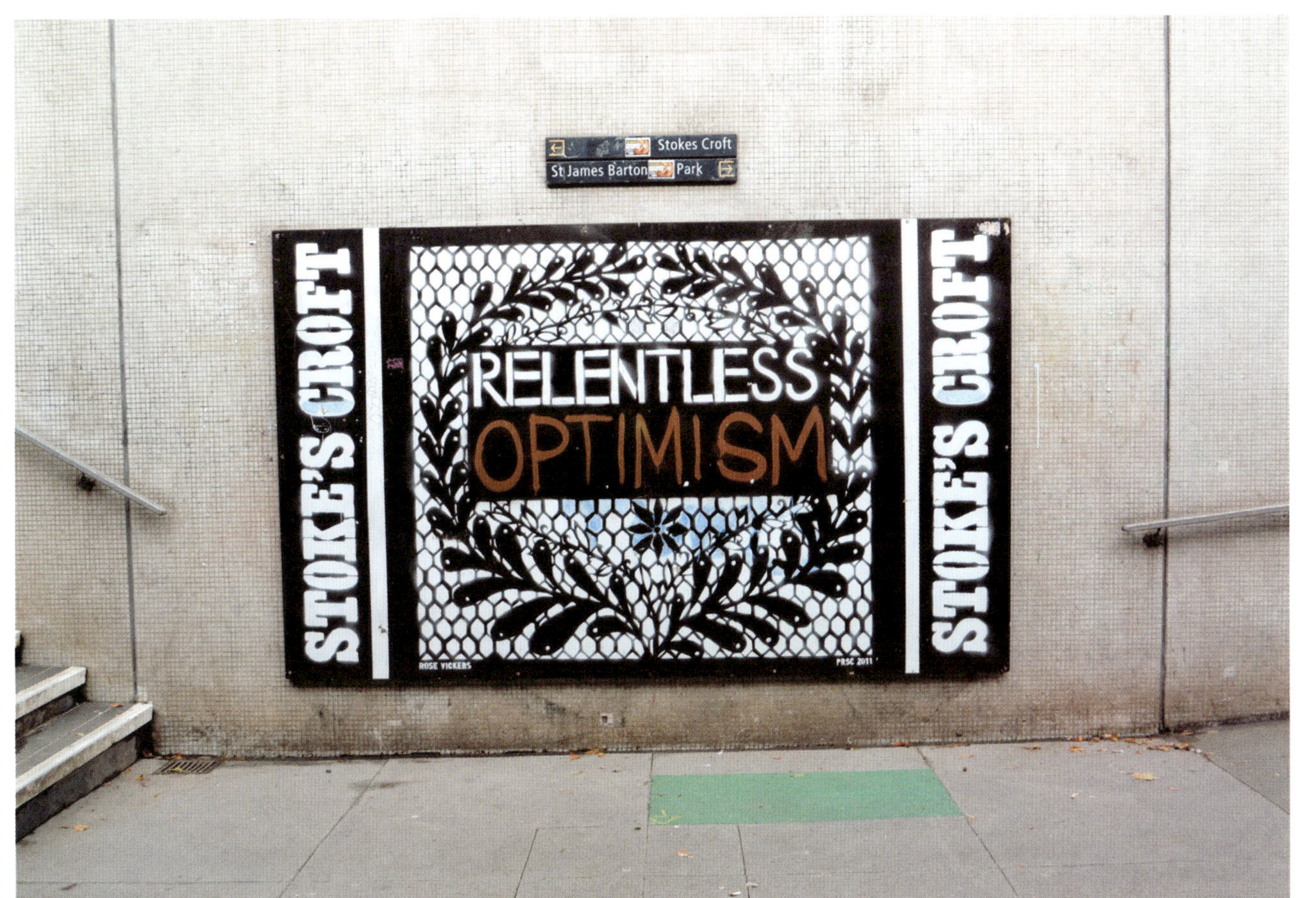

Unknown Shoreditch, London ← and **Rose Vickers** Stokes Croft, Bristol ↑

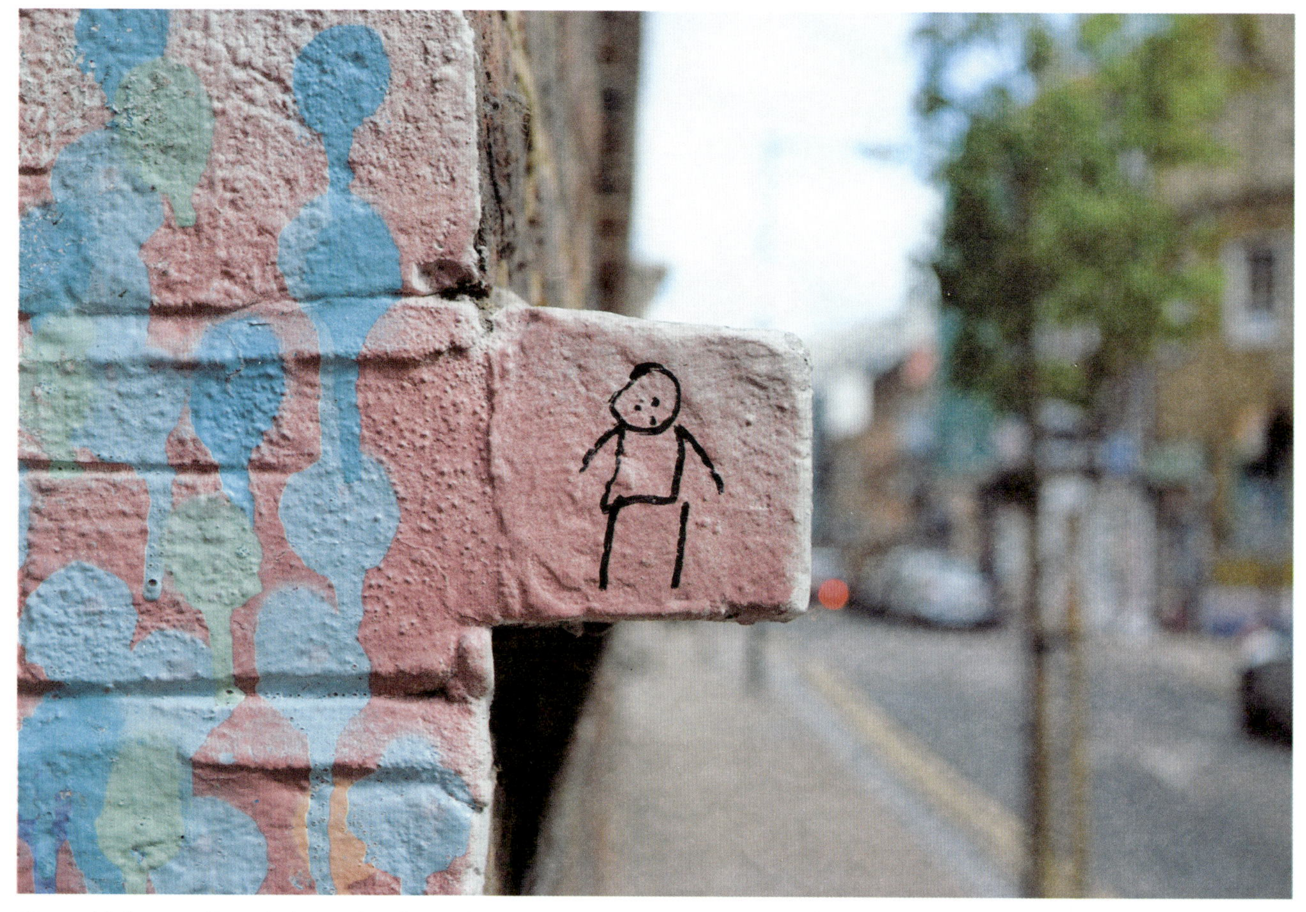

Unknown Shoreditch, London ↑ and **Unknown** Hackney Wick, London →

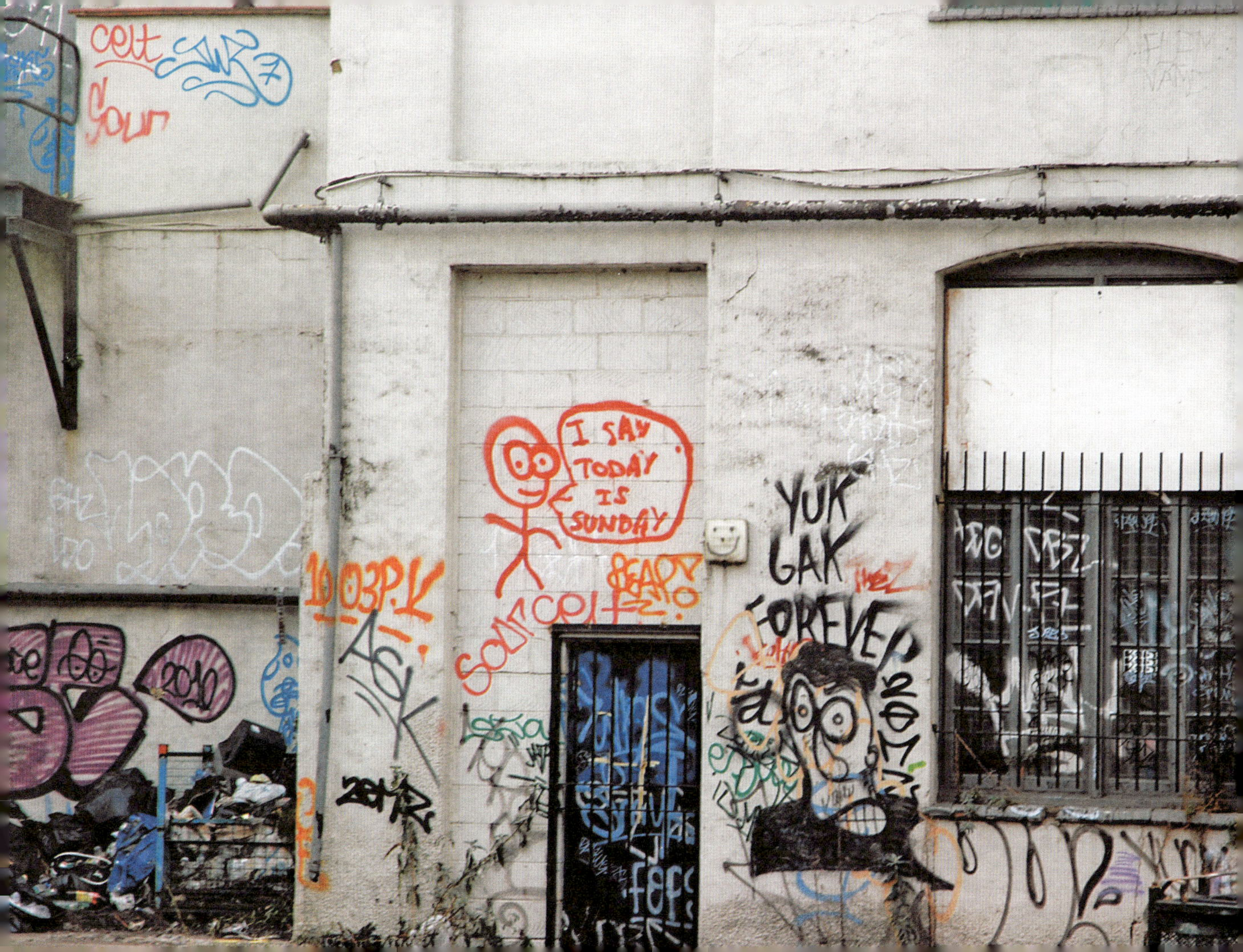
I SAY TODAY IS SUNDAY
YUK GAK FOREVER

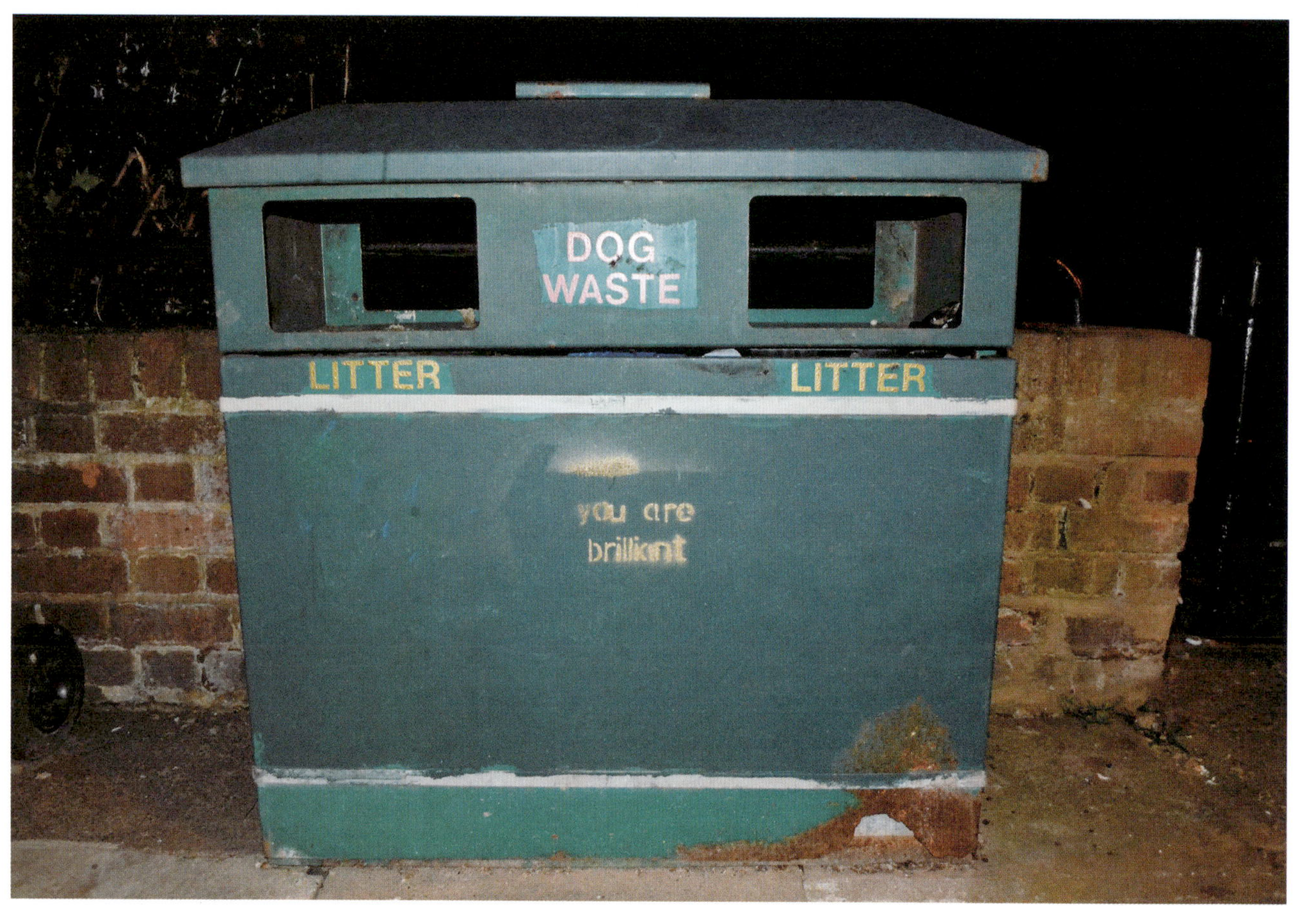

 Unknown Stoke Newington, London ↑

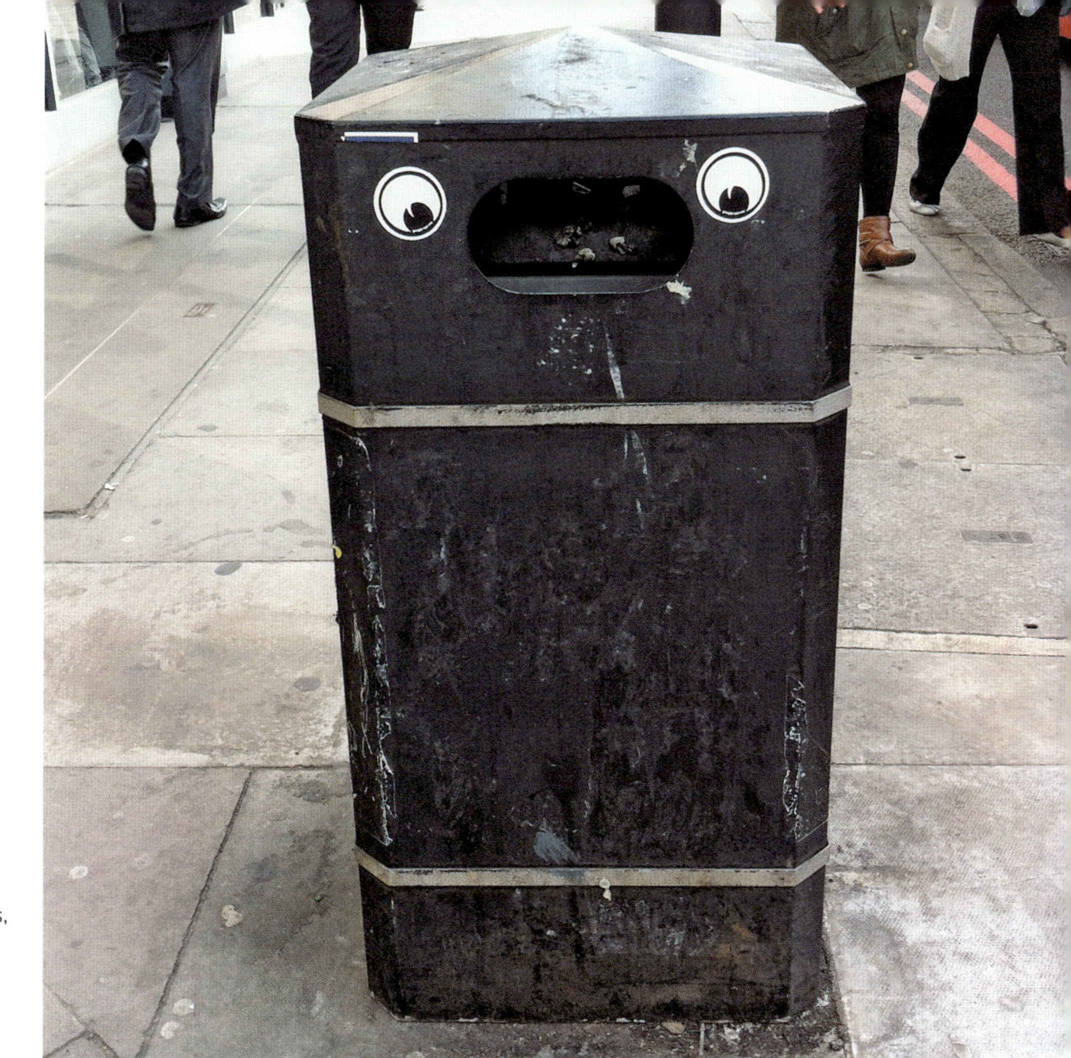

Googly Eye Cru Spitalfields, London →

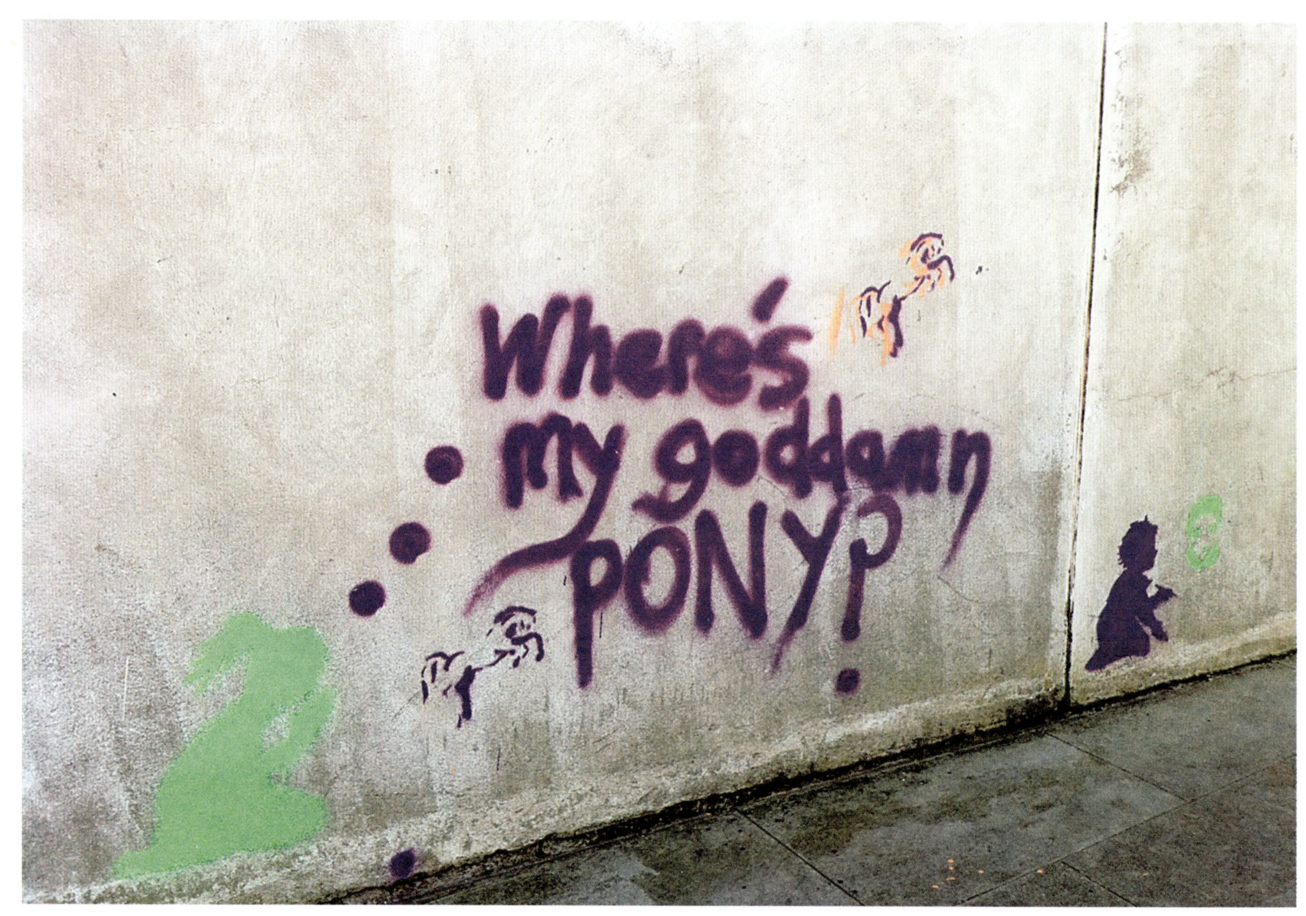

 Unknown Old Course Golf Club, St Andrews ↑ and **Unknown** Brick Lane, London →

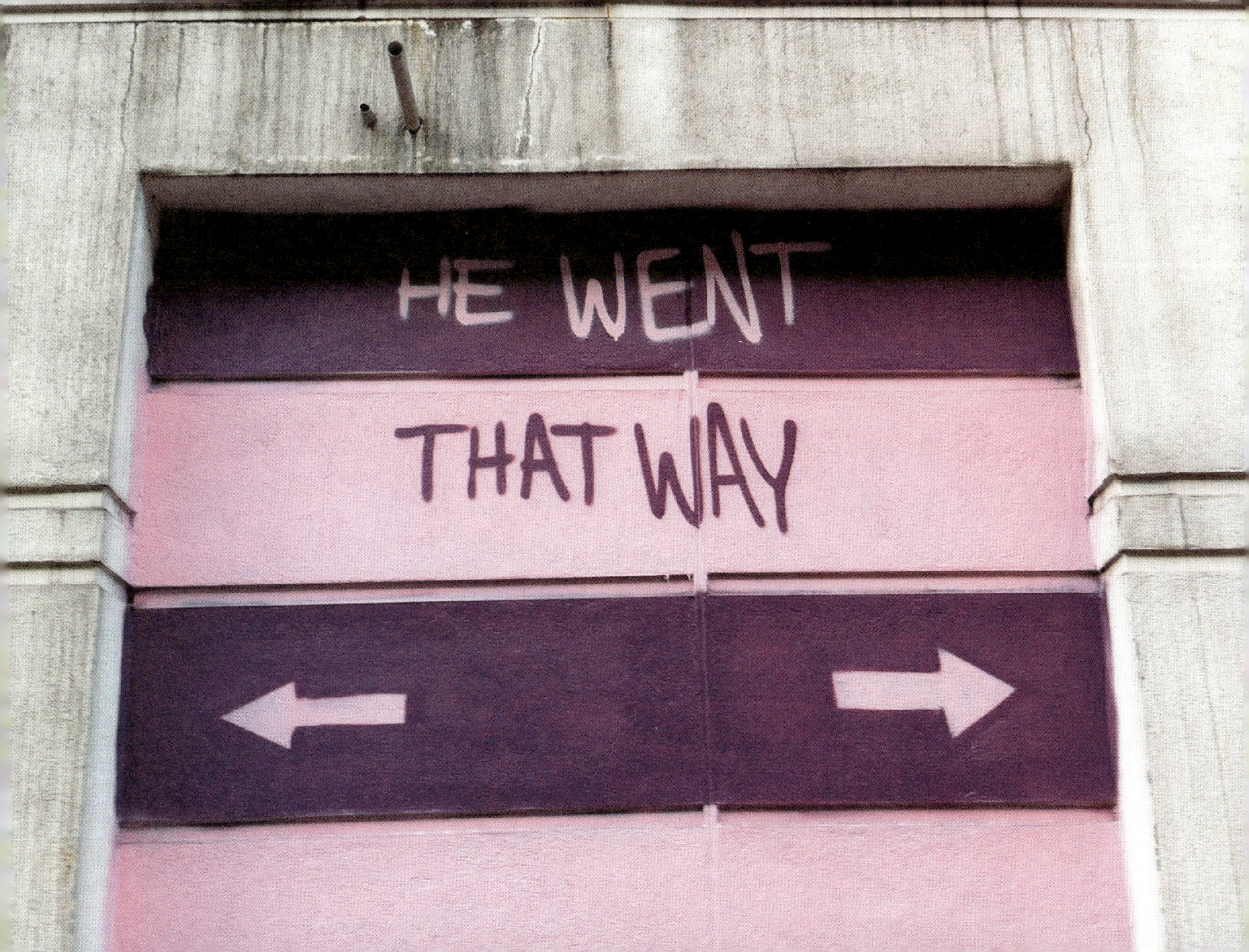
HE WENT
THAT WAY

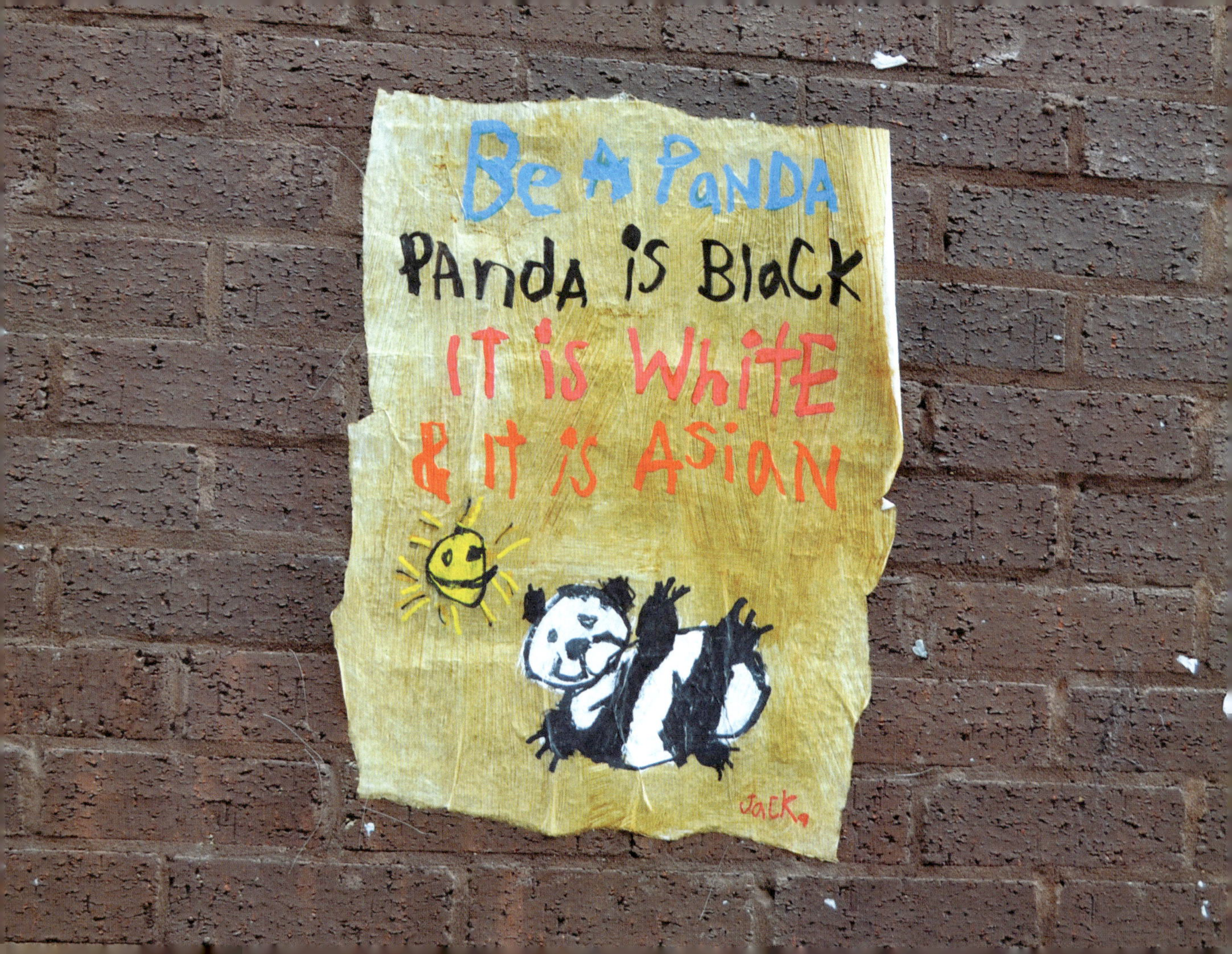
Be A PANDA
PANDA IS BLACK
IT IS WHITE
& IT IS ASIAN
JACK

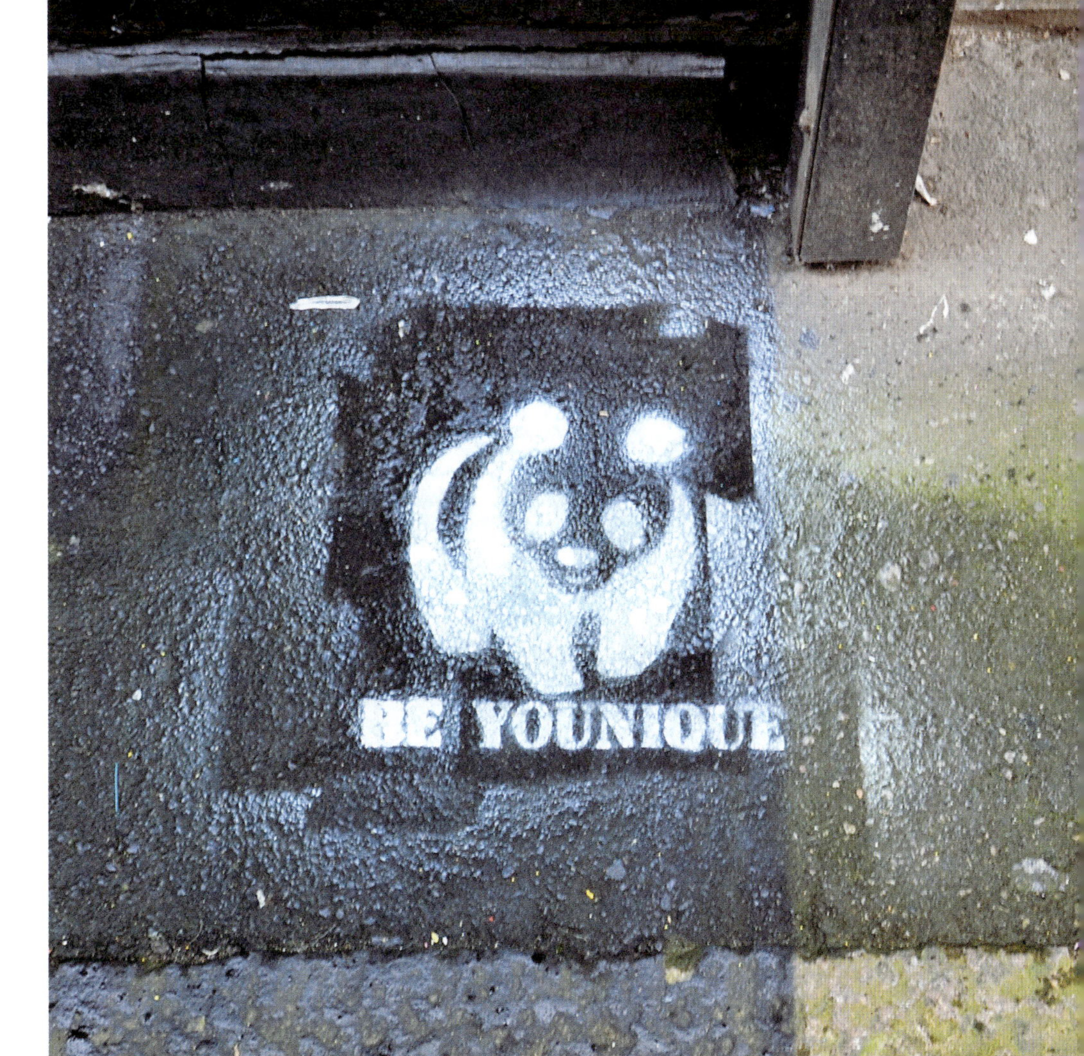

Unknown Shoreditch, London ← and **Unknown** Shoreditch, London →

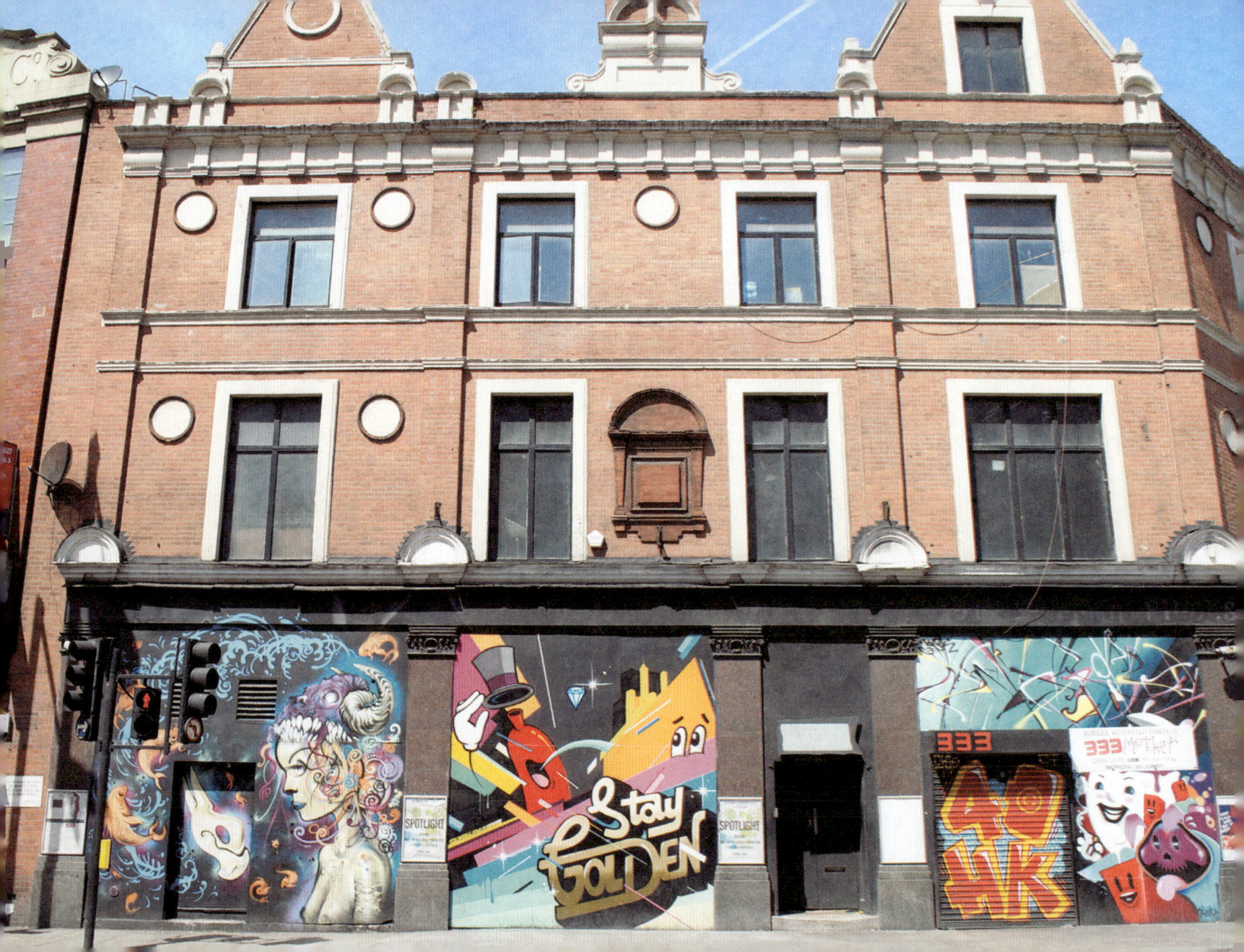

Stay
GOLDEN
SPOTLIGHT
SPOTLIGHT
333

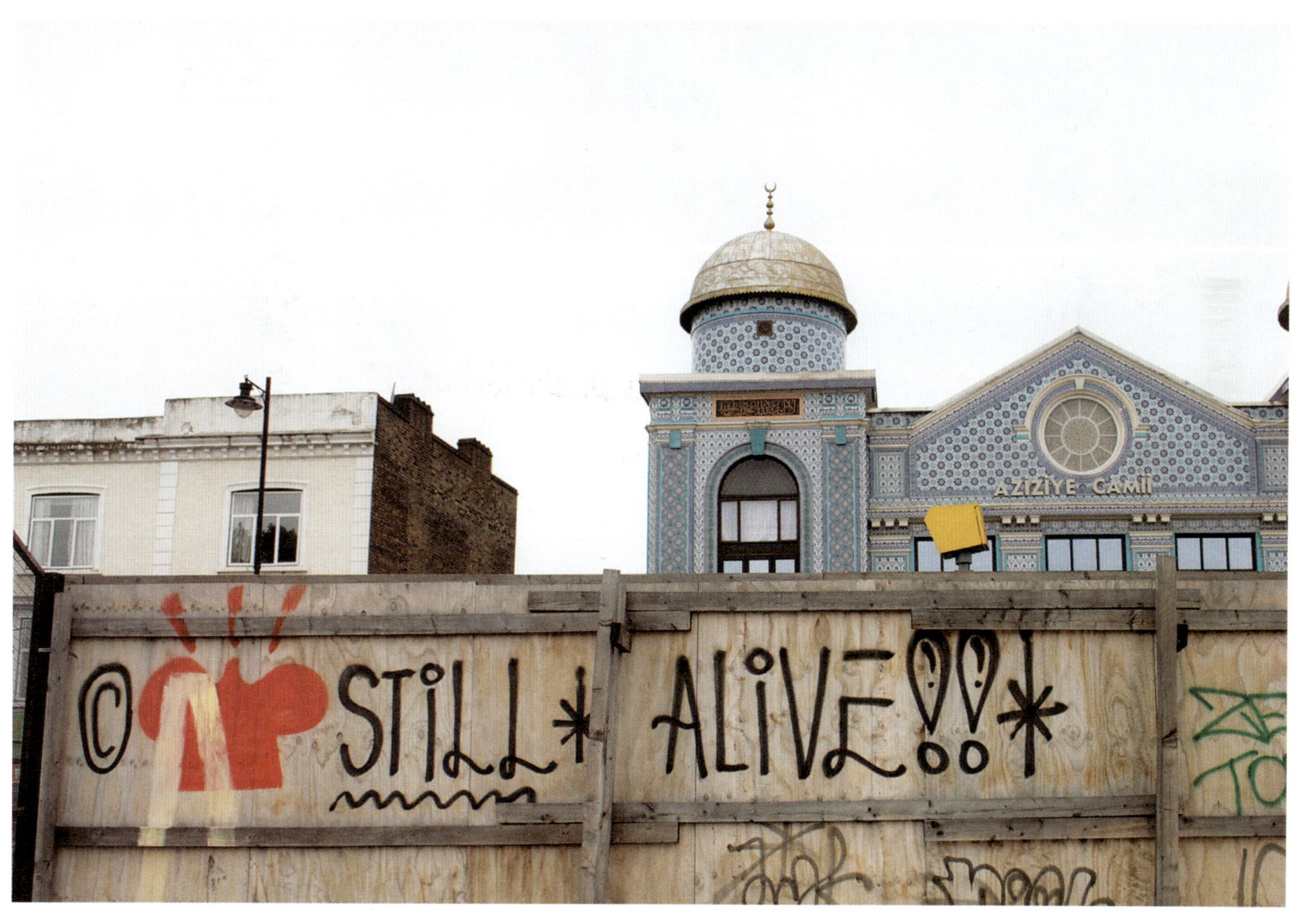

Remi/Rough & Dabs & Myla Old Street, London ← and **Sickboy** Stoke Newington, London ↑

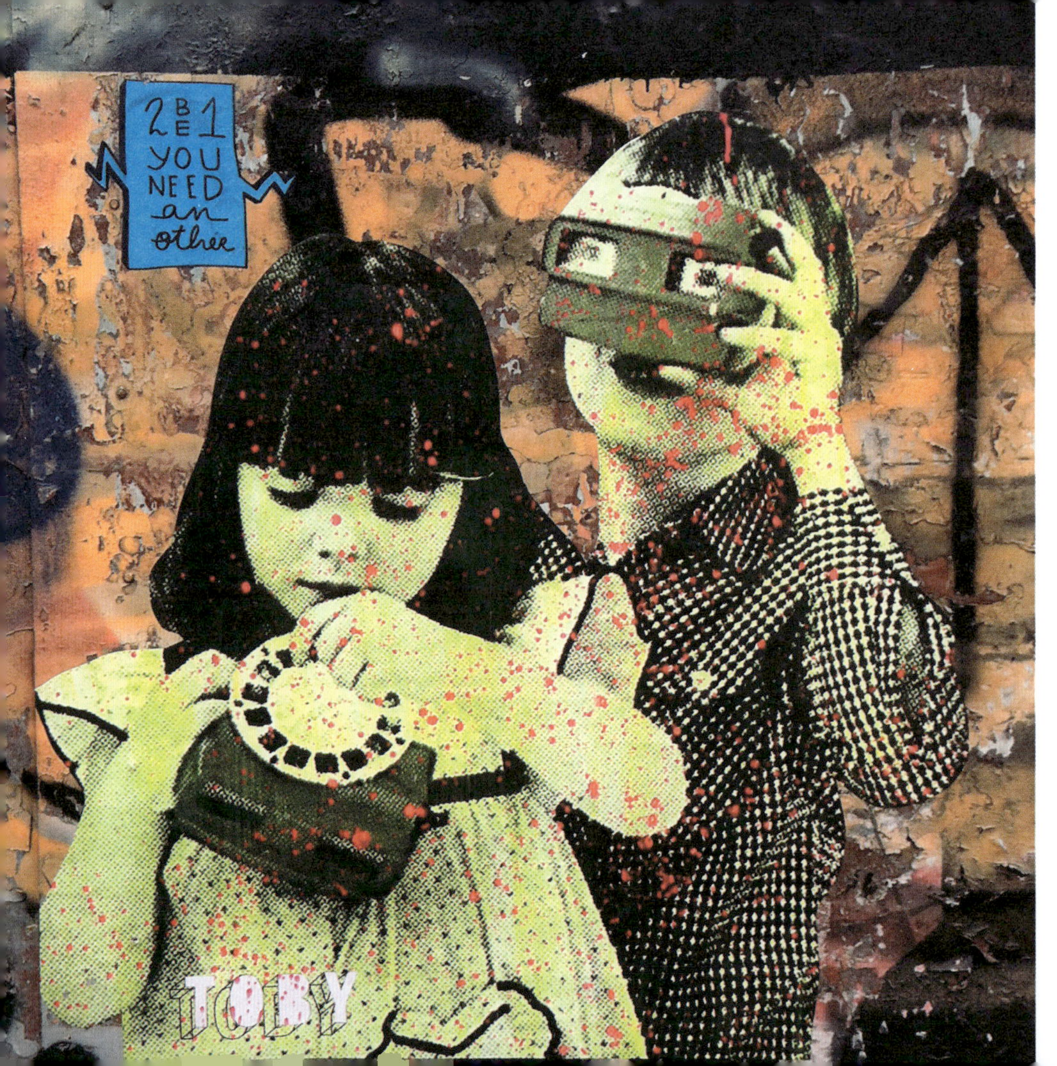

Toby Brick Lane, London ←

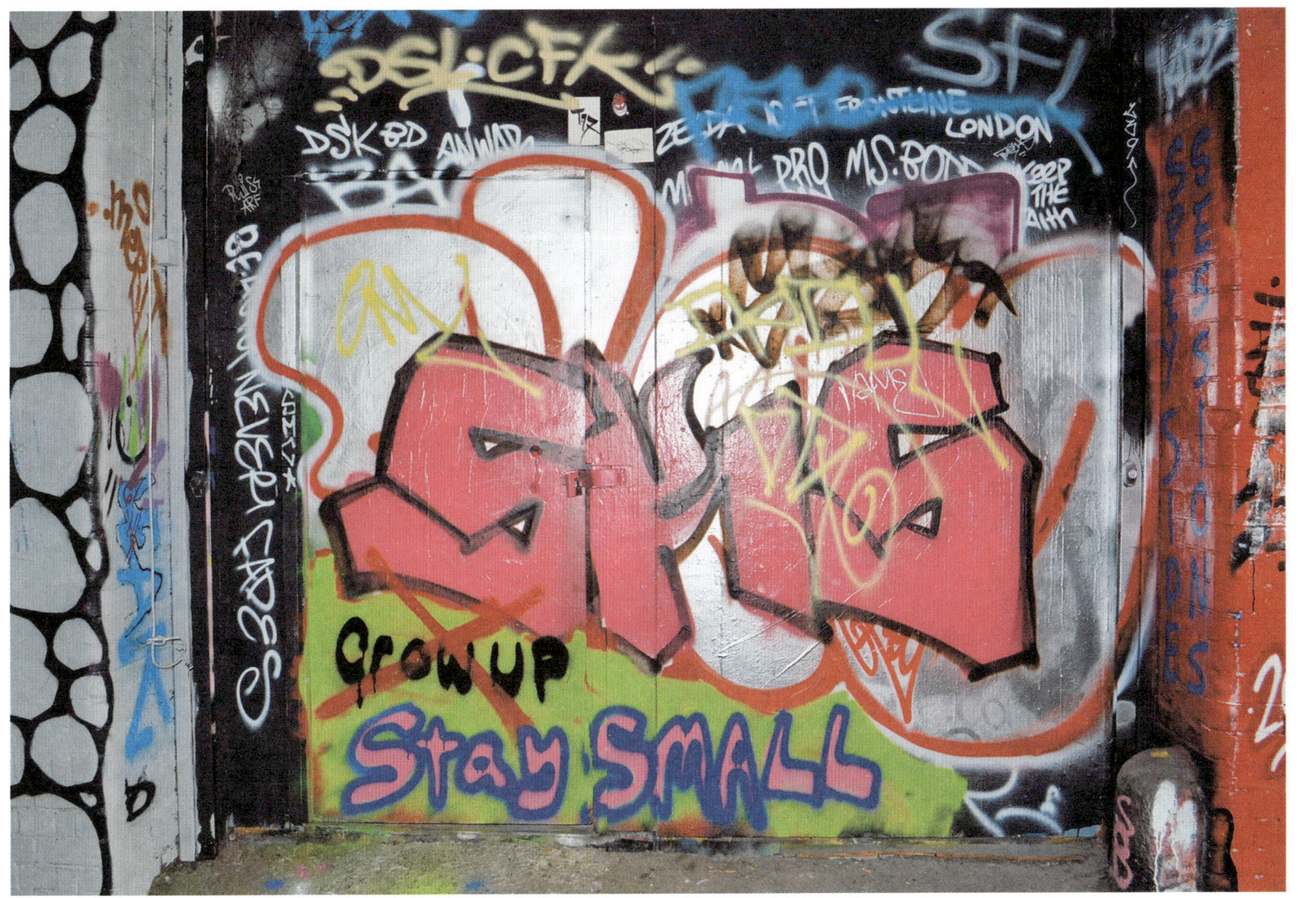

Unknown Leake Street Tunnel, London ↑

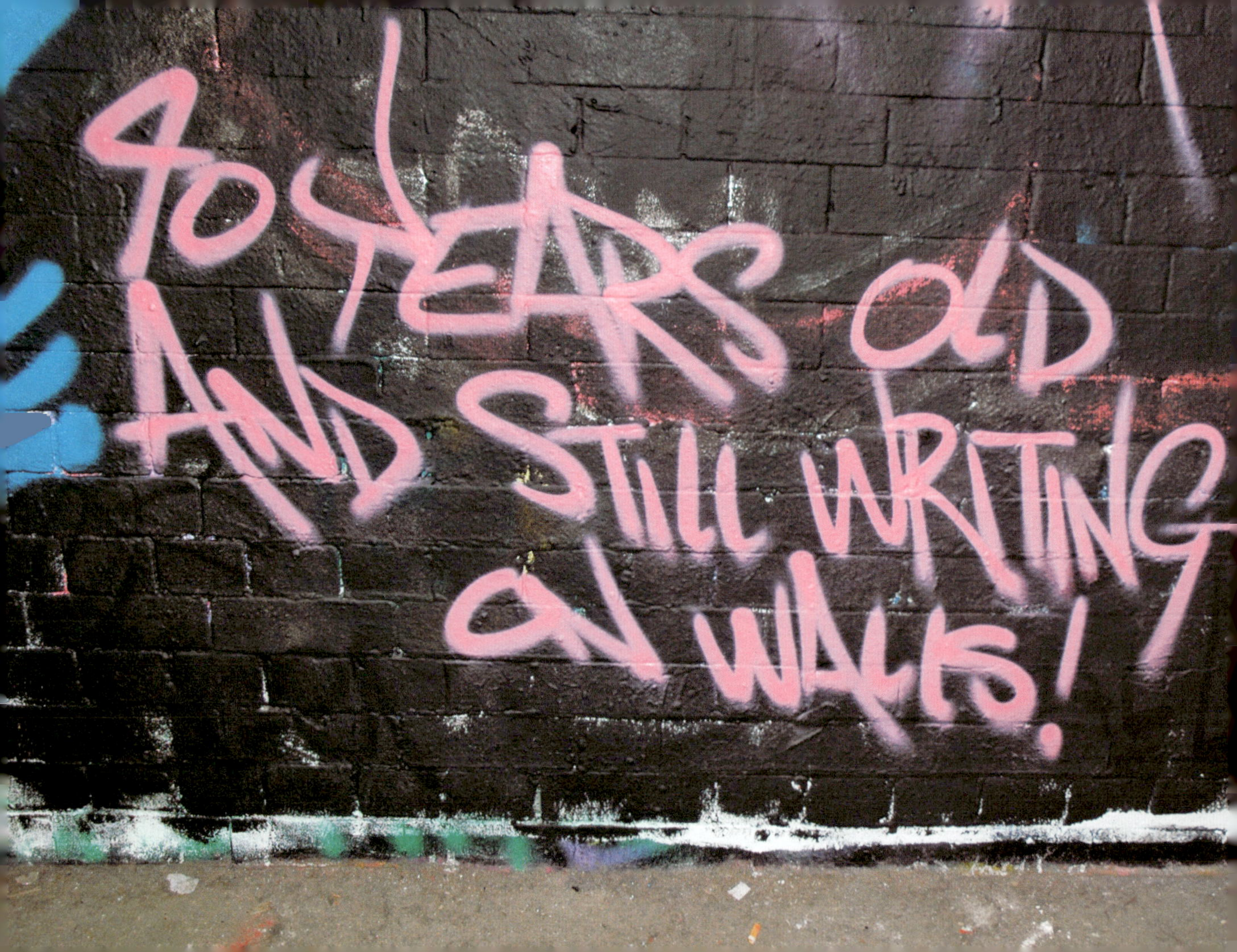
40 YEARS OLD
AND STILL WRITING
ON WALLS!

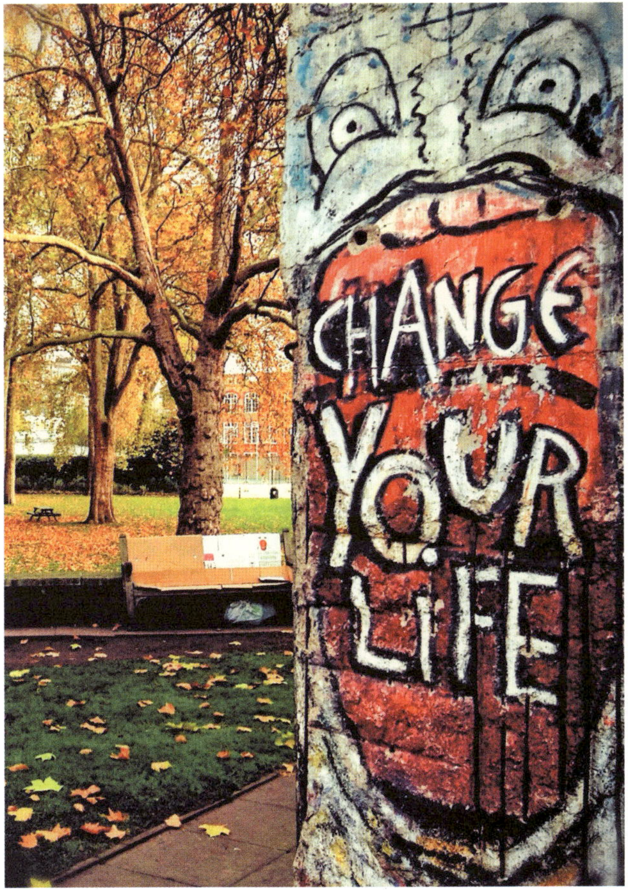

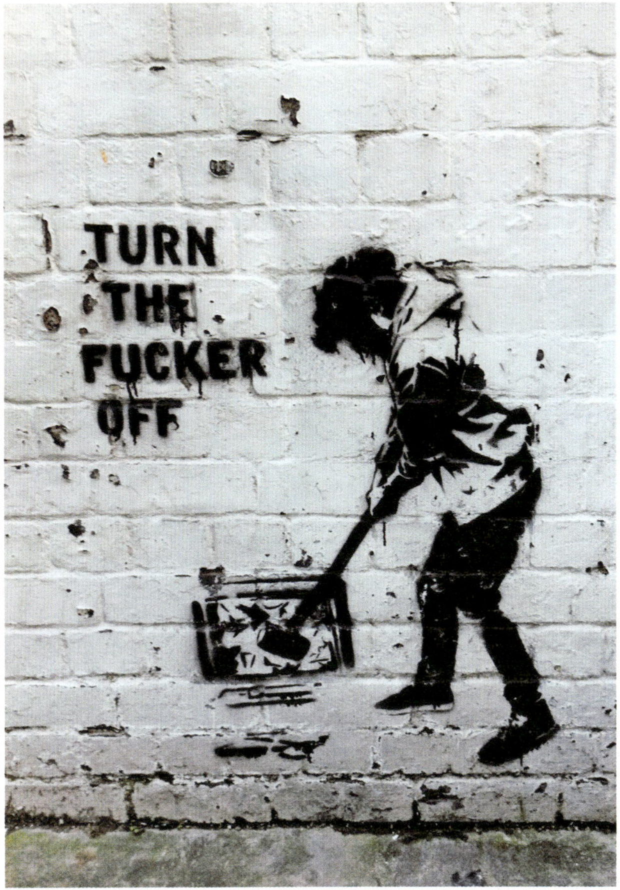

Unknown Leake Street Tunnel, London ← and **Unknown** Lambeth, London, **Unknown** Brick Lane, London ↑

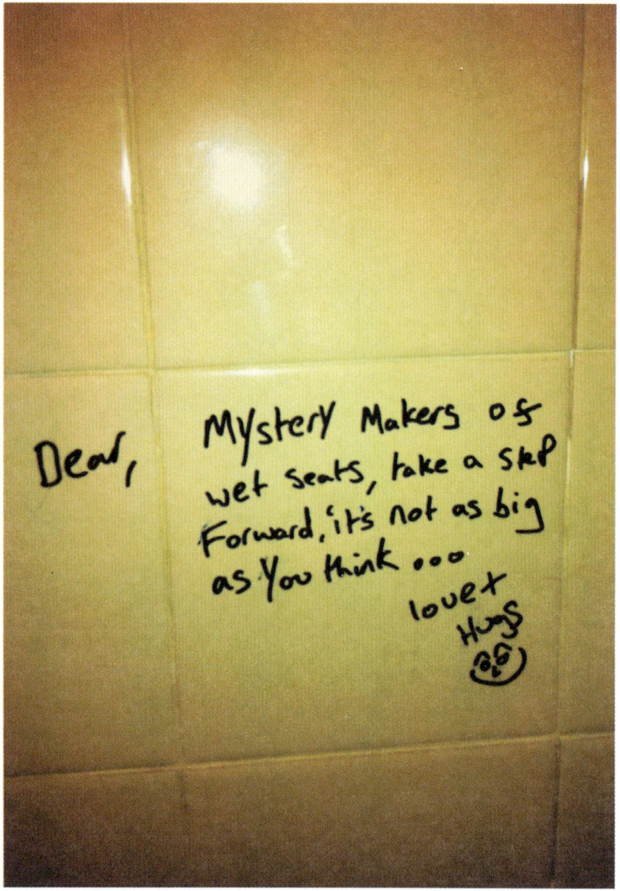

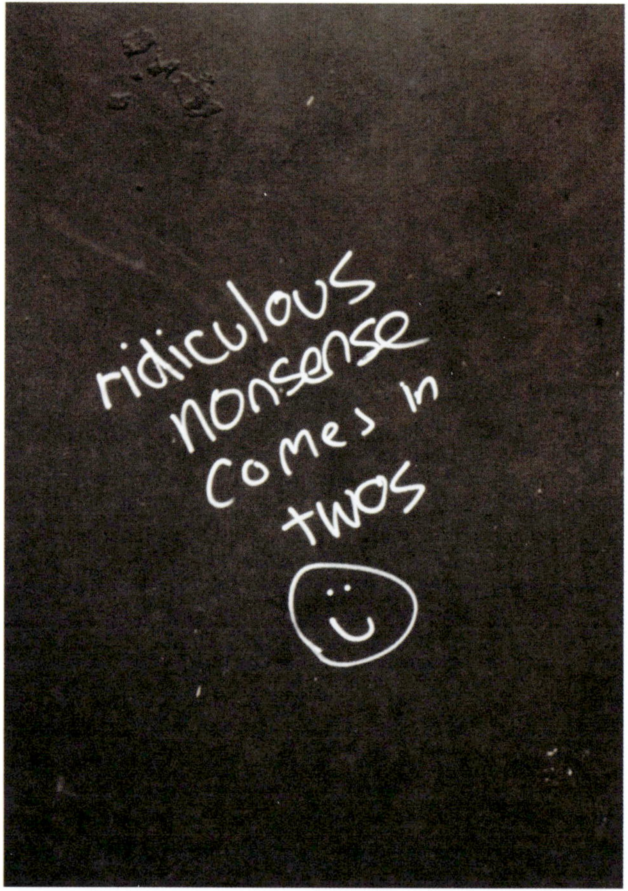

Unknown Waterloo, London, **Unknown** Islington, London ↑ and **Unknown** Oxford Road, Manchester →

It was the Best of Days
Said the Sun to the
sky.

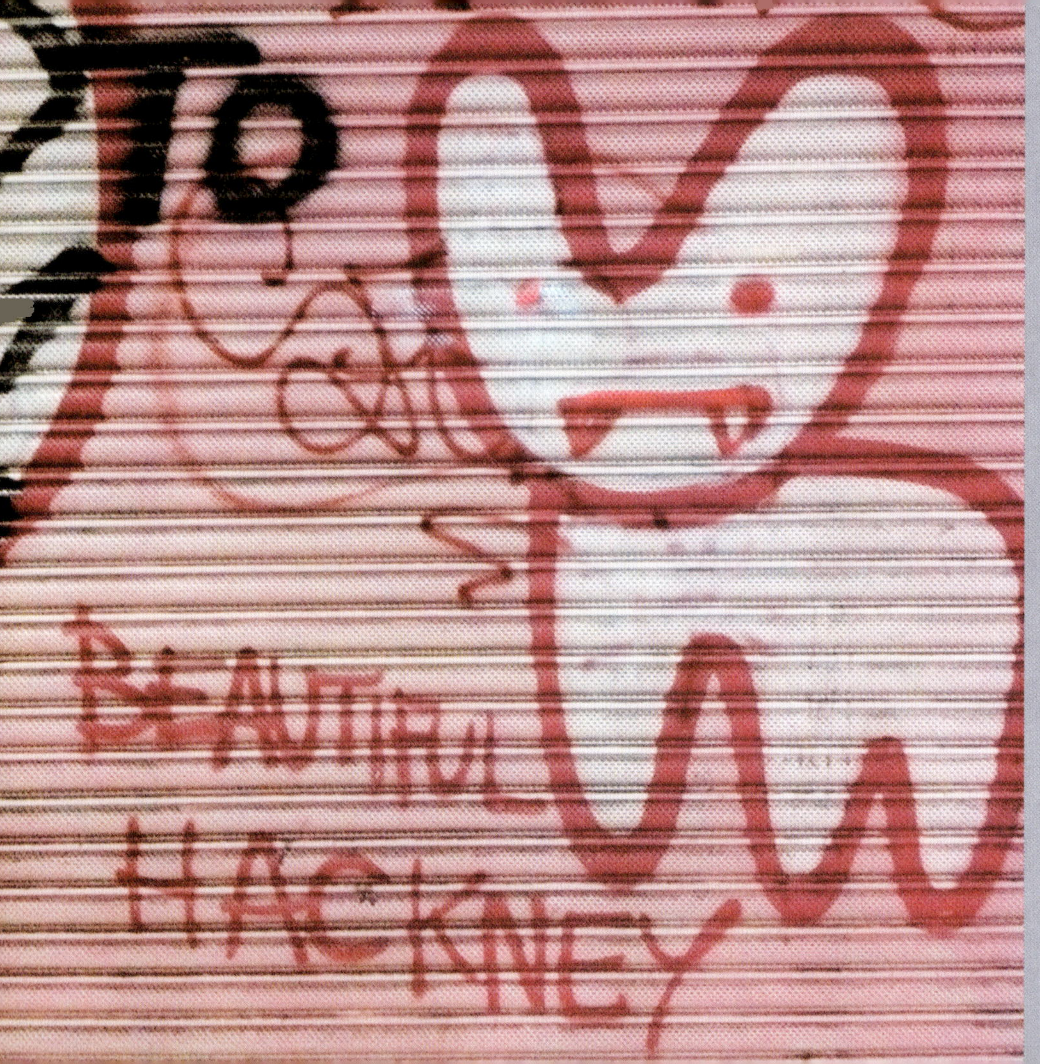

Pure Evil

Pure Evil isn't very evil – he's actually quite a nice man. He paints just like a ten-year-old and enjoys painting vampire rabbits and other weird stuff all over the world. He also now runs his own gallery: Pure Evil Gallery in East London.

Pure Evil Hackney, London ←

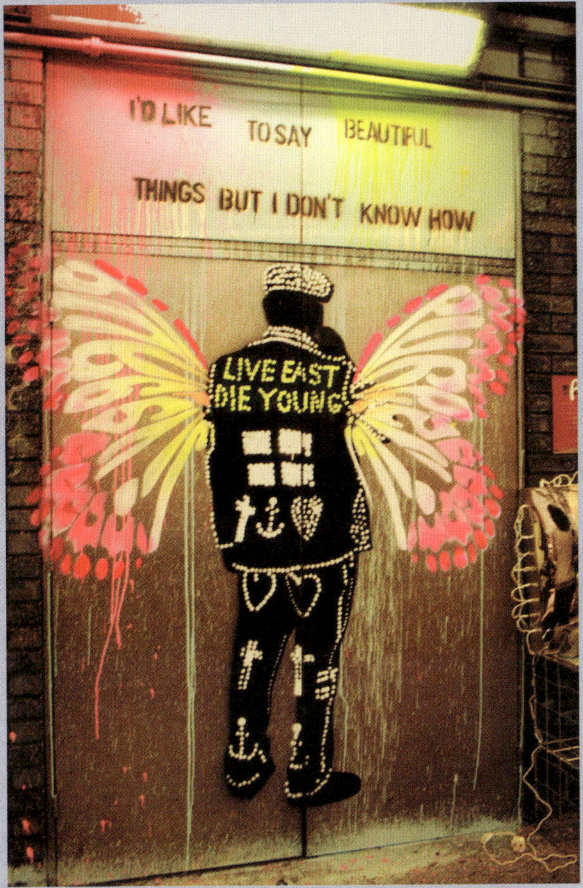

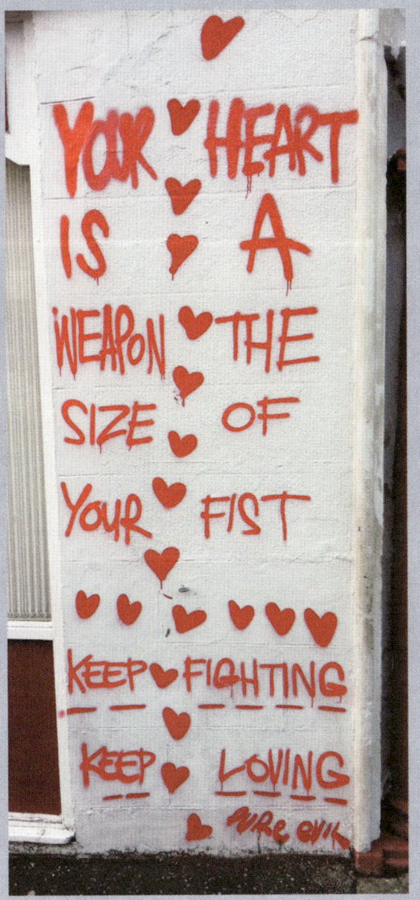

Pure Evil Leake Street Tunnel, London and Lisburn, Belfast ↑

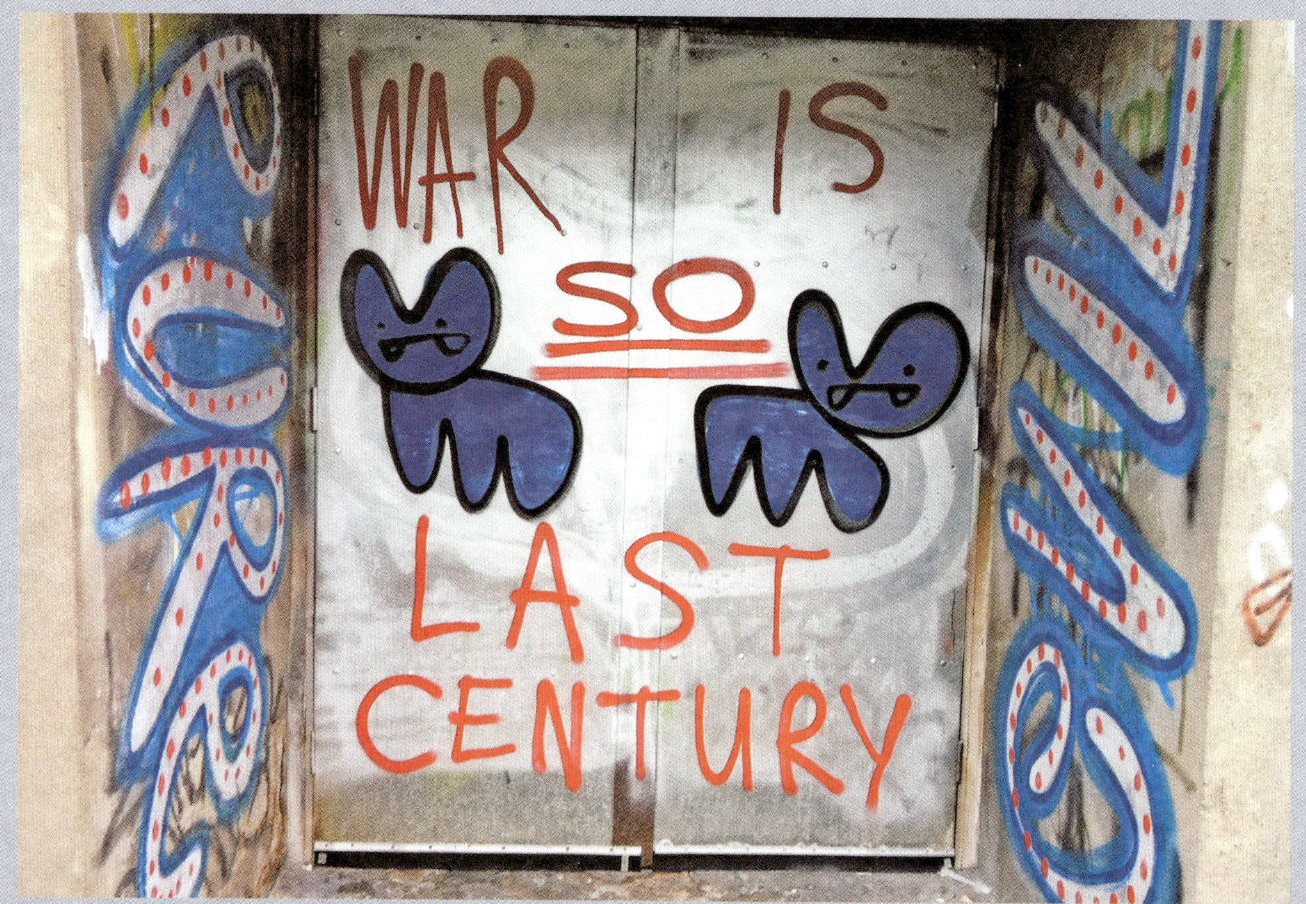

Pure Evil Lisburn, Belfast ↑

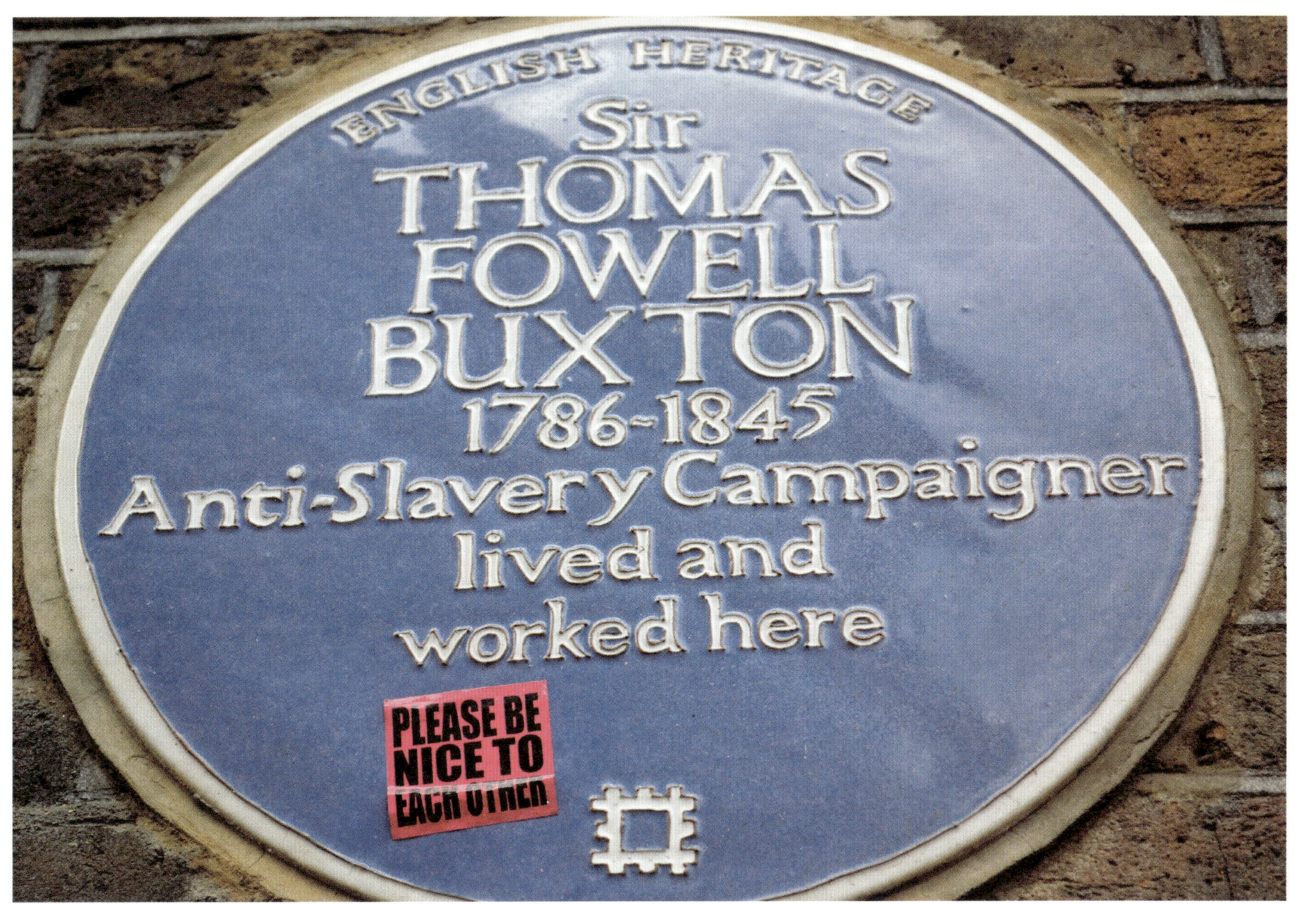

Unknown Brick Lane, London ↑

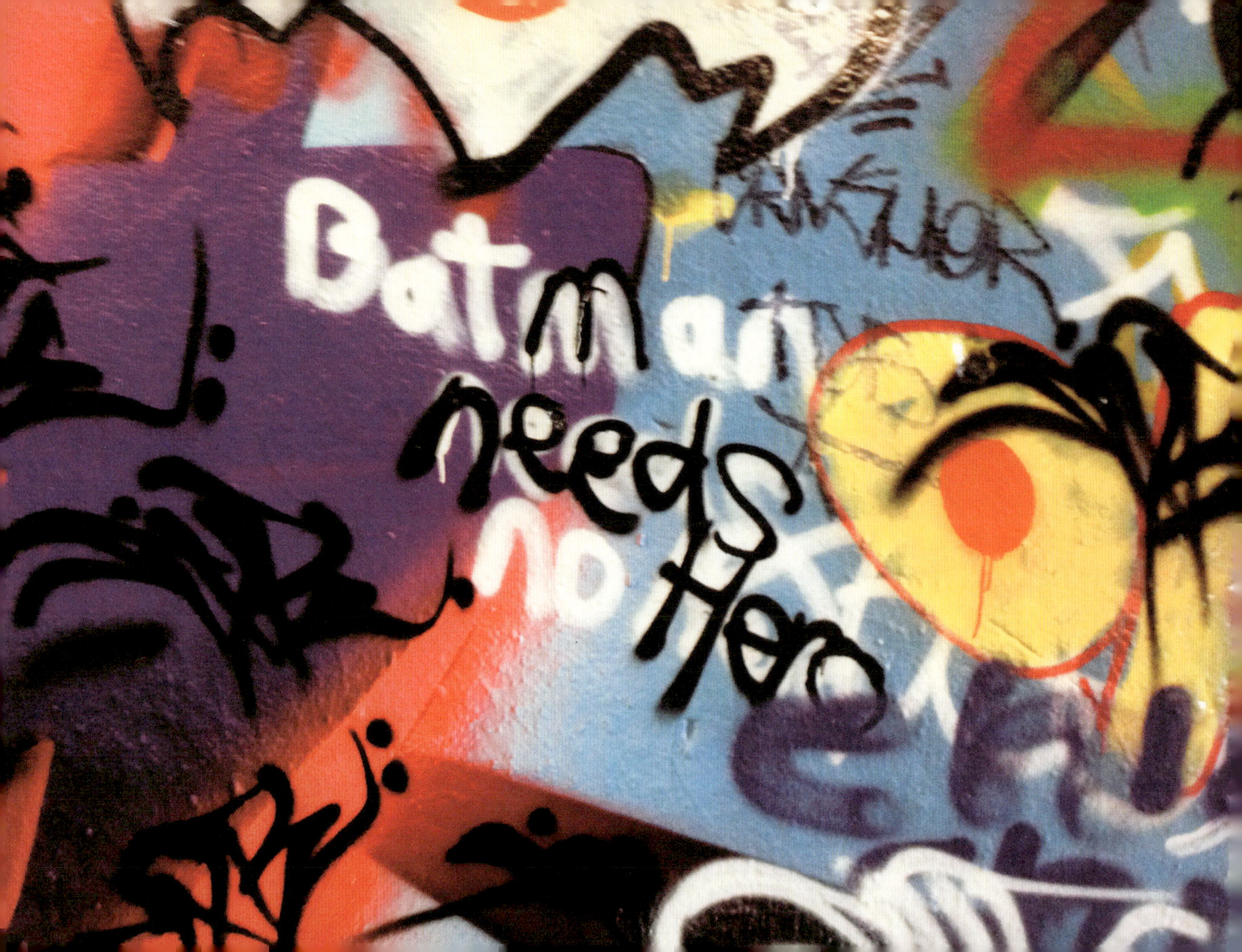
Batman needs no Hero

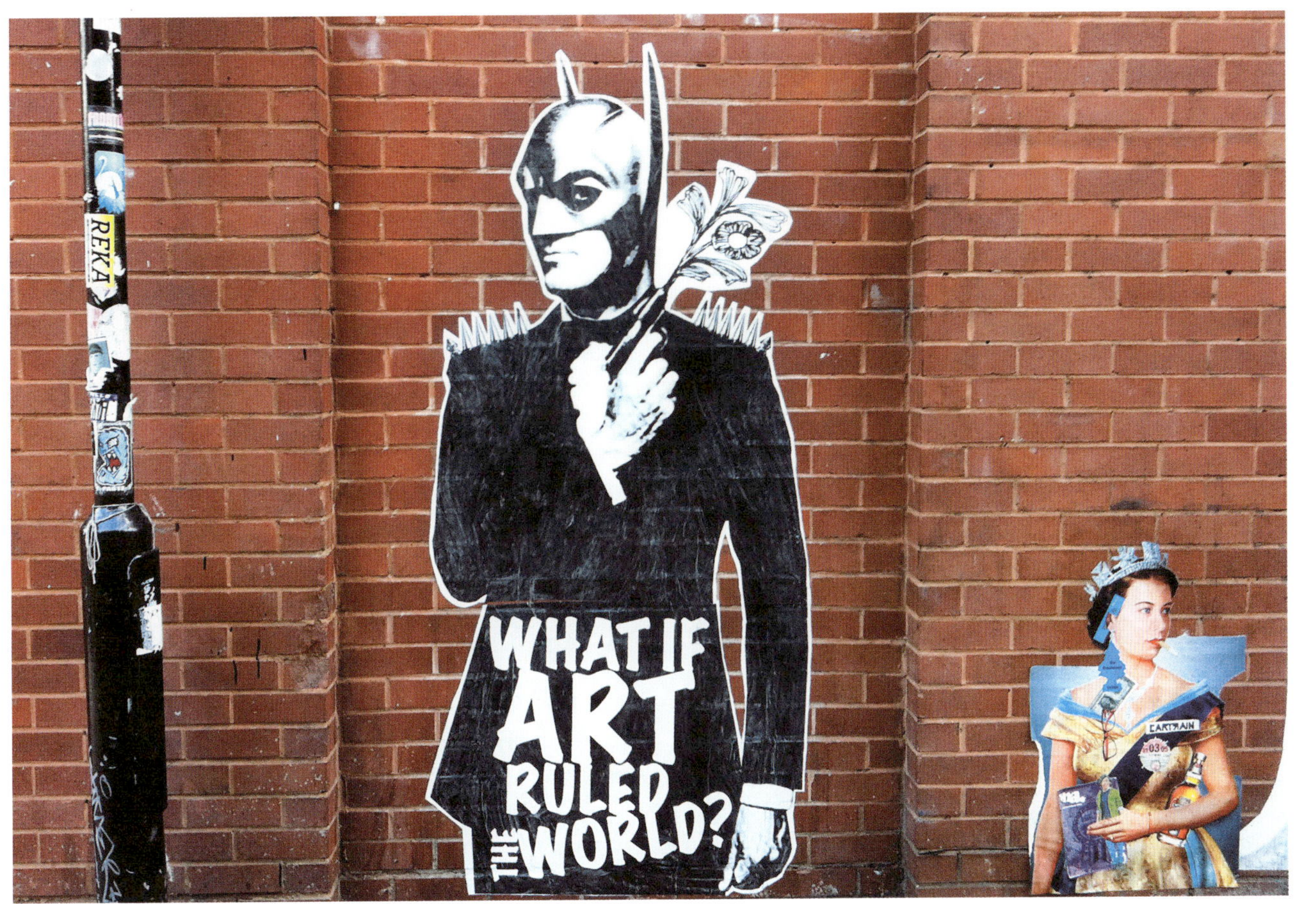

Unknown Leake Street Tunnel, London ← and **Stikki Peaches** Shoreditch, London ↑

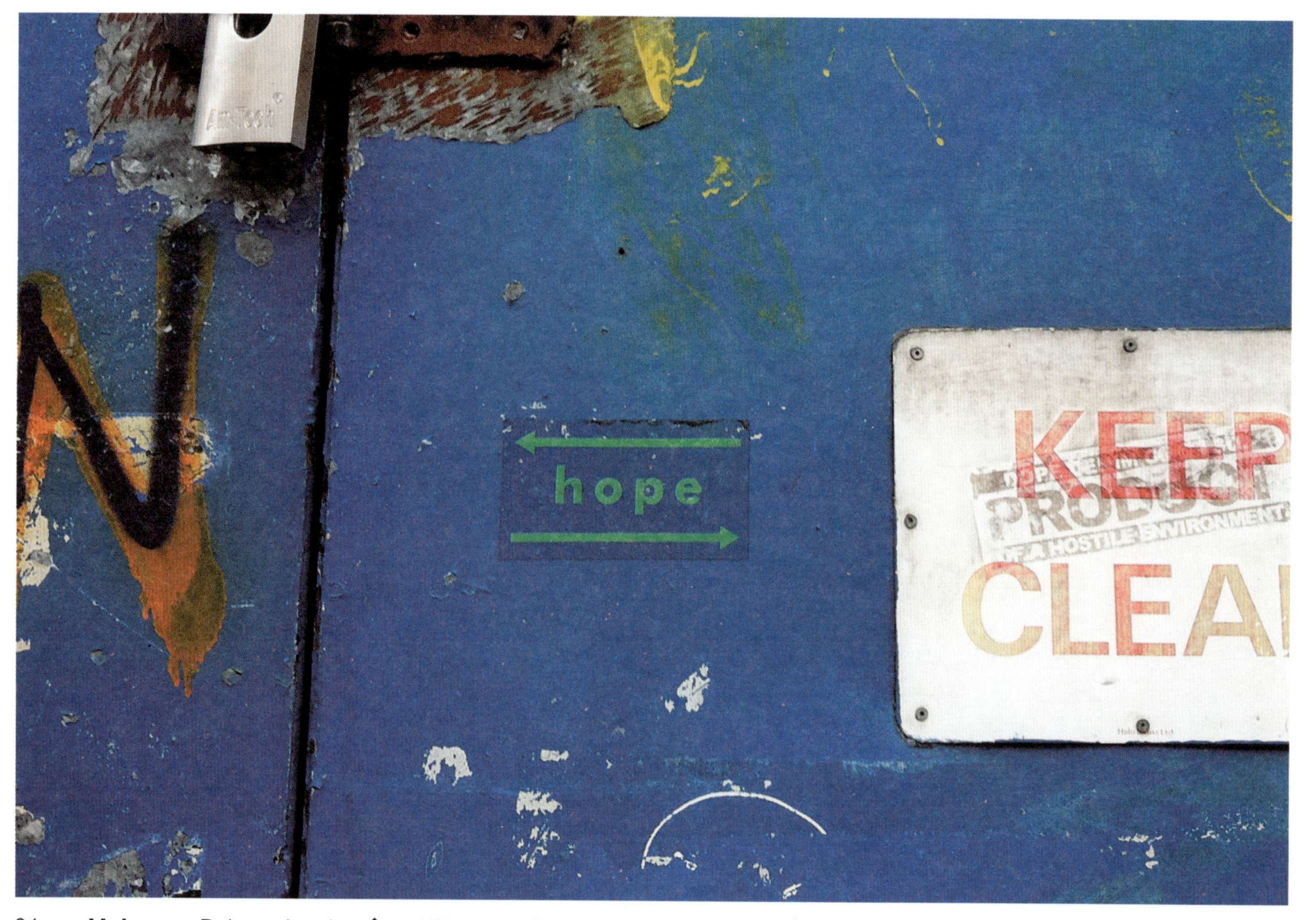

Unknown Dalston, London ↑ and **Expanded Eye** Brick Lane, London →

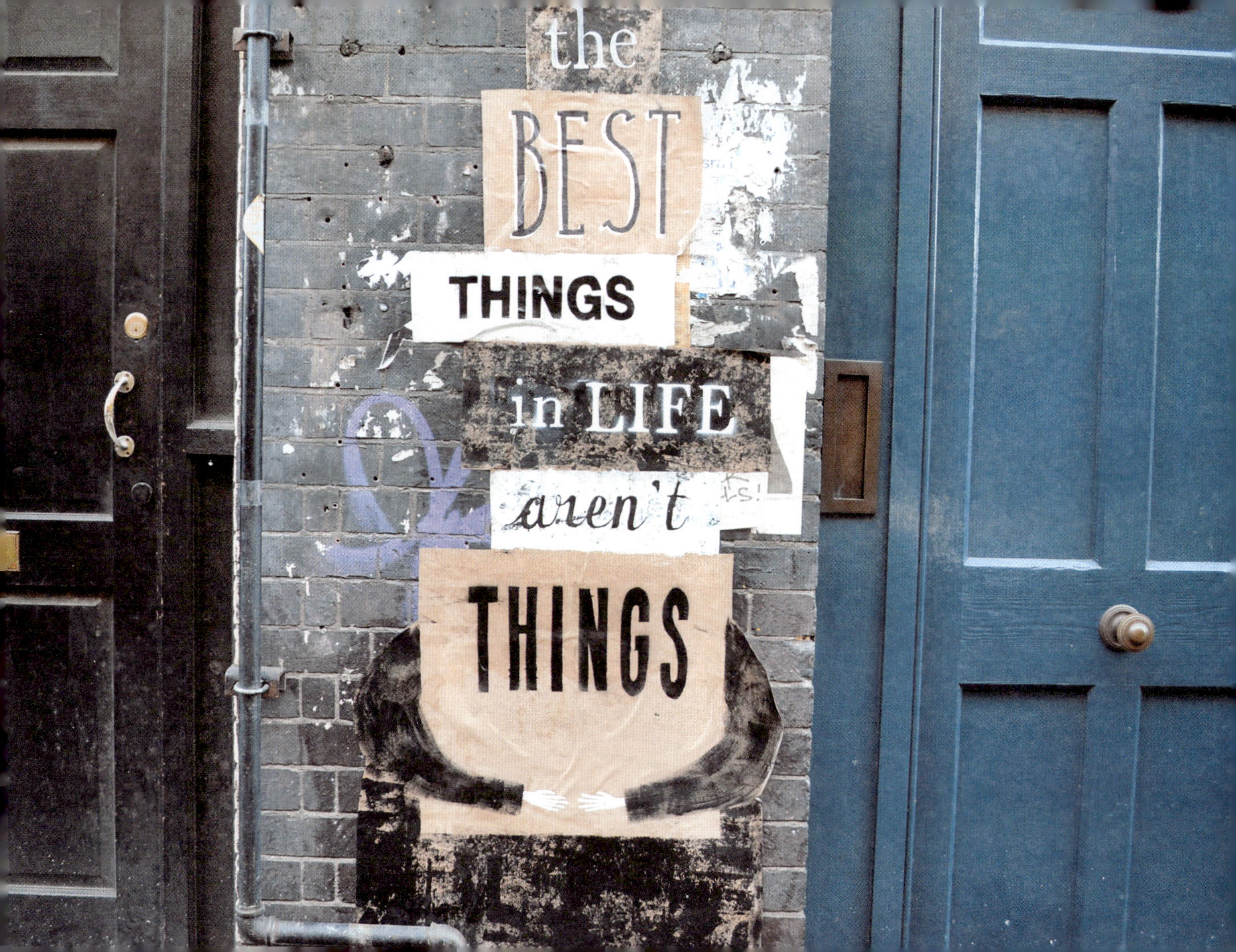
the
BEST
THINGS
in LIFE
aren't
THINGS

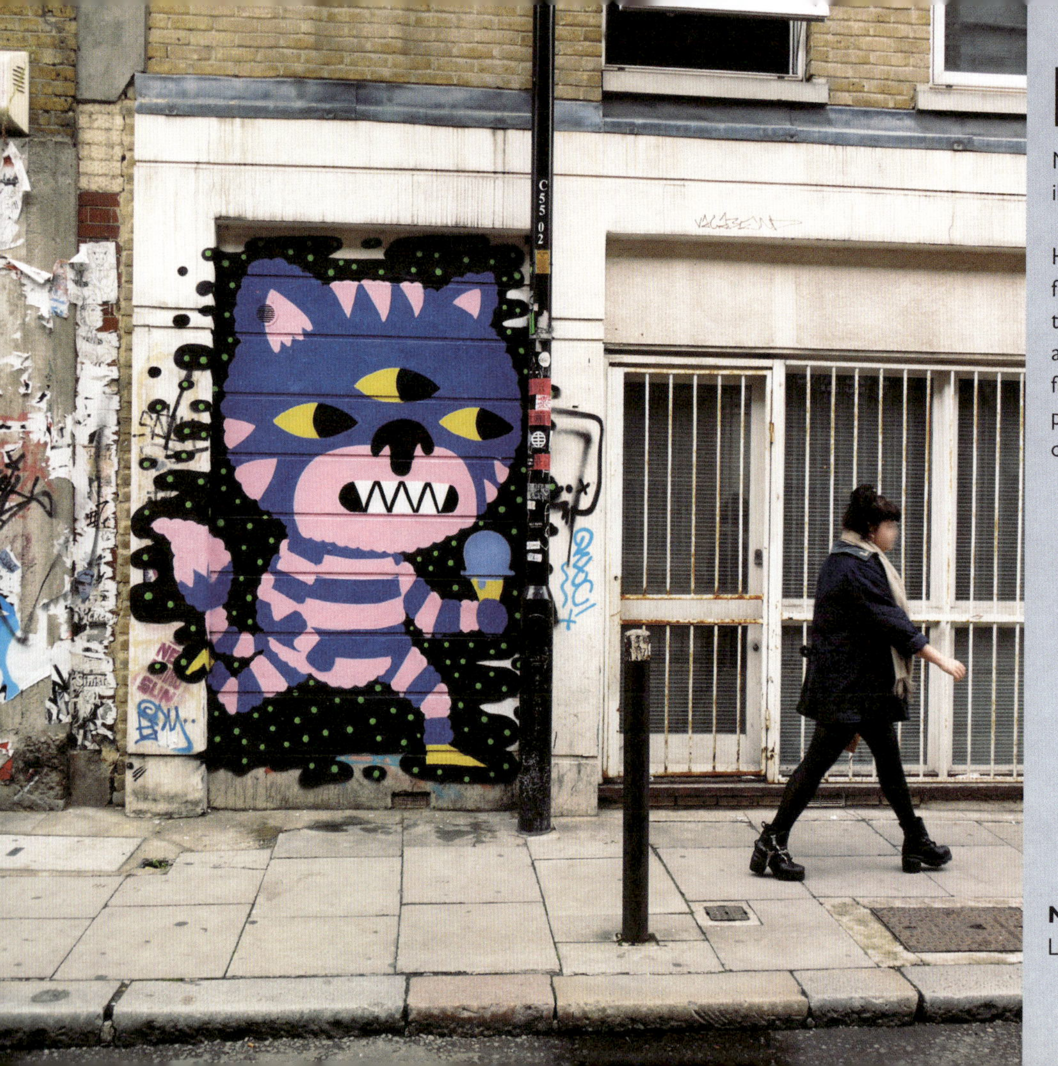

Malarky

Malarky is a street painter, illustrator and skateboarder

Half of the time he can be found putting colour onto the streets of grey London and the other half you can find him drinking a beer and painting a truck in the sunshine of Barcelona.

Malarky Shoreditch, London ←

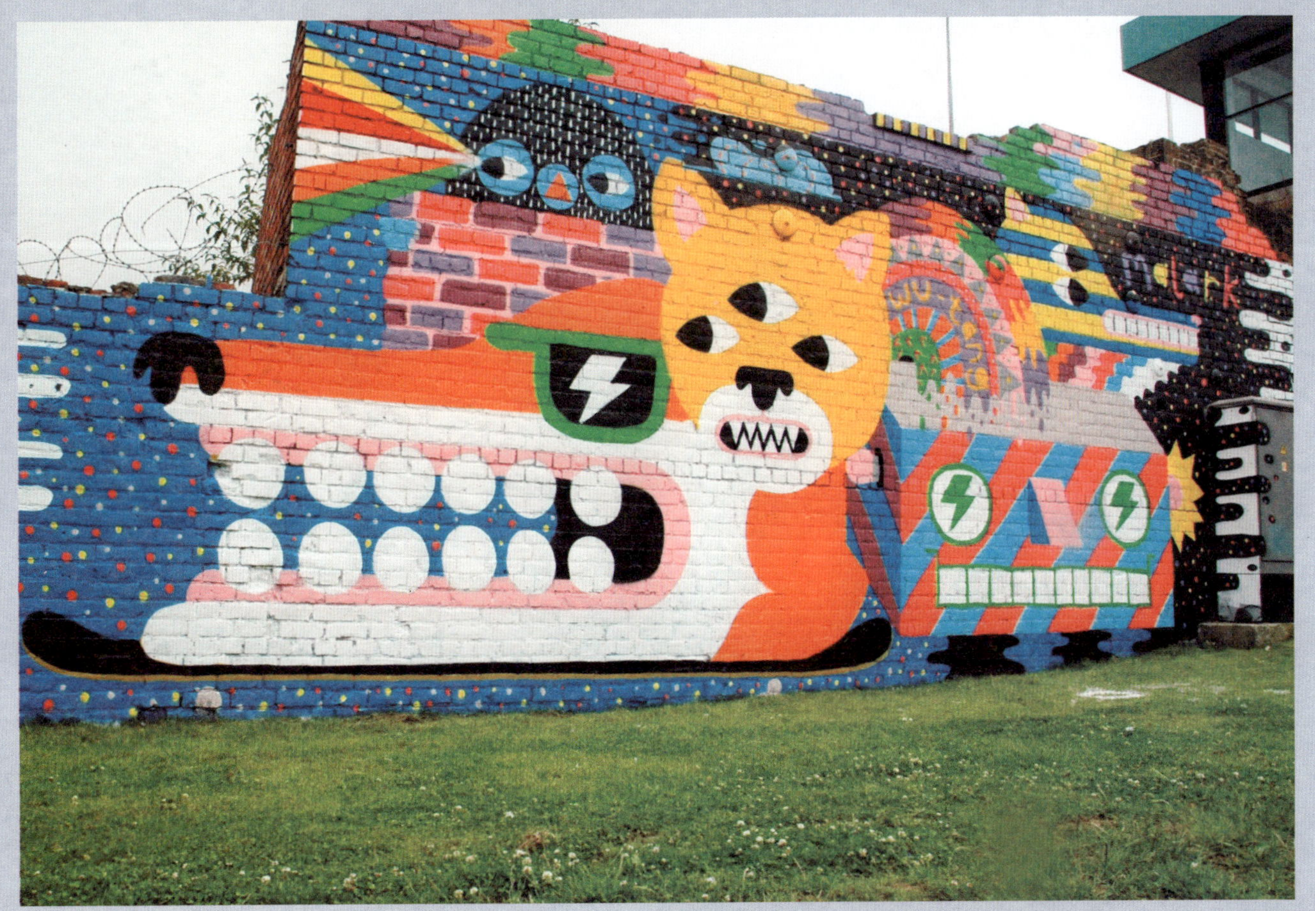

Malarky Gateshead ↑

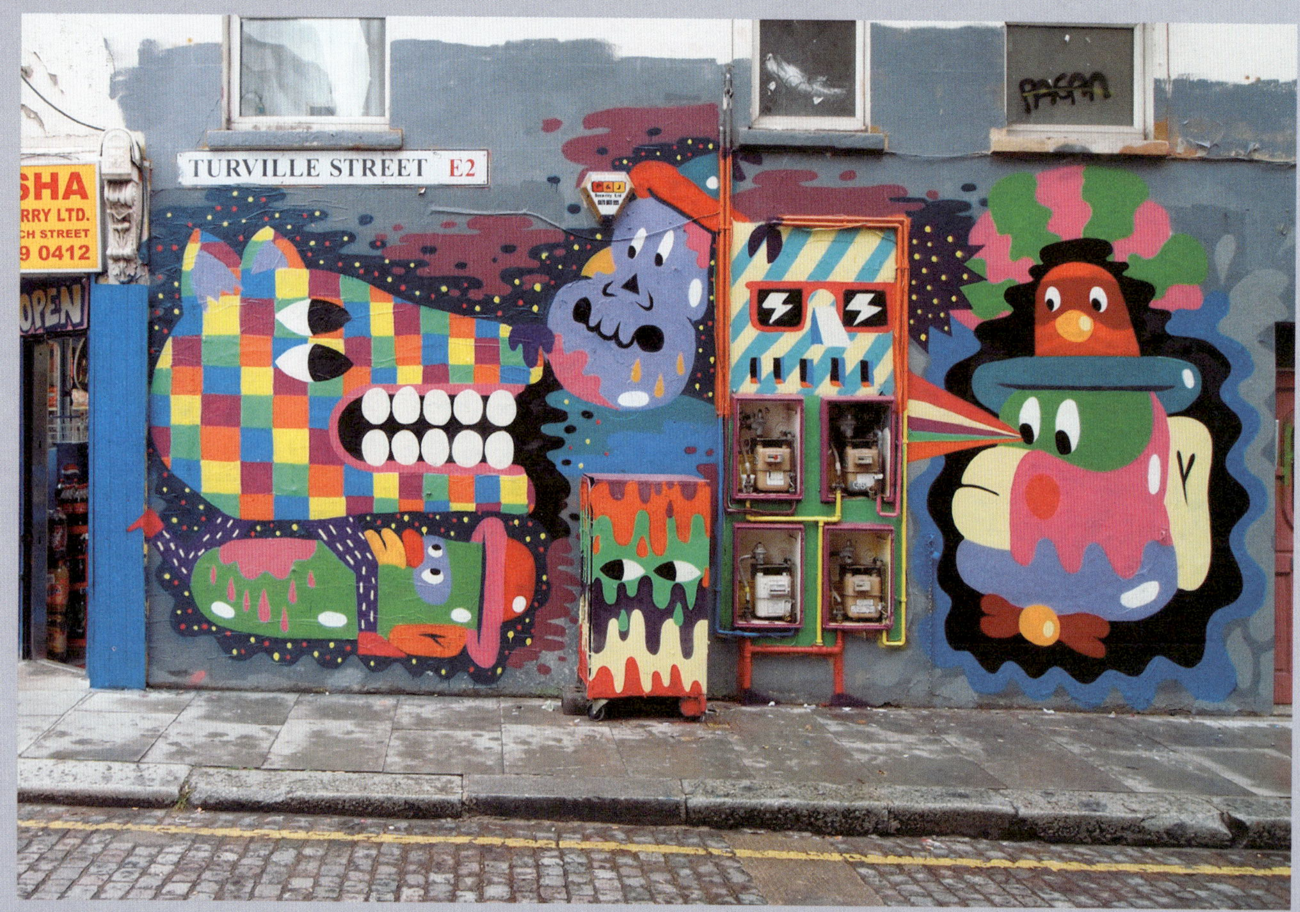

 Malarky Shoreditch, London ↑

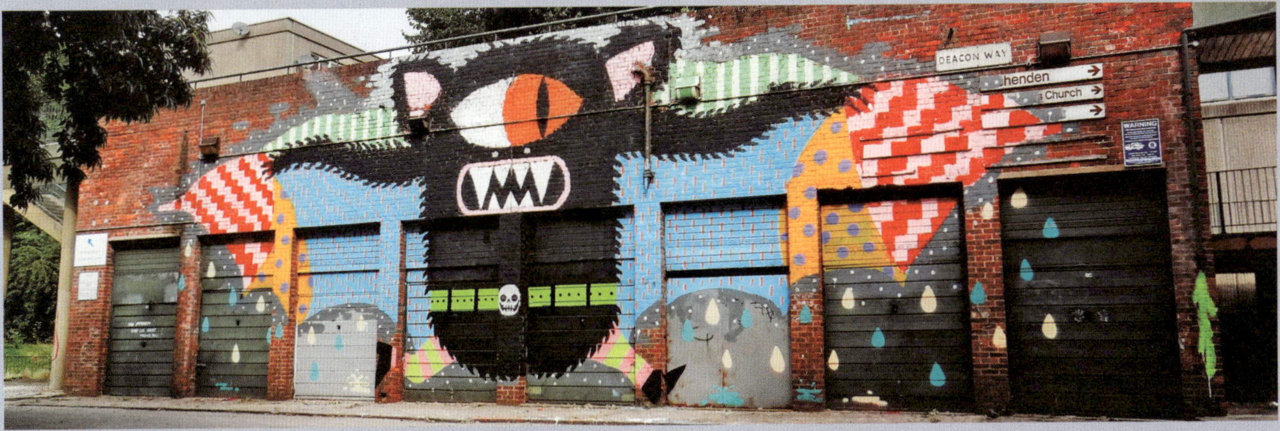

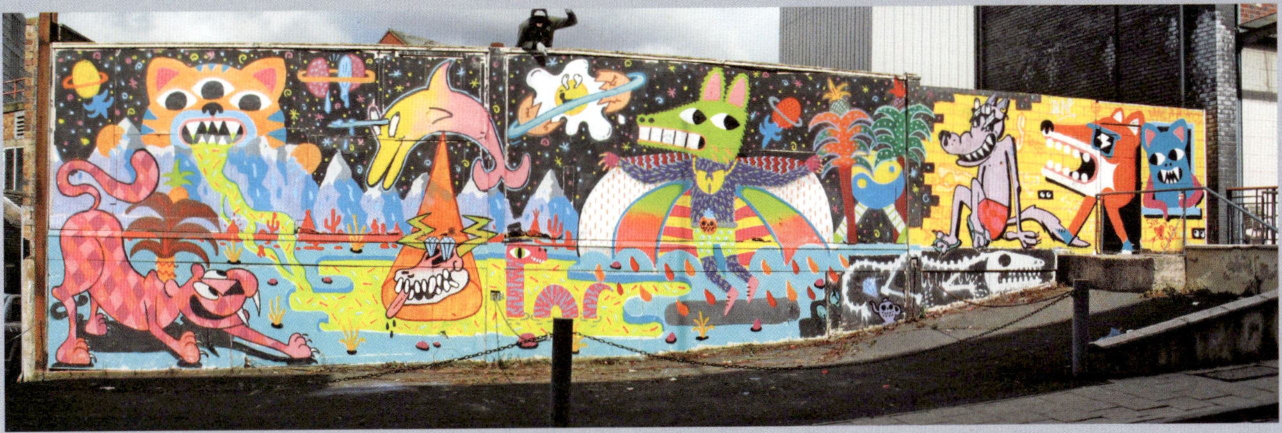

Malarky Elephant and Castle, London and Hanley, Stoke-on-Trent ↑

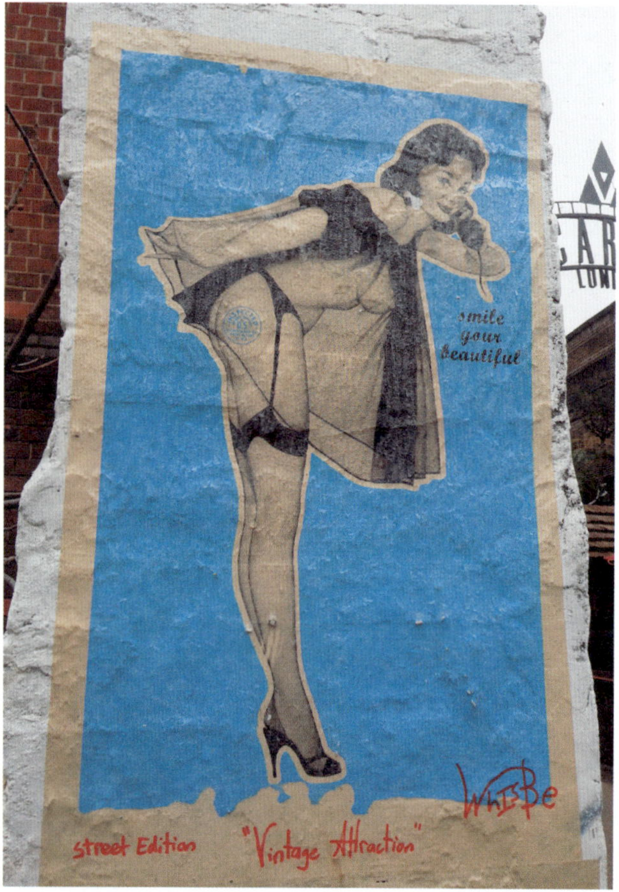

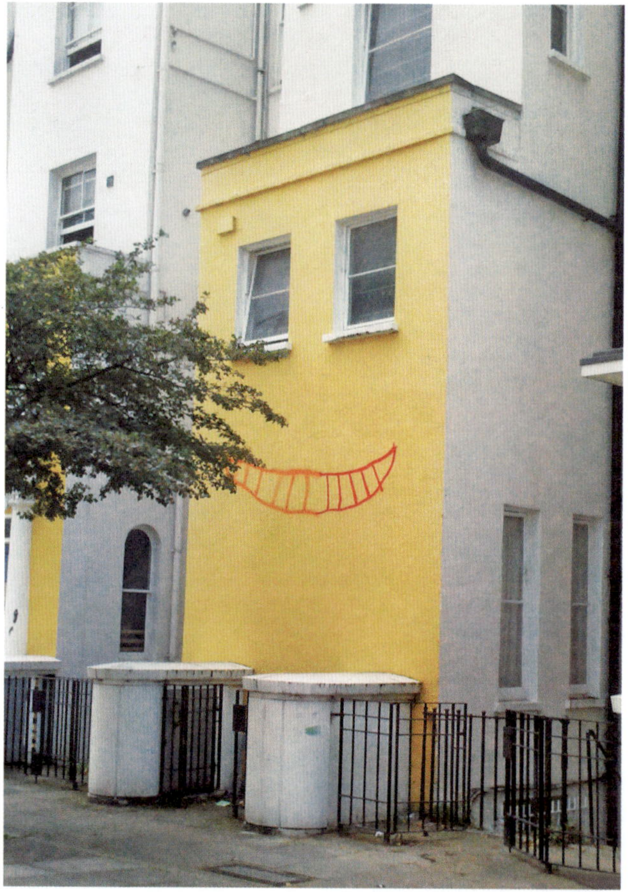

 WhisBe Shoreditch, London, **Unknown** Notting Hill, London ↑

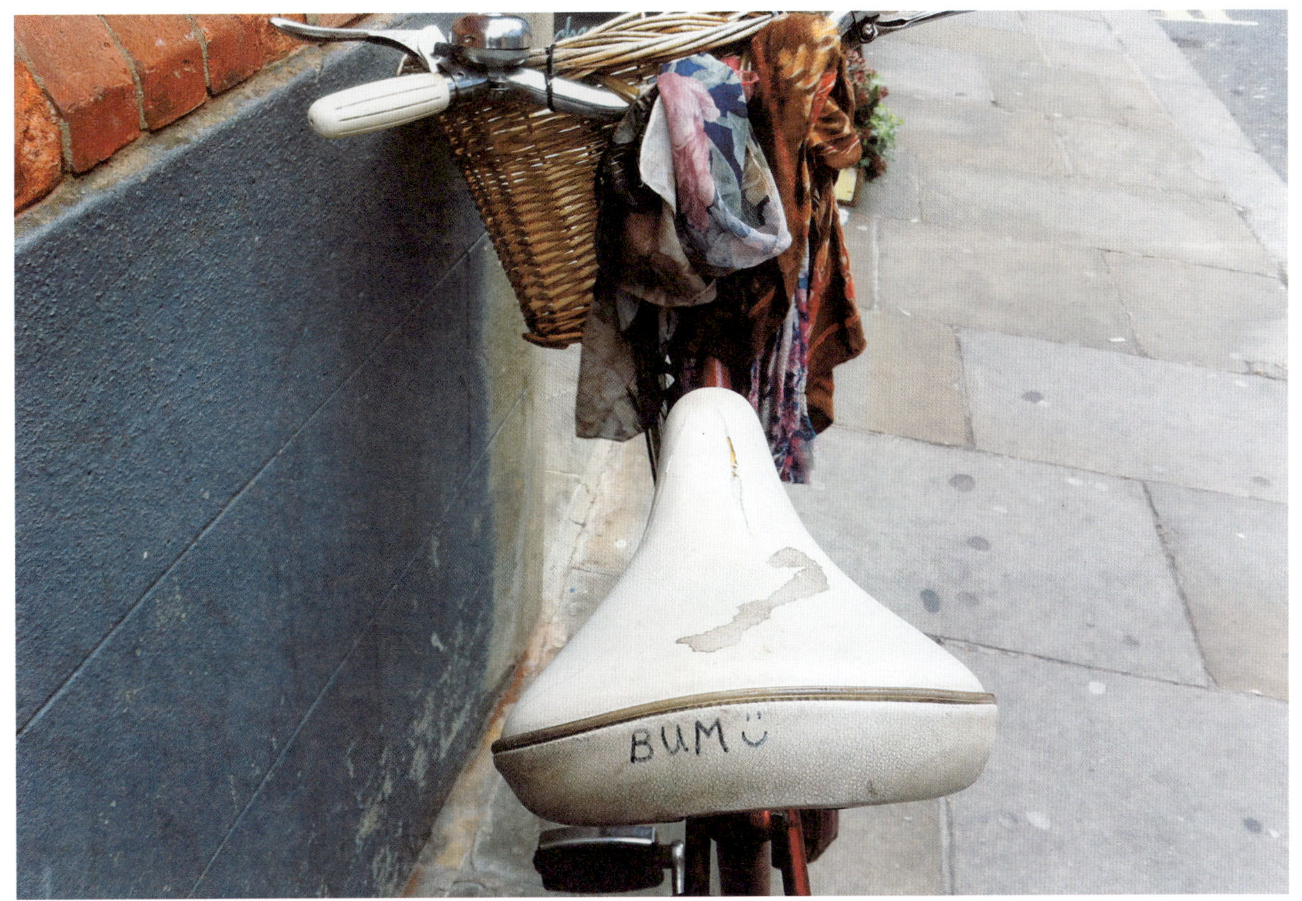

Unknown Spitalfields, London ↑

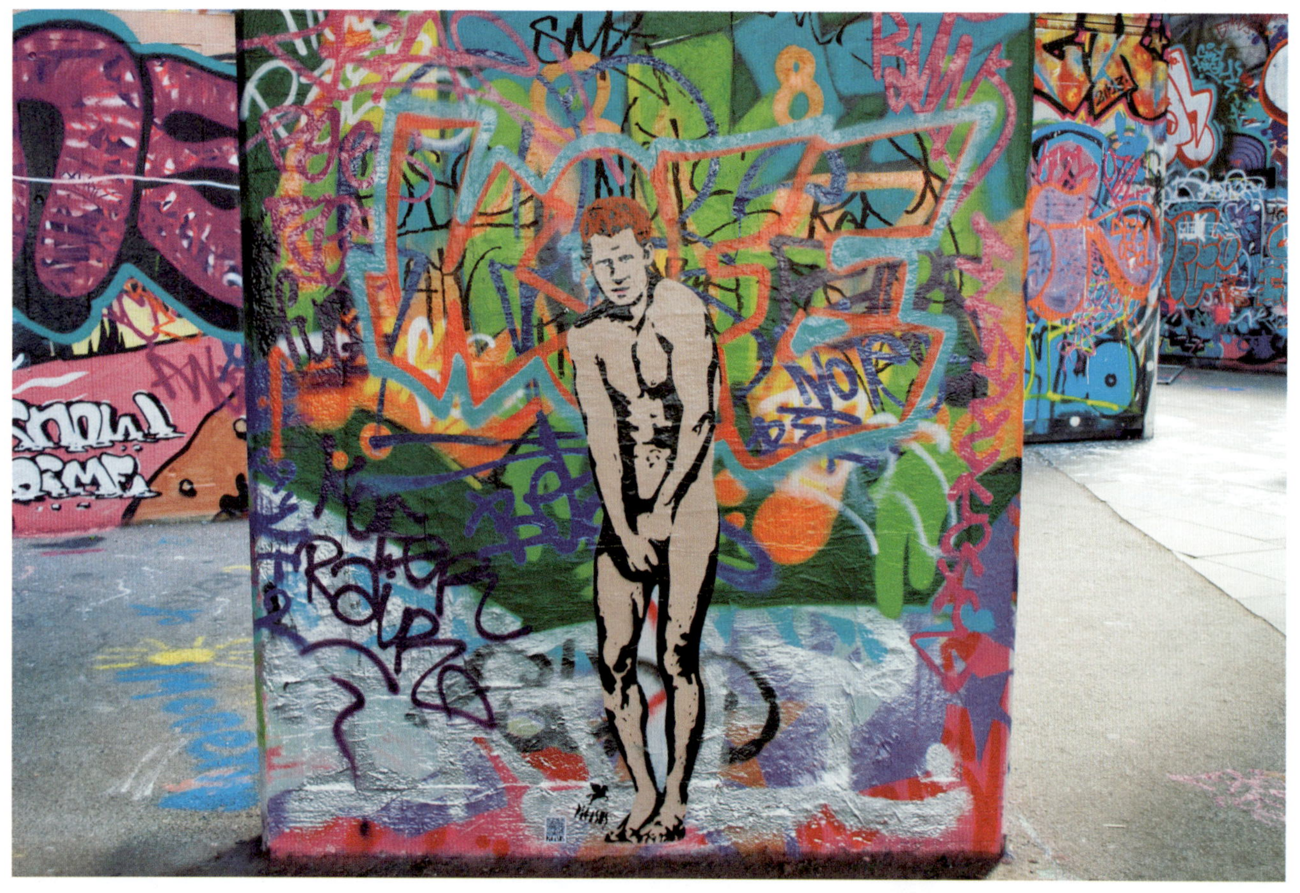

 Pegasus Southbank, London ↑ and **Unknown** Bethnal Green, London →

NICE
NIPS

Kid Acne

Kid Acne spent his formative years painting graffiti, creating fanzines and making limited release records on his own 'Invisible Spies' imprint. Nowadays, his artwork can be seen throughout the globe – both inside and outside the gallery, in wheatpastes and murals from New York to Azerbaijan. His signature style has adorned products for the world's leading brands, while the man himself continues to paint epic slogans in sub-zero temperatures.

And he still has acne.

Kid Acne Hoult's Yard, Newcastle upon Tyne ↓ and Shoreditch, London →

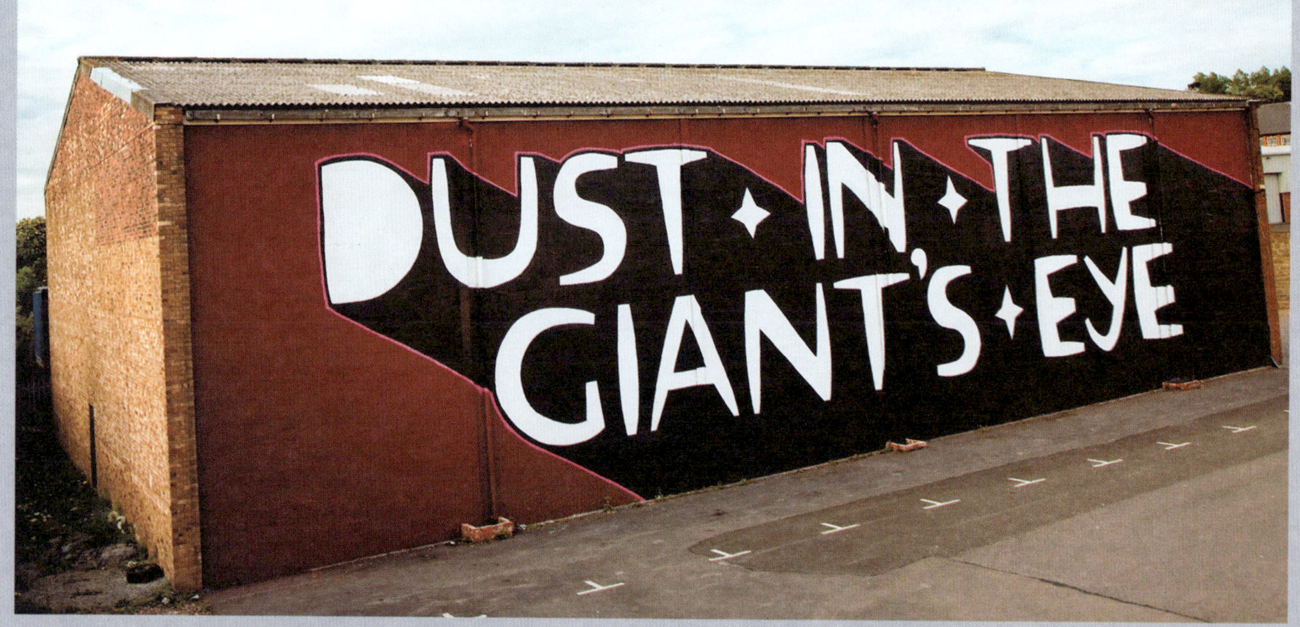

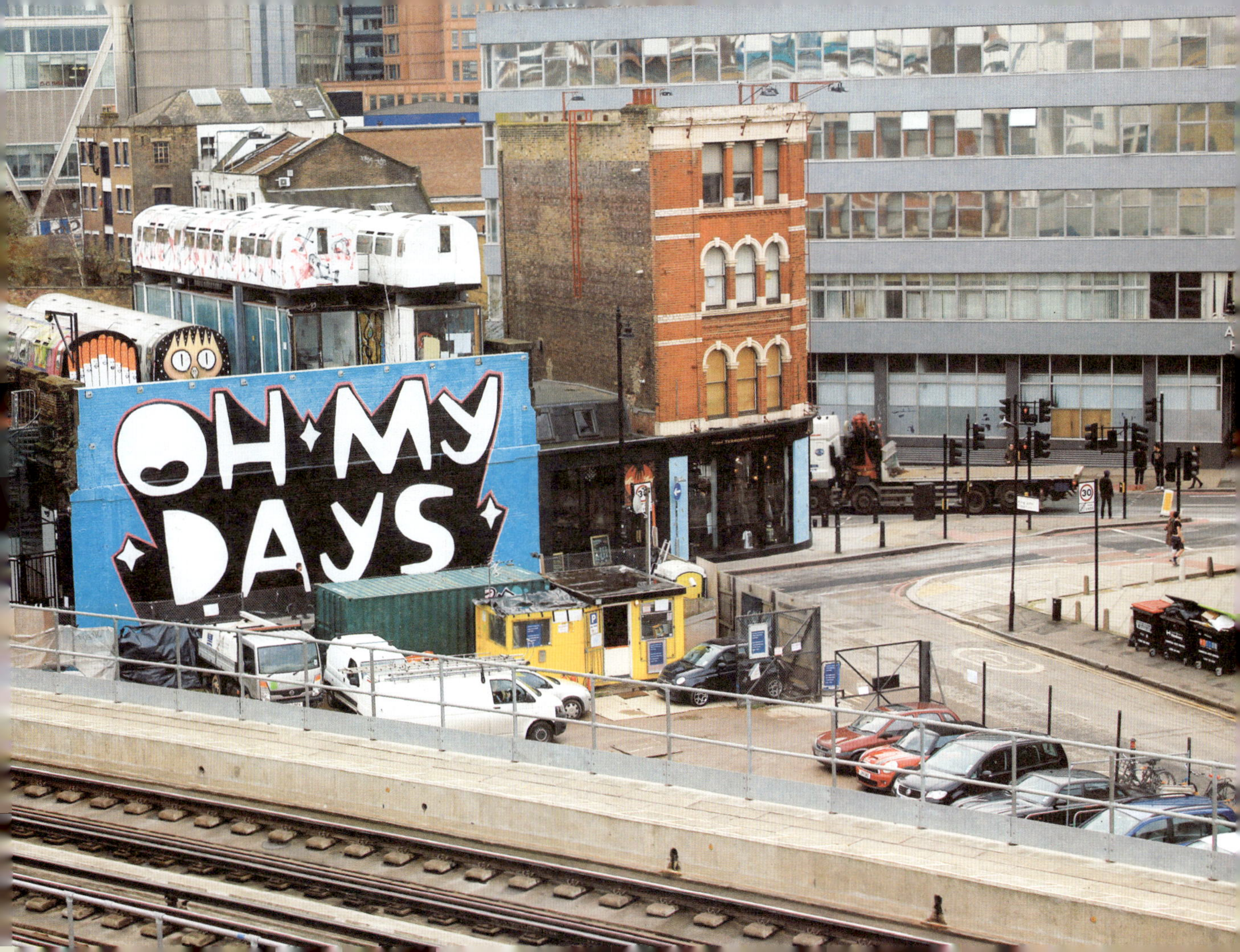
OH MY
DAYS
30

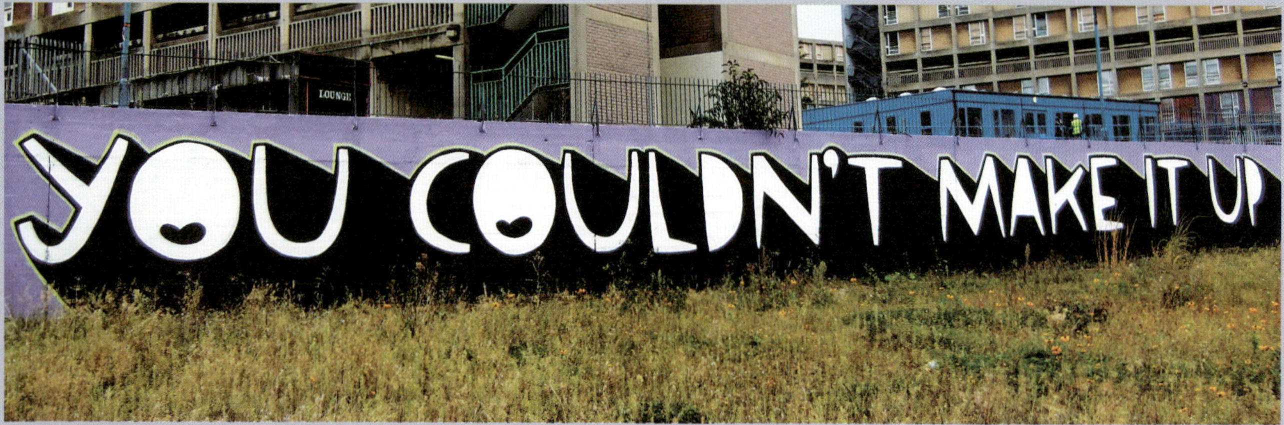

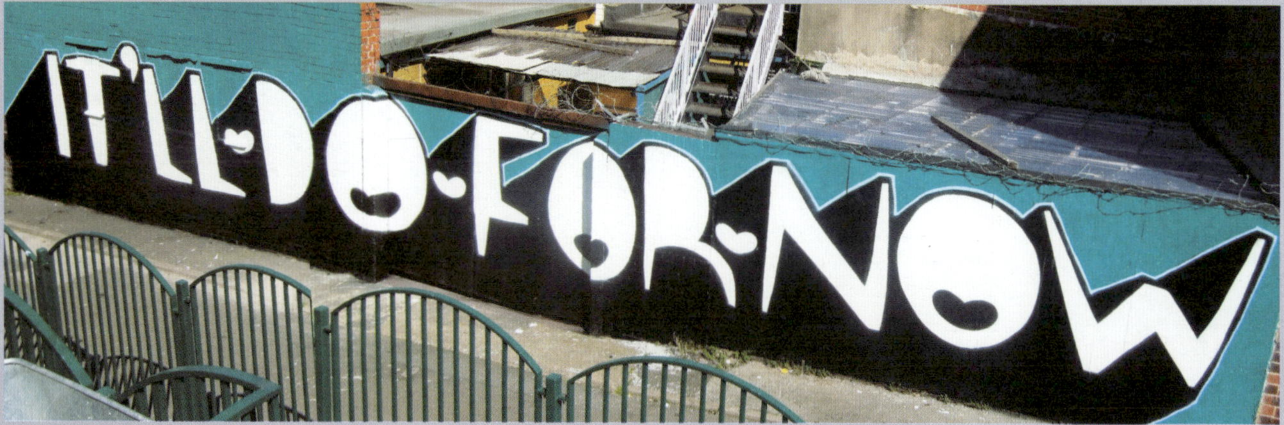

Kid Acne Park Hill, Sheffield and Sharrow, Sheffield ↑

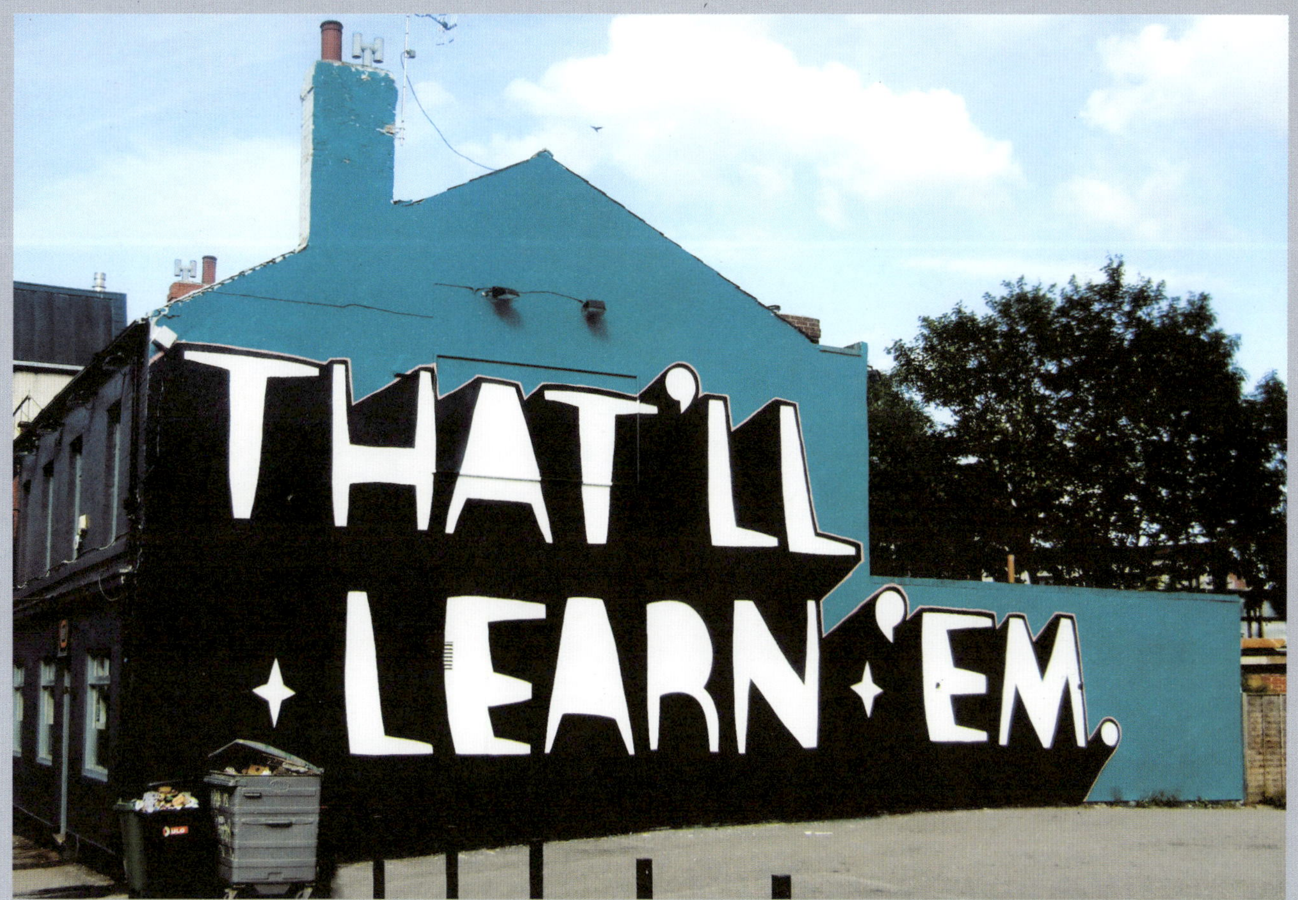

Kid Acne London Road, Sheffield ↑

Just
Be
You

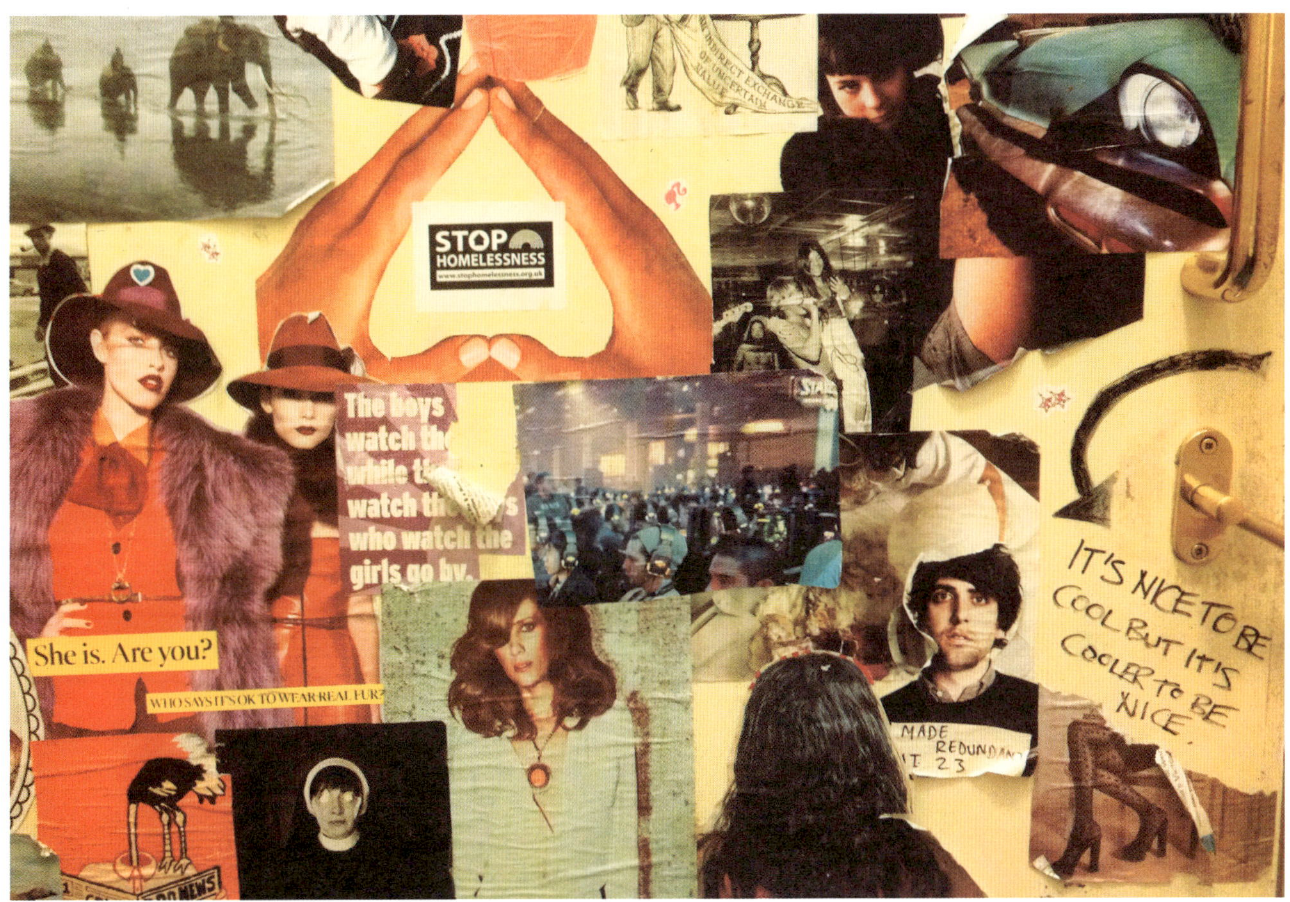

Unknown Leake Street Tunnel, London ← and **Unknown** Leith, Edinburgh ↑

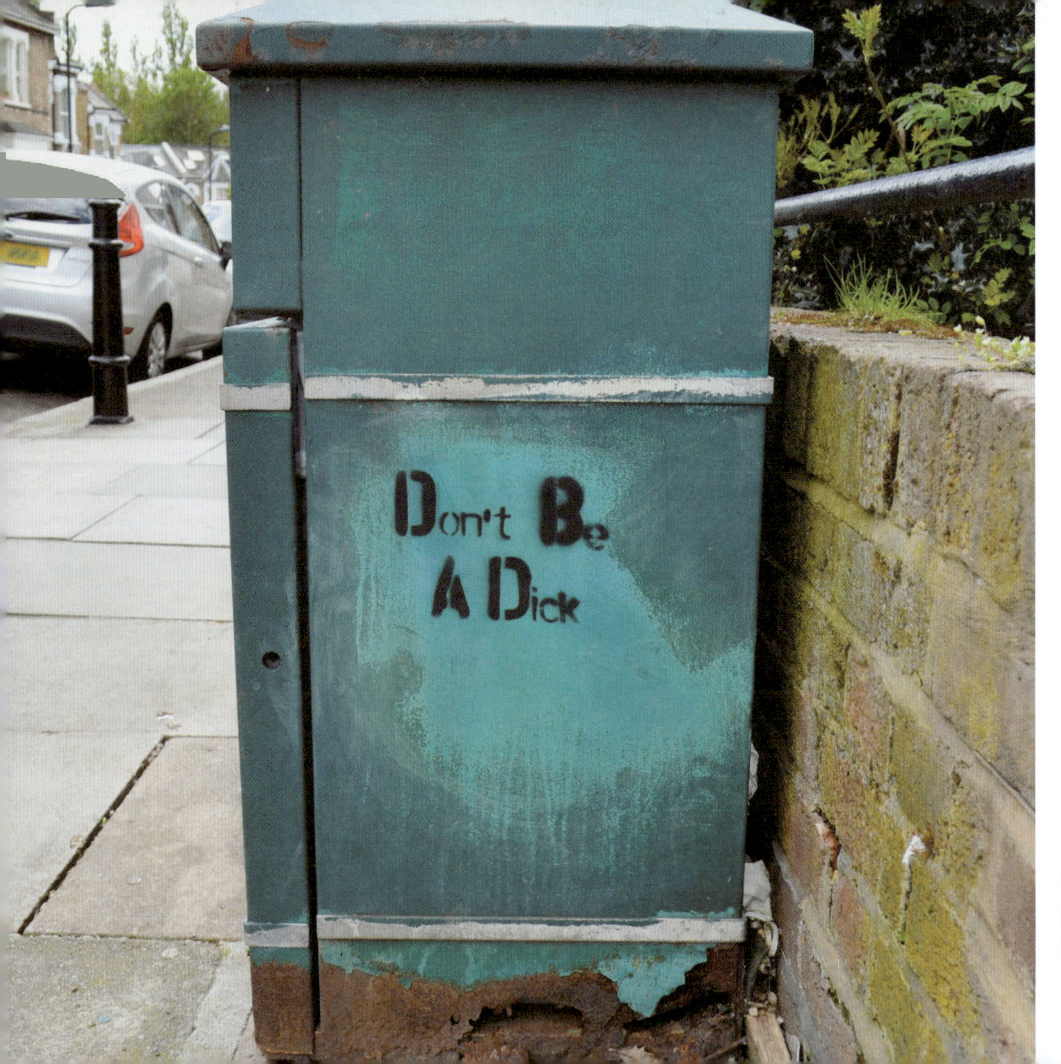

Unknown Stoke Newington, London ← and **Solo One** Nelson Street, Bristol →

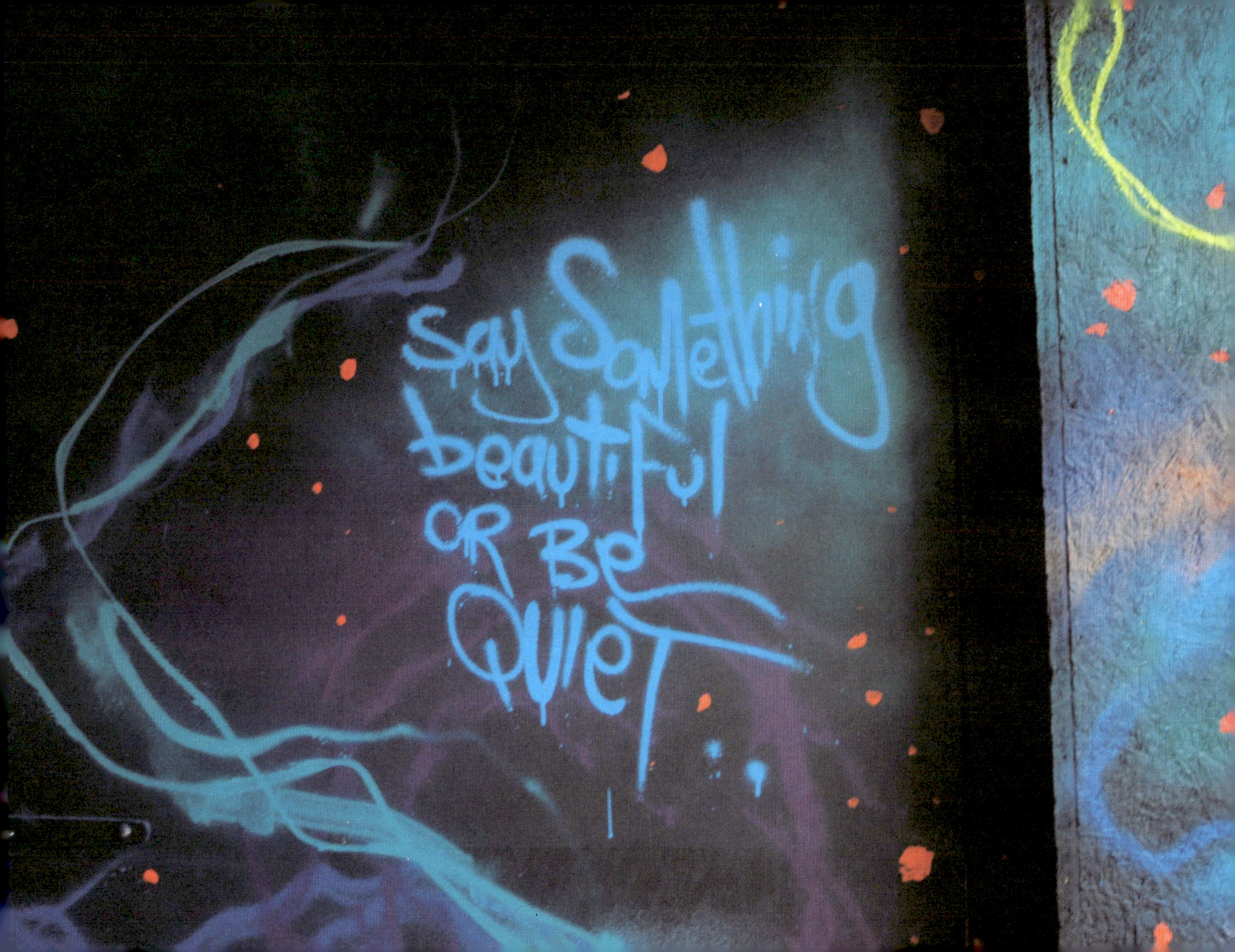
say Something
beautiful
OR Be
Quiet

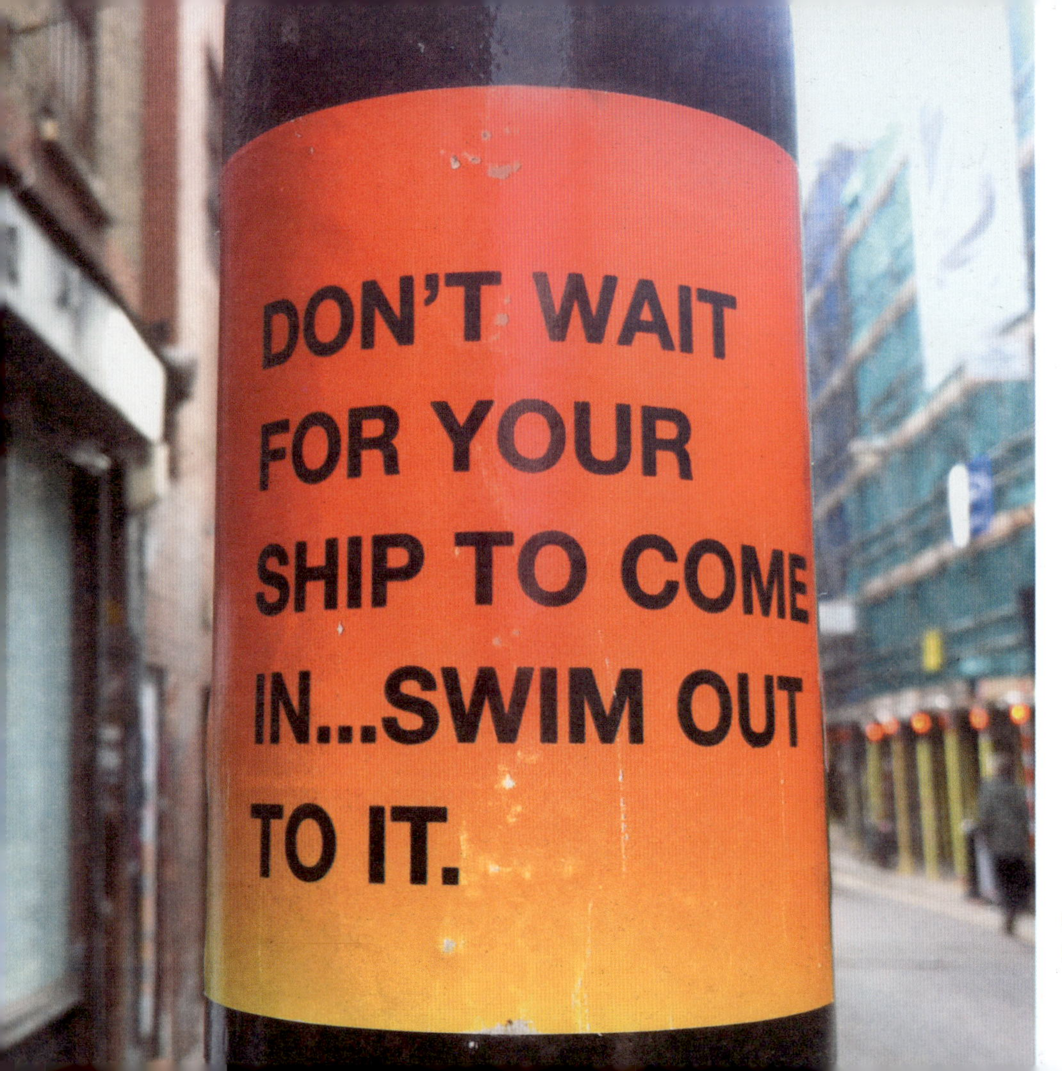

Unknown Shoreditch, London ←

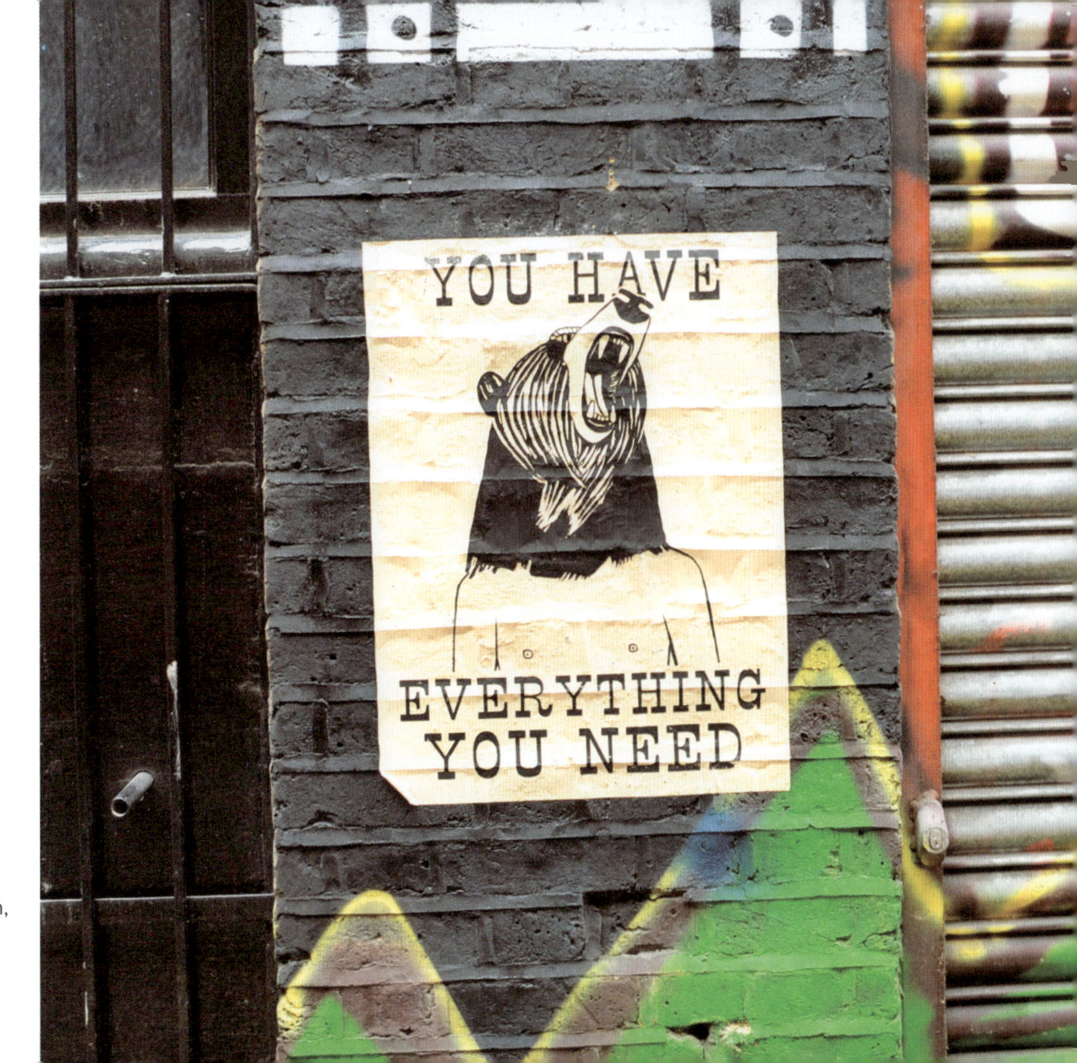

Deedee Cheriel Shoreditch, London →

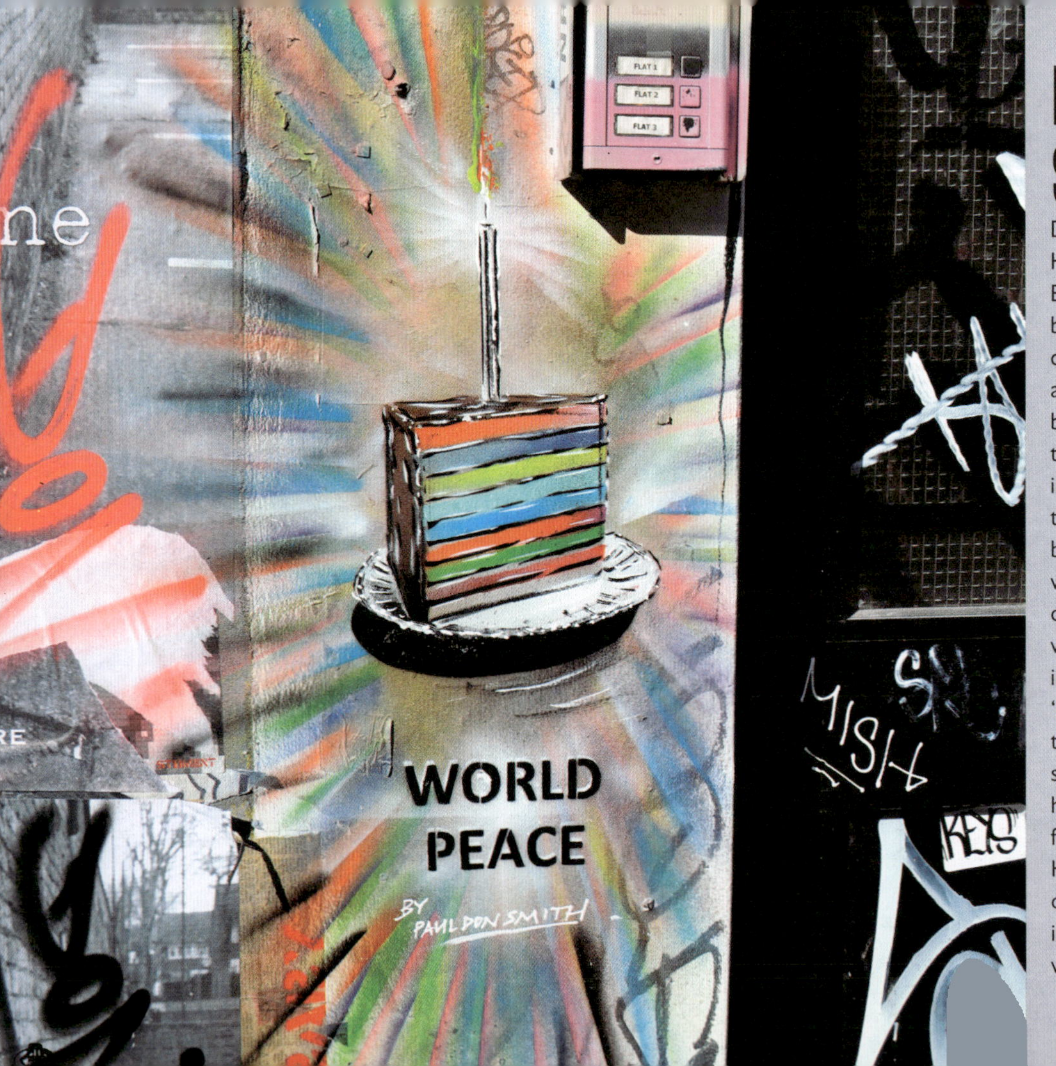

Paul Don Smith

Don started out in 1985. He'd been brought up in Borneo and, when he came back to England, he felt the confines of the concrete jungle around him. But this was to be a blessing: He looked at the stone and concrete walls in a different light and saw them as vast spaces ready to be painted. Moving spaces were even better; trains, like cheetah in the wild, were fast, went everywhere and, most importantly, were always 'spotted'. He quickly learnt that a jungle kid could fast settle into his new pack when he earned himself respect from his name and 'got up'. He was just 12. Old habits die hard and street art is as important to him now as it was then.

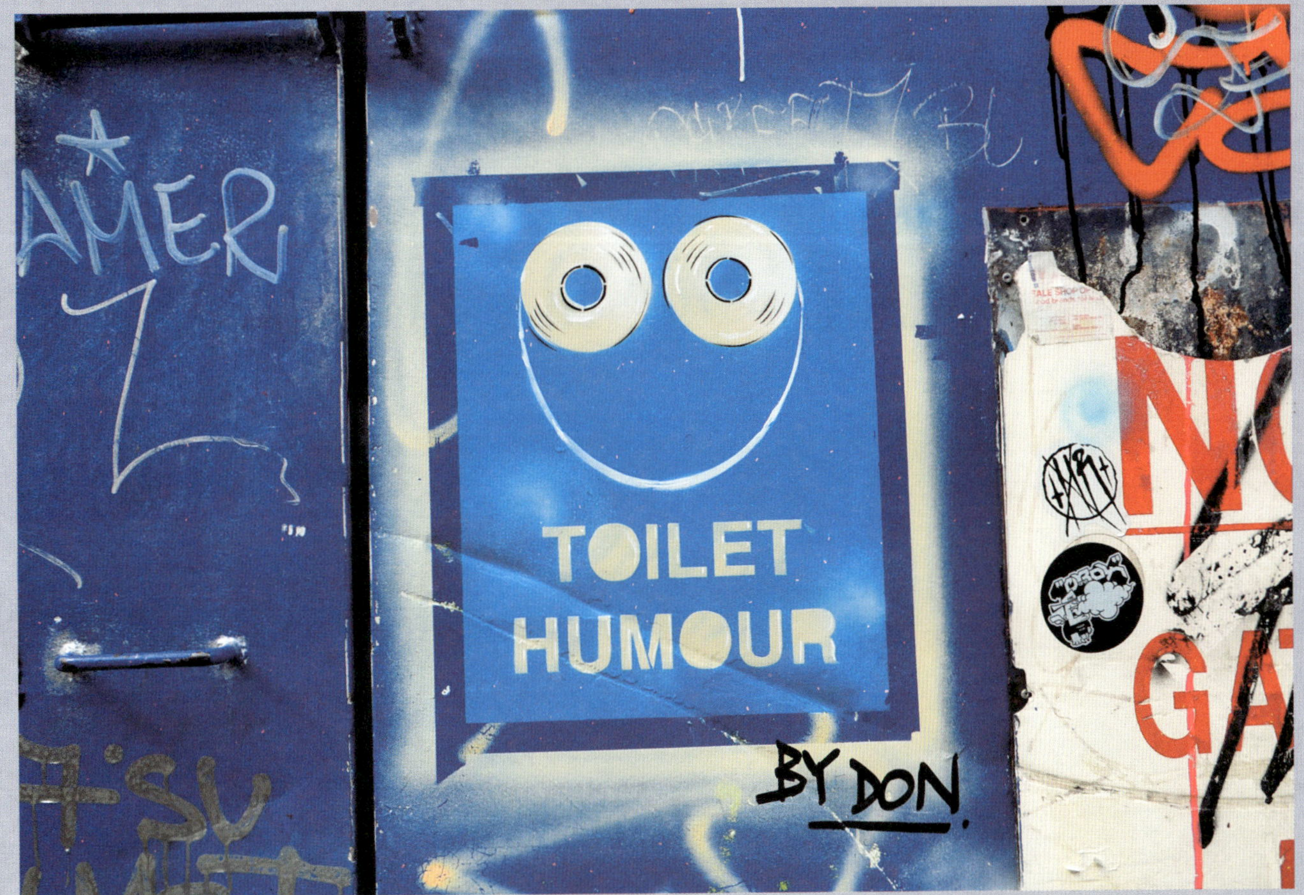

Paul Don Smith Shoreditch, London ← Shoreditch, London ↑

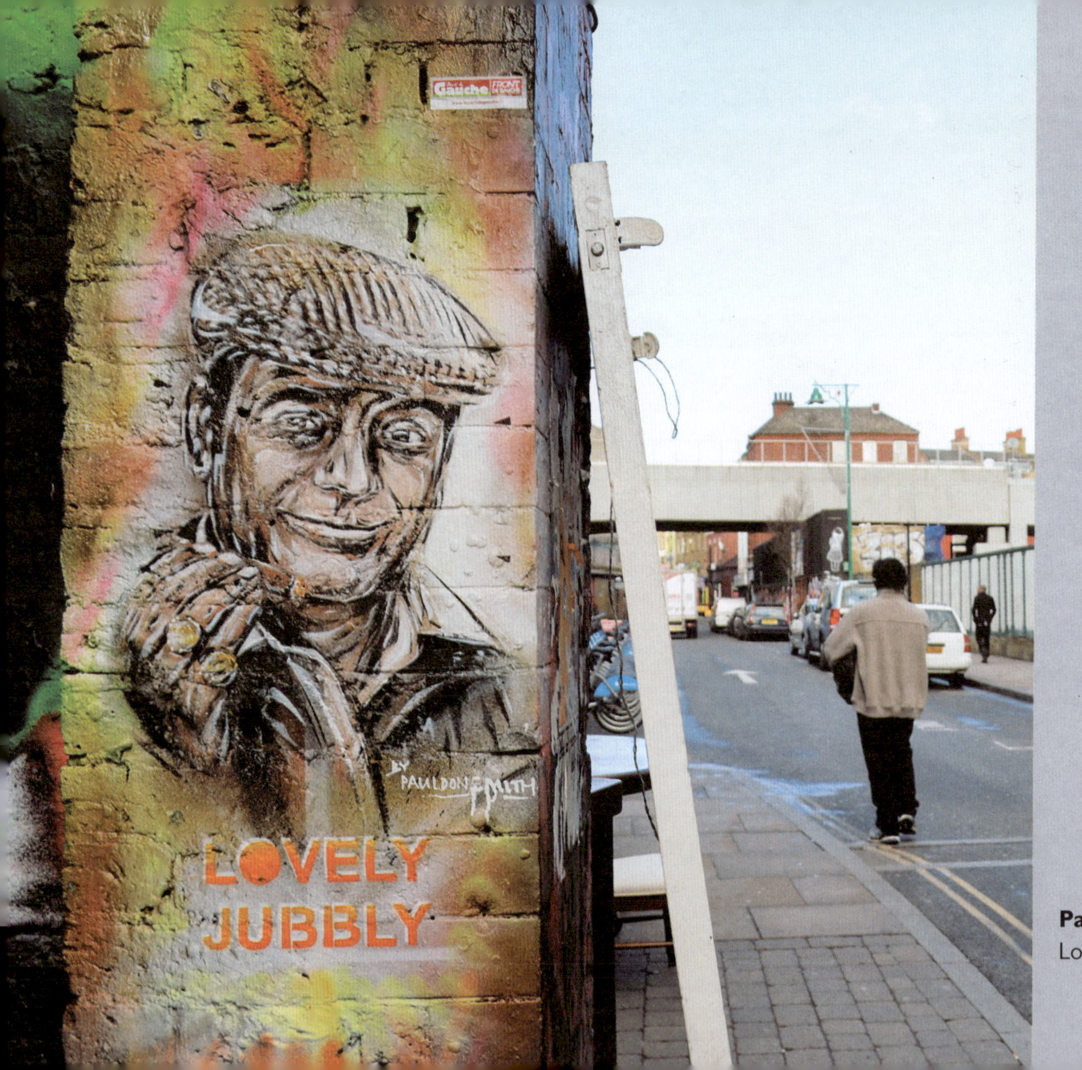

Paul Don Smith Brick Lane, London ←

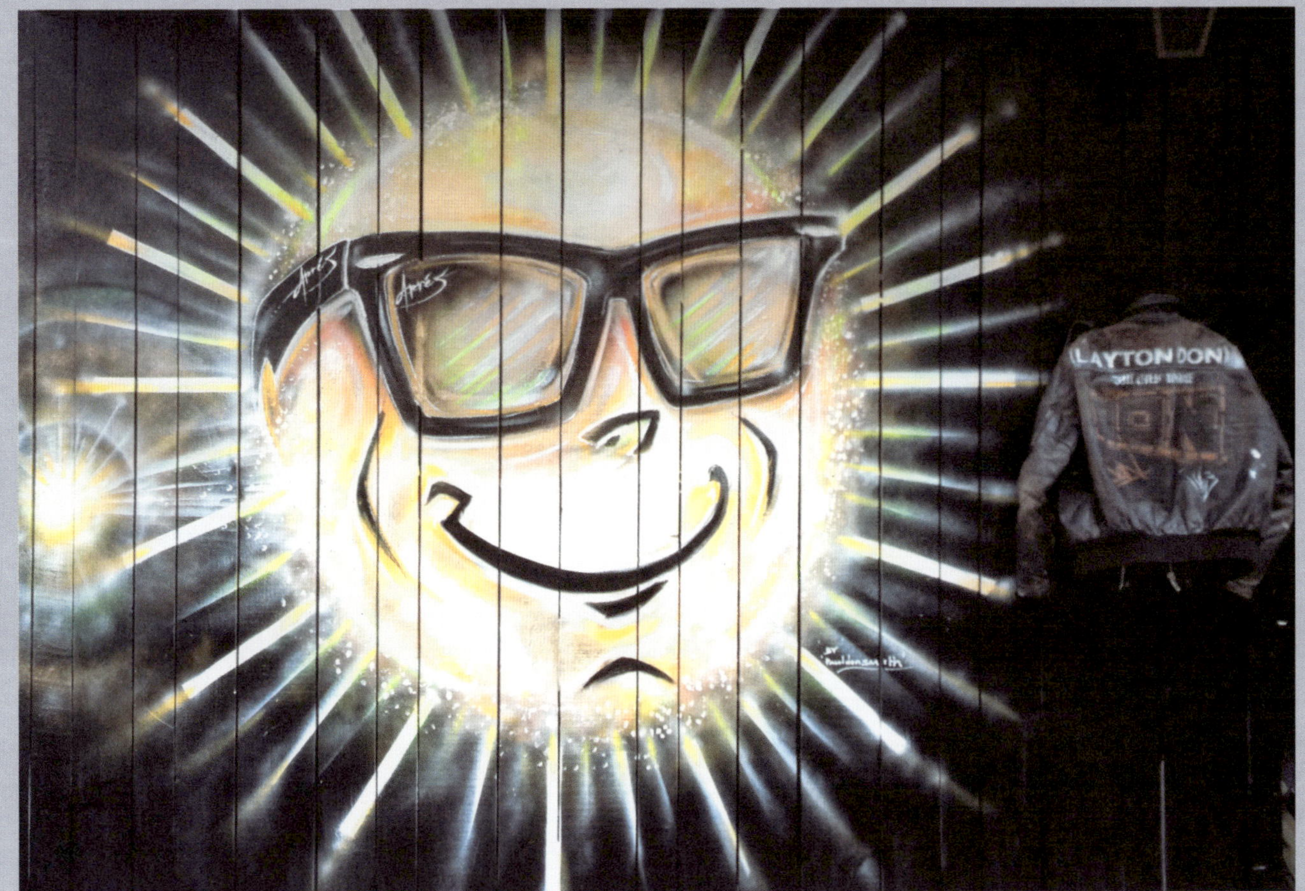

Paul Don Smith Oxford Street, London ↑

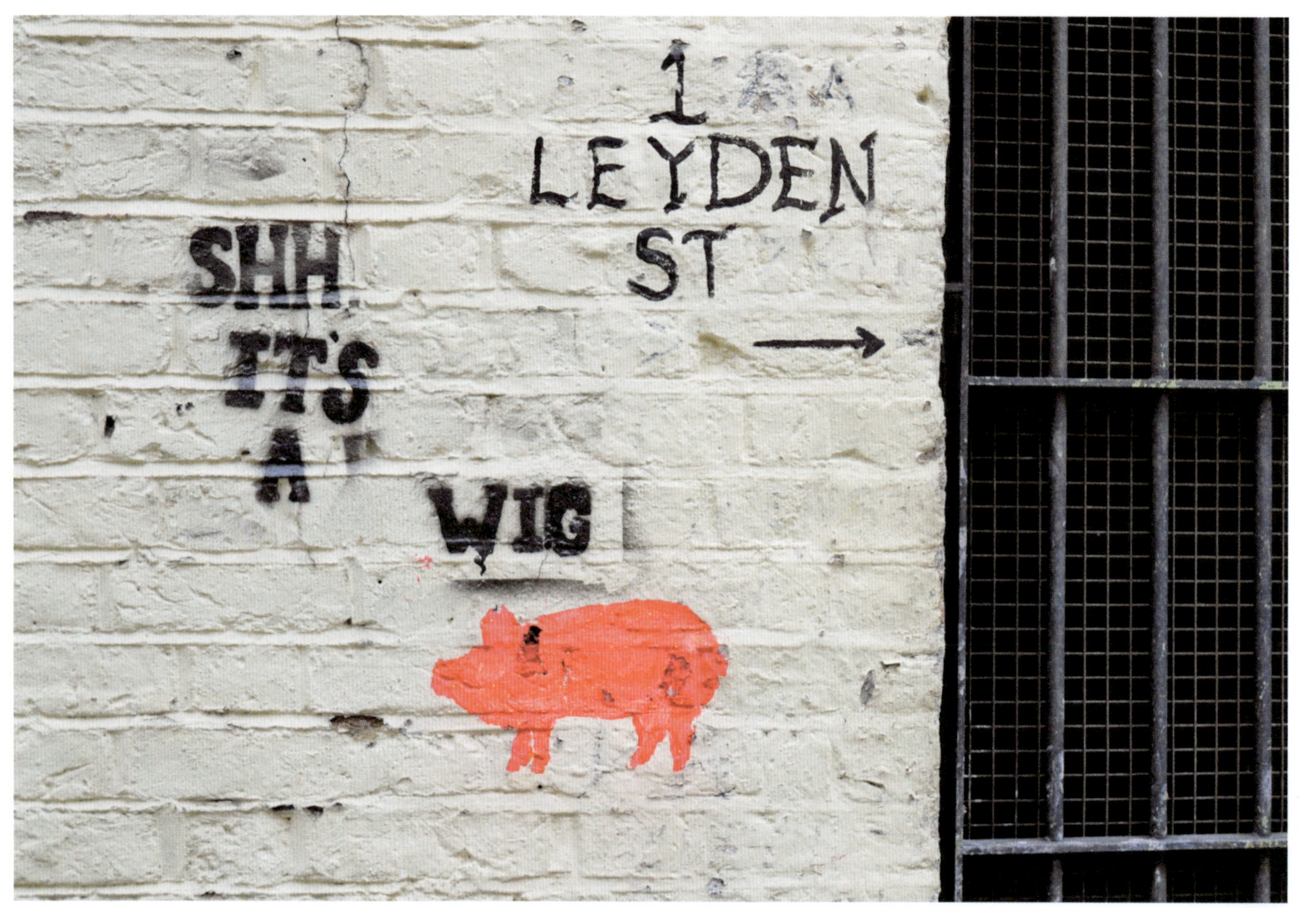

 Unknown Aldgate, London ↑

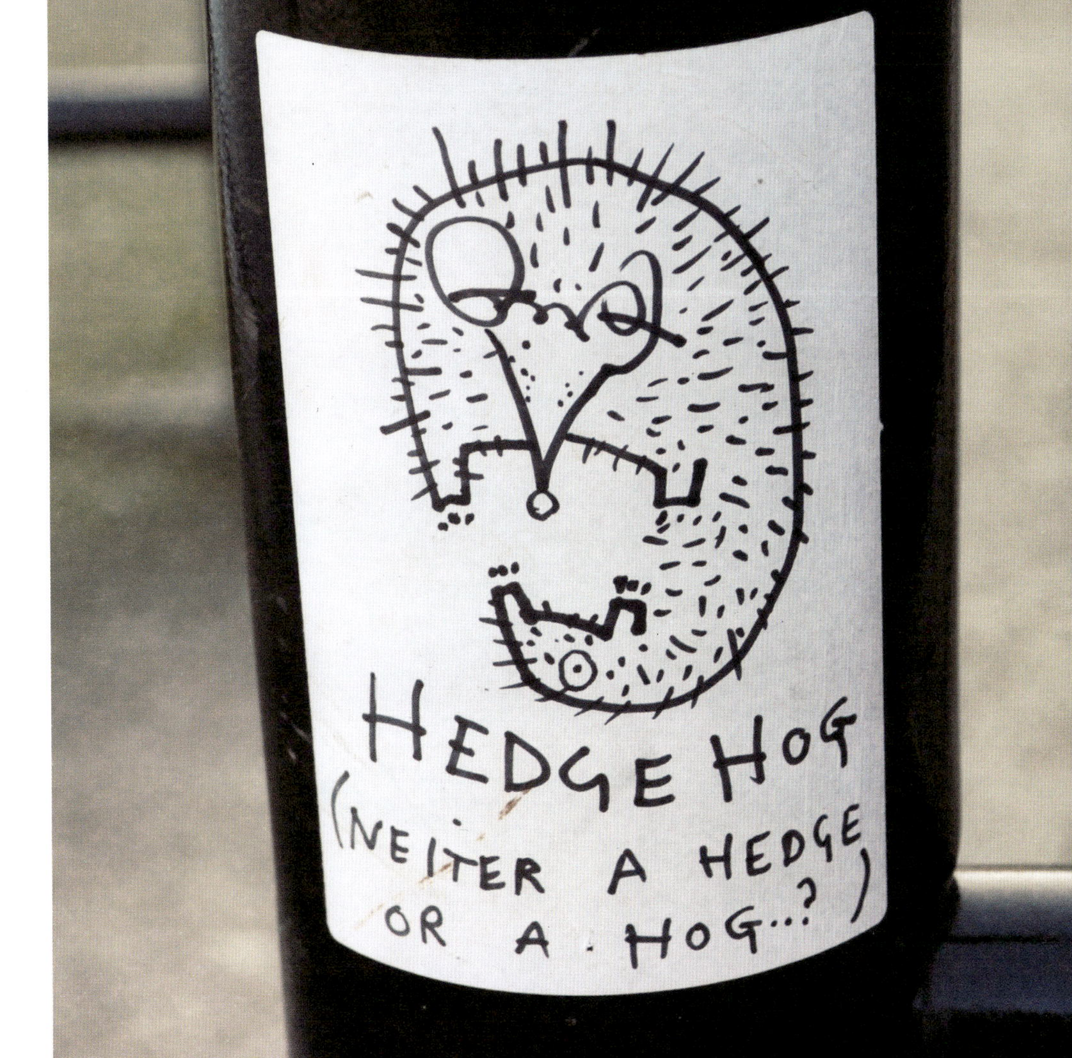

Edwin Hackney Wick, London →

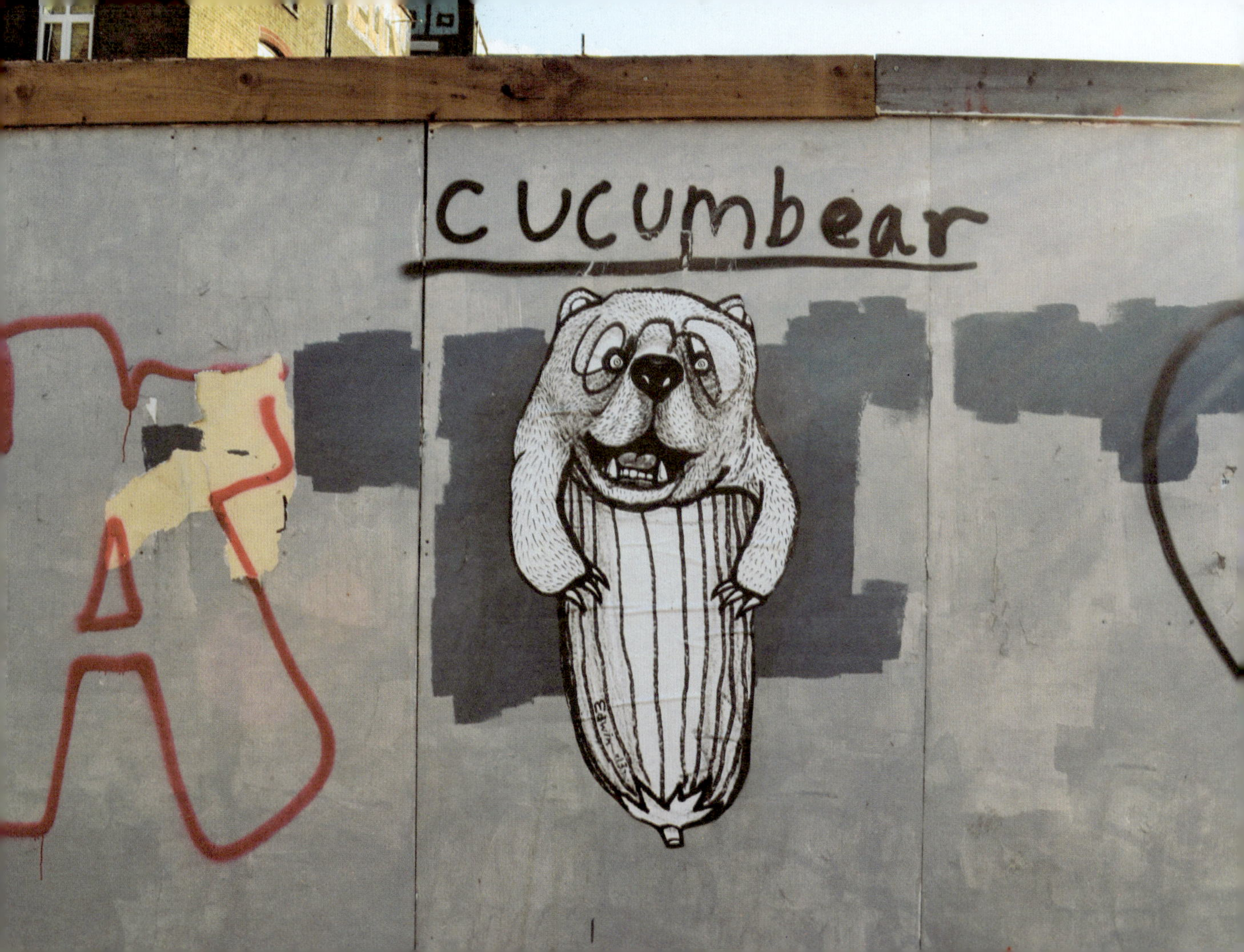
cucumbear

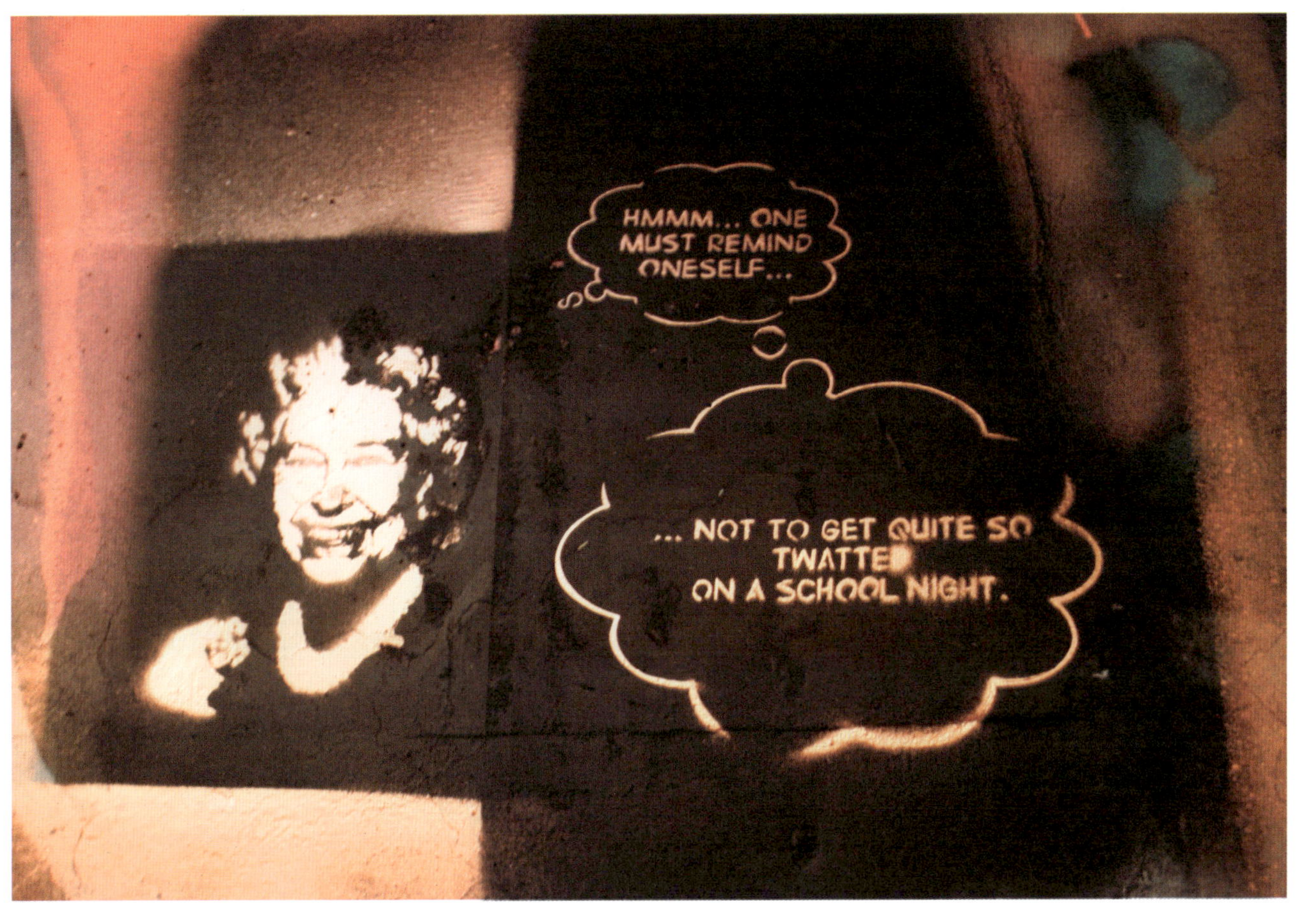

Edwin Hackney Wick, London ← and **Unknown** Leake Street Tunnel, London ↑

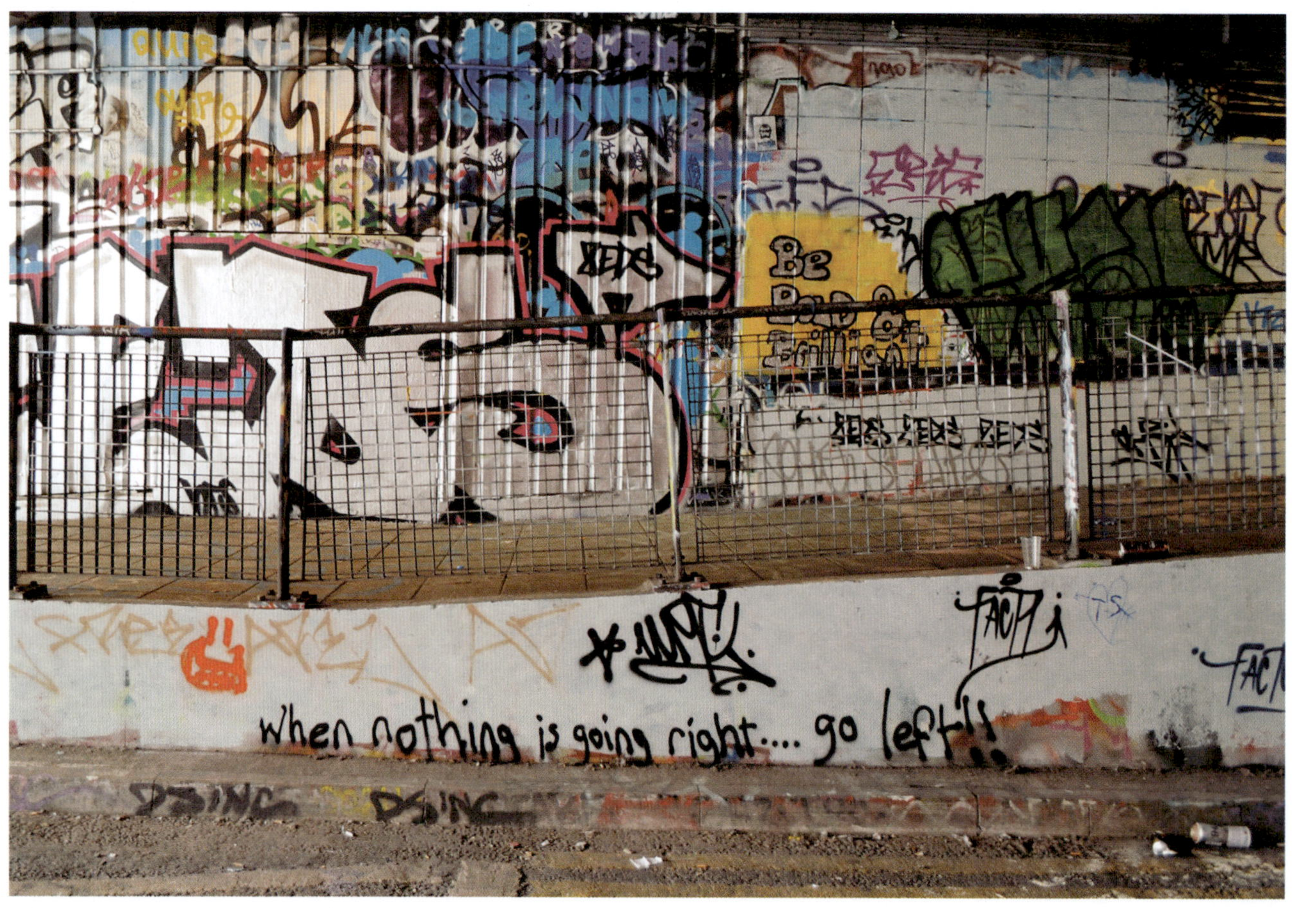

 Unknown Leake Street Tunnel, London ↑

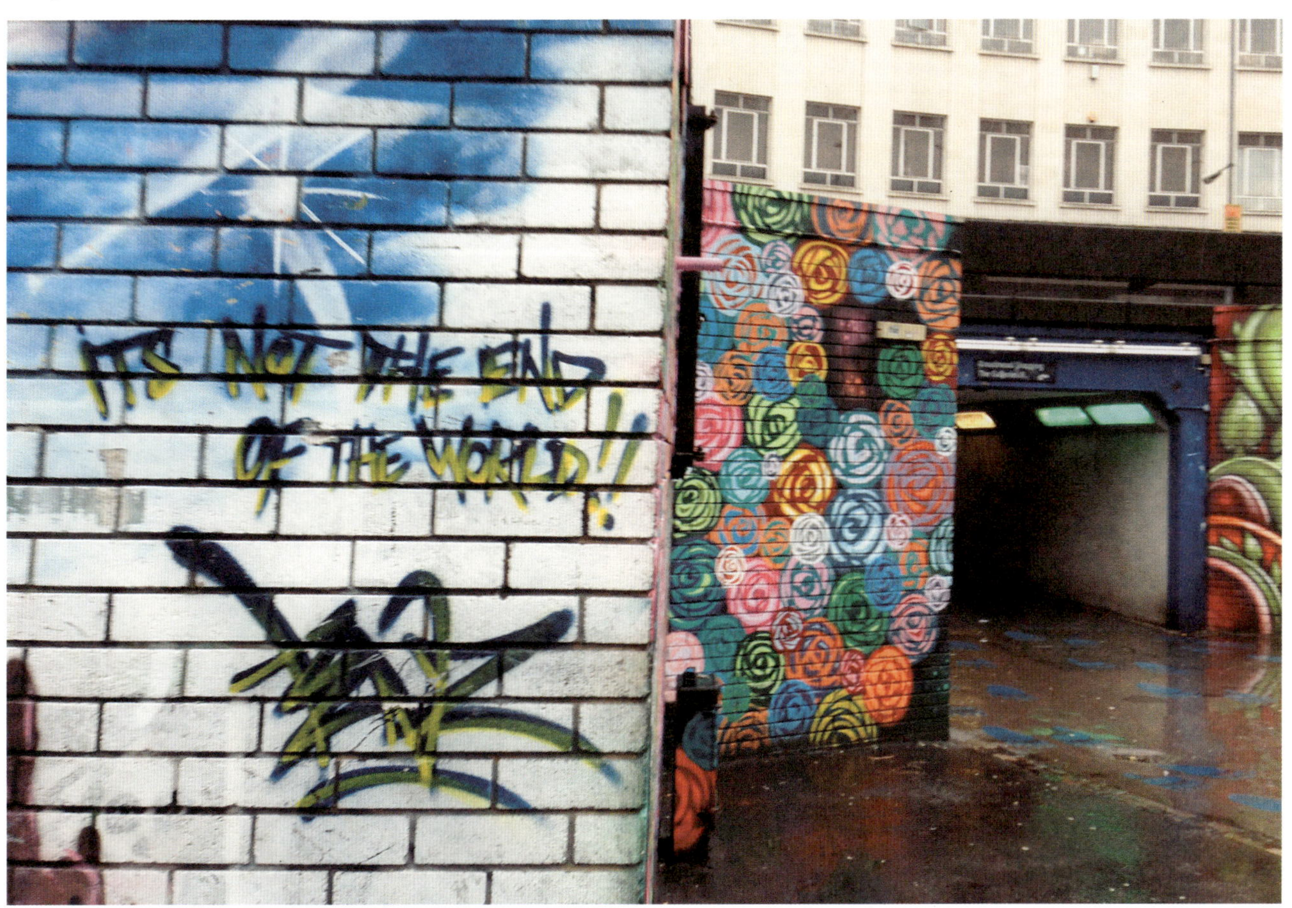

Unknown Stokes Croft, Bristol ↑

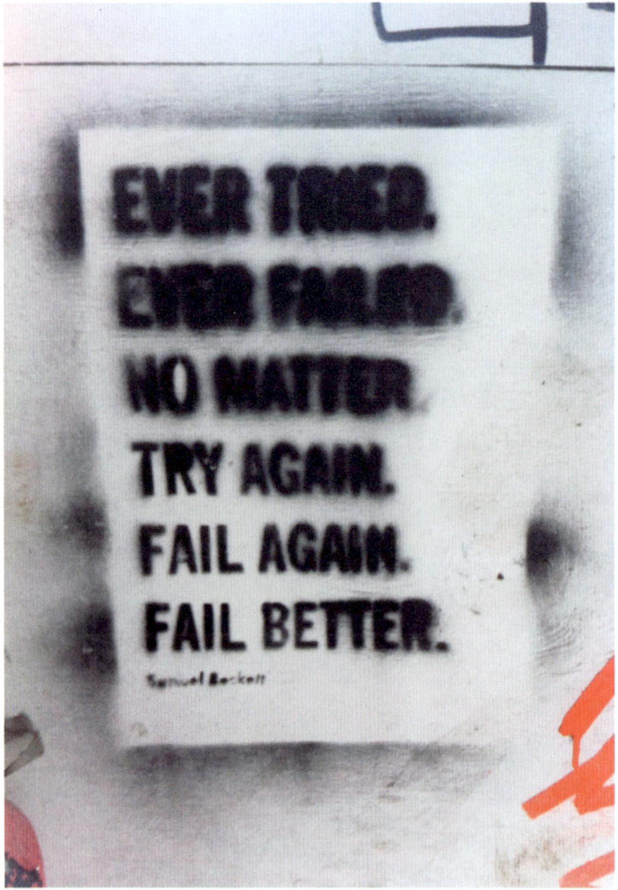

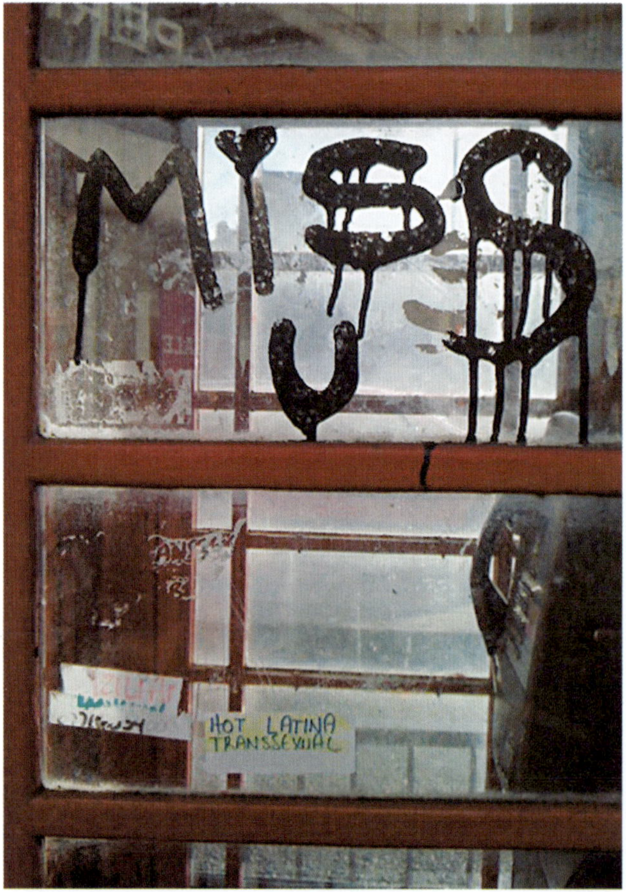

Fail Better Shoreditch, London, **Unknown** Tottenham Court Road, London ↑ and **Unknown** Shoreditch, London →

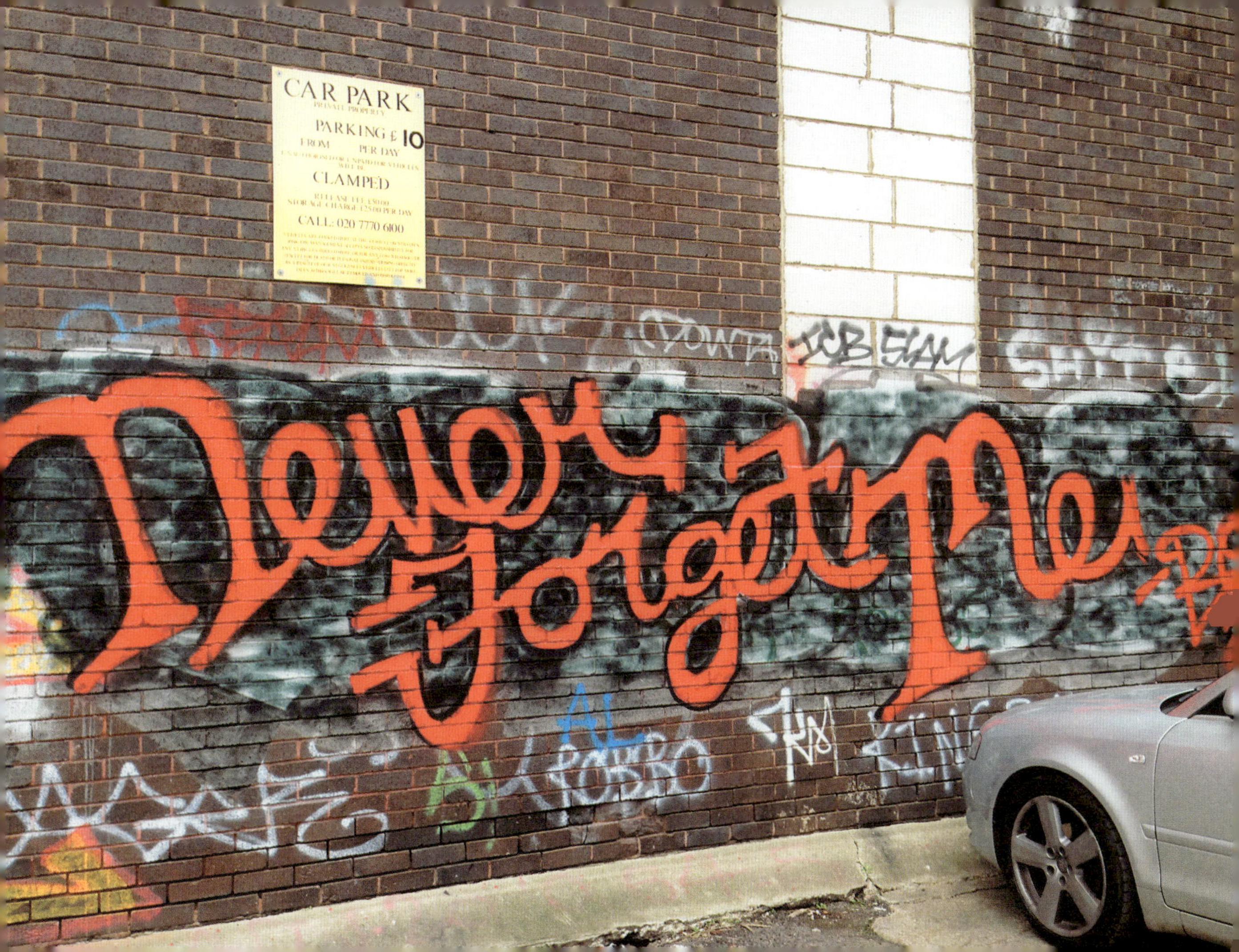
CAR PARK
PARKING £ 10
FROM
PER DAY
CLAMPED
CALL: 020 7770 6100
Never Forget Me

Acknowledgments

Thank you to all the brilliantly talented artists for your colourful brains, painty hands and for wanting to be involved in this little book. Thank you too to all the anonymous writers and scribblers. Thank you for putting smiles on our chops:

Animaux Circus www.animauxcircus.co.uk
As One www.asonearts.com
Ben Eine www.einesigns.co.uk
Binty Bint www.bintybint.com
Bortusk Leer www.bortusk.com
Camille Walala www.camillewalala.com
Dabs & Myla www.dabsmyla.com
David Shillinglaw www.davidshillinglaw.co.uk
Deedee Cheriel www.deedeecheriel.com
Dones www.donesgraffiti.com
Dscreet www.facebook.com/dscreetartist
Edwin www.theedwin.tumblr.com
ESPO www.firstandfifteenth.net
Expanded Eye www.expandedeye.co.uk
Googly Eye Cru www.thegooglyeyecru.com
Graffiti Life www.graffitilife.co.uk
Hin www.hin-art.com
Hunto www.huntoland.com
Ian Stevenson www.ianstevenson.co.uk
Jody www.digital-fire.co.uk
Kid30 www.smallkid.co.uk
Kid Acne www.kidacne.com
Levingos levingos@hotmail.com
Malarky www.malarko.com
Martina O'Shea www.martinaoshea.com
Milo Tchais www.milotchais.carbonmade.com
Mobstr www.mobstr.org
Morley www.iammorley.com
My Dog Sighs www.mydogsighs.co.uk
Pablo Delgado www.pablodelgadomc.com
Paul Don Smith www.pauldonsmith.com
Pegasus www.pegasusstreetart.com
Philipp Jordan www.teddiesinspace.com
Pure Evil www.pureevil.me
Remi/Rough www.remirough.com
Rose Vickers rosievickers@yahoo.co.uk
Sickboy www.thesickboy.com
Stikki Peaches www.stikkipeaches.tumblr.com
Throne throne.art@hotmail.co.uk
Toby www.flickr.com/photos/tobyuk/
WhisBe WhIsBeArt@gmail.com

Thank you to all the *Happy Graffiti* followers and contributors for your thumbs, eyes and ears. Please do keep sending your photos in. All the photos in this book were taken by *HGHQ* apart from the following:

5 My Dog Sighs
7 Lins McRobie
13 Camille Walala
17 Arlen Figgis
22 Mark Hat
24 Bortusk Leer
25 Bortusk Leer
26 Bortusk Leer
28 Ben Lavell
31 Levingos
32 Throne
33 Martina O'Shea
34 Tim Galbraith
36 Kid30
41 Throne
43 Solo One
48 Morley
49 Morley
50 Morley
51 Morley
53 Solo One
57R Beth Simons
63 Jenny Harvey
65 Sophia Fox
66 Binty Bint
67 Binty Bint
68 Binty Bint
69 Binty Bint
76 Aileen Thomson
82 Mark Hat
85L Felipe Bencini
86L Malcolm Croft
87 Jenny Harvey
89L Simona Sarafudinova
89R Pure Evil
90 Pure Evil
96 Malarky
97 Malarky
98 Malarky
99 Malarky
100 Lauren Newman
104 Kid Acne
105 Kid Acne
106 Kid Acne
107 Kid Acne
109 Roberta Pia
121 Simona Sarafudinova
122 Emma Cooke
124R Karen 'Biv' Webb
128 Harley Birch

Thank you to

Becky Thomas, for looking out for me.
Alison and everyone at Octopus, for making this book look nice and getting it into your paws.
Stevie Star, for painting 'SMILE' on that wall in that creepy lane all those years ago.
My boss lady, for being patient with me.
Mum and Dad, for always being supportive and for generally being brilliant.
My brother Steve, for getting me into this new fangled internet nonsense.
Betty McGill, for just being you – Snap Snap.

And to all my beautiful and wonderful friends for being a giant bunch of funny bastards and loveable rogues – you are a constant source of love and laughing for me and I feel very lucky to have you all in my life. I couldn't have made this silly book without you all.

Contact us

If you'd like to join the *Happy Graffiti* revolution, we would love to hear from you! Whether it's sending us a photo of something you've spied or just to say hello – come and give us a wave at one of our many online homes:

www.happygraffiti.com
hello@happygraffiti.com
www.facebook.com/happygraffiti
Twitter @Happeegraffiti
Instagram @Happygraffiti

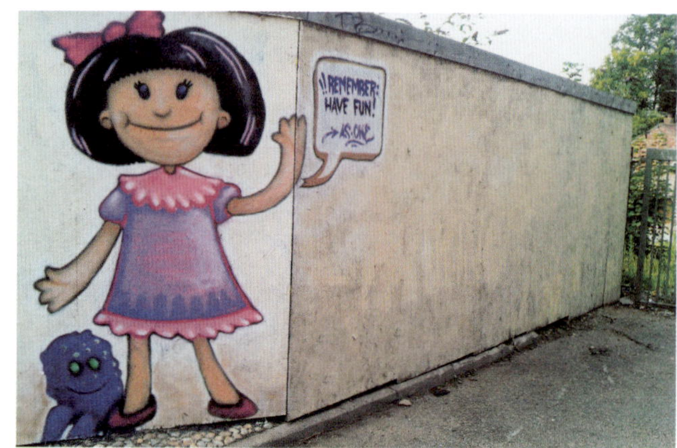

As One Pottergate Street, Norwich ↑